LITTLE WOMEN AT 150

Children's Literature Association Series

LITTLE WOMEN AT 150

Edited by **Daniel Shealy**

UNIVERSITY PRESS OF MISSISSIPPI | JACKSON

The University Press of Mississippi is the scholarly publishing agency of the Mississippi Institutions of Higher Learning: Alcorn State University, Delta State University, Jackson State University, Mississippi State University, Mississippi University for Women, Mississippi Valley State University, University of Mississippi, and University of Southern Mississippi.

www.upress.state.ms.us

The University Press of Mississippi is a member of the Association of University Presses.

Copyright © 2022 by University Press of Mississippi
All rights reserved

First printing 2022

∞

Library of Congress Cataloging-in-Publication Data

Names: Shealy, Daniel, editor.
Title: Little Women at 150 / edited by Daniel Shealy.
Other titles: Children's Literature Association series.
Description: Jackson : University Press of Mississippi, 2022. | Series: Children's Literature Association series | Includes bibliographical references and index.
Identifiers: LCCN 2021048486 (print) | LCCN 2021048487 (ebook) | ISBN 9781496837981 (hardback) | ISBN 9781496837998 (trade paperback) | ISBN 9781496838018 (epub) | ISBN 9781496838001 (epub) | ISBN 9781496838032 (pdf) | ISBN 9781496838025 (pdf)
Subjects: LCSH: Alcott, Louisa May, 1832–1888. Little women. | Alcott, Louisa May, 1832–1888—History and criticism. | Children's literature—19th century—History and criticism.
Classification: LCC PS1018 .L58 2022 (print) | LCC PS1018 (ebook) | DDC 813/.4—dc23/eng/20211209
LC record available at https://lccn.loc.gov/2021048486
LC ebook record available at https://lccn.loc.gov/2021048487

British Library Cataloging-in-Publication Data available

For Joel Myerson

Contents

ix   Acknowledgments

3   Introduction
      Daniel Shealy

18   Class, Charity, and Coming of Age in *Little Women*
      John Matteson

37   Louisa May Alcott's Emersonian Use of *The Pilgrim's Progress*:
      Little Women as Palimpsest
      Roberta Seelinger Trites

65   "Faithfulness Itself": The Imperative for Hannah Mullet in *Little Women*
      Sandra Harbert Petrulionis

89   Mobilizing the Little Women: Images of Transport and the Domestic
      Beverly Lyon Clark

114   "This Was Something Altogether New": On Jo March's Adulthood
      and *Little Women*'s Final Chapters
      Anne K. Phillips

140 Marriage in the Nineteenth Century: The Influence of Margaret Fuller's "The Great Lawsuit" on *Little Women*
CHRISTINE DOYLE

162 Louisa May Alcott, Ethel Turner, and Some Little Women Down Under
JOEL MYERSON

180 Louisa May Alcott, Major Author: *Little Women* and Beyond
GREGORY EISELEIN

205 About the Contributors

209 Index

ACKNOWLEDGMENTS

Research for *Little Women at 150* was supported in part by funds from the Foundation of the University of North Carolina at Charlotte and from the State of North Carolina. I would like to acknowledge the support of the Department of English and Nancy A. Gutierrez, dean of the College of Liberal Arts and Sciences at UNC-Charlotte.

I am also grateful to Katie Keene at the University Press of Mississippi for the opportunity to publish this book. Mary Heath, editorial associate at the press, provided help in the early stages, always answering numerous queries promptly and cheerfully. Valerie Jones, the book's project editor, offered generous support in seeing the book through the press. Kelly Burch's exemplary copyediting helped improve the volume.

Thanks also goes to my children, Luke and Hannah. Their love makes all the work worthwhile.

A special thanks goes to Andrea Eugster for her encouragement all along the way. From the time our paths crossed at Orchard House in Concord, her support has been inspirational and transformative.

As this book was in press, sad news arrived that Beverly Lyon Clark had passed away suddenly on March 18, 2021. A professor of English at Wheaton College for forty-four years, Bev was a wonderful teacher, a brilliant scholar, and a generous friend. Her scholarship in children's literature, and Louisa May Alcott in particular, will endure and continue to aid and inspire new generations of students, literary critics, and scholars for years to come. Sadly, on November 19, 2021, Joel Myerson also died suddenly. Joel was a Carolina

Distinguished Professor, Emeritus, at the University of South Carolina, where he began his academic career in 1971. He edited or authored over sixty books and was an esteemed scholar of nineteenth-century American literature, publishing works on Emerson, Whitman, Fuller, Dickinson, and Hawthorne. Together, Joel and I, often with Madeleine B. Stern, edited five books on Louisa May Alcott. Joel was such a large presence in my own life—a teacher, a mentor, but most of all, a good friend. I was delighted when both Bev and Joel agreed to contribute to *Little Women at 150*, as I knew their work would only strengthen the book as a whole. Amy March, in *Little Women*, declares, "I want to be great, or nothing." Beverly Lyon Clark and Joel Myerson *were* "great."

Little Women at 150

Introduction

Daniel Shealy

In 1922, Nathaniel Hawthorne's son, Julian, reminiscing about Louisa May Alcott, his friend and neighbor in Concord, Massachusetts, writes that "a few months ago I saw a moving picture based upon [*Little Women*]; the picture was not so good as the book, but it drew big audiences all over the country, and paid more money to the producers, no doubt, than Louisa herself ever made out of the book" (190). The film was most likely the now-lost silent version released by Paramount-Artcraft in January 1919, starring Dorothy Bernard as Jo March. Produced by William A. Brady, who had also produced the popular 1912 Broadway play of the novel, this adaptation of *Little Women* was even filmed partially in Concord. The image of Julian Hawthorne, who once claimed to be the inspiration for the character of Laurie, watching the escapades of the March sisters in a darkened theater is somewhat haunting. The time warp that the black-and-white celluloid images brought to the mind of Hawthorne, then in his midseventies, comes across clearly in his recollection. This early twentieth-century episode not only shows how the 1868–69 novel was becoming part of the culture of modern times in the United States but also demonstrates how time was quickly passing. Soon the people who grew up with Louisa May Alcott and her sisters in Concord, like Julian, would be gone. Hawthorne ends his brief account of the film by observing how Alcott's *Little Women* endures: "There is a popularity of more than fifty years, a Victorian success lasting over to our revolutionary and sophisticated twentieth century, and still vigorous and unafraid. A book written just after our Civil War, and keeping sweet and good all through the World War, and likely to survive the next cataclysm, whatever that might be. Nothing short of genius could achieve such a result" (190). Now, 150 years after its initial publication, *Little Women* still survives and still looms large on the US literary landscape and in the American conscious. Ironically, Louisa May Alcott's greatest success came from a novel that she never seemed to consider her best literary work.

In *Jo's Boys* (1886), the final volume in the March family trilogy, Alcott writes of her main character's unexpected literary success:

> A book for girls being wanted by a certain publisher, [Jo] hastily scribbled a little story describing a few scenes and adventures in the lives of herself and sisters . . . and with very slight hopes of success sent it out to seek its fortune. . . . The hastily written story, sent away with no thought beyond the few dollars it might bring, sailed with a fair wind and a wise pilot at the helm straight into public favor, and came home heavily laden with an unexpected cargo of gold and glory. (46)

She goes on to note: "A more astonished woman probably never existed than Josephine Bhaer when her little ship came into port with flags flying, cannon that had been silent before now booming gayly, and, better than all, many kind faces rejoicing with her, many friendly hands grasping hers with cordial congratulations" (46). Readers, of course, recognize that Jo's literary success was really Alcott's own experience with the publication of *Little Women*.

In October 1868, the month of the book's publication, Alcott thanked Mary E. Channing Higginson, wife of the abolitionist, soldier, and author Thomas Wentworth Higginson, for taking the time to congratulate her: "I am glad my 'Little Women' please you, for the book was very hastily written to order, & I had many doubts about the success of my first attempt at a girl's book. . . . Your husband gave me the praise which I value most highly when he said the little story was 'good, & American'" (*Selected Letters* 118). However, her reference to *Little Women* as "the little story" in her reply to Mrs. Higginson indicates that she did not consider it great literature—a feeling one might understand given the literary environment she grew up with in Concord and Boston. But her father, Bronson Alcott, the transcendentalist poet and philosopher, reflected on Higginson's letter in his journal—and on his daughter's reaction: "This is high praise, and should encourage her to estimate, as I fear she has not properly, her superior gifts as a writer" (*Journals of BA* 391). Two years later, while holding Conversations in Ohio, he wrote home to Louisa, informing her "of the enthusiasm with which her [*Little Women*] is here received . . . all of which she will be slow to accept, cannot even comprehend" (404). But, as Bronson suggests, it appears Alcott never fully grasped the significance of her accomplishment since eleven months before her death, in April 1887, she told a newspaper reporter that she "yet hope[d] to write a few of the novels which have been simmering in my brain while necessity & unexpected success have confined me to juvenile literature" (*Selected Letters* 307–8). Not only did she seem to view "juvenile" fiction as inferior, but she also initially resisted writing the novel that continues to endure after 150 years since its initial publication.

When Thomas Niles, the editor at Roberts Brothers Publishers of Boston, approached Louisa May Alcott in September 1867 and asked her to write a "girls book," Alcott promised to "try" it (*Journals* 158). However, she put off her attempt for months while she composed other fiction and corrected proofs for *Morning-Glories, and Other Stories*, a collection of twelve fantasy tales. In addition to *Morning-Glories*, she wrote blood-and-thunder thrillers for Frank Leslie—"$50 and $100 for all I will send him"—and penned two stories each month for *The Youth's Companion* (162). At the same time, she was under contract to Horace B. Fuller to edit the children's periodical *Merry's Museum*, a position she assumed in October of 1867 for $500 a year. Her "girls book" was put on the back burner. As 1868 began, Alcott noted in her journal that she had earned $1,000 from her writing the previous year, and as her first hyacinth bloomed that January, she felt it was "a good omen" for her impoverished family: "Perhaps we are to win after all, and conquer poverty, neglect, pain, and debt, and march on with flags flying into the new world with the new year" (162). Five months later, in May 1868, her father spoke to Thomas Niles on Louisa's behalf "about a fairy book" (165). After all, fairy tales and fantasy stories were easy for the thirty-five-year-old author to write. Her first book, *Flower Fables* (1854) had been a small collection of peaceful, nature fantasy tales, and after the minor success of *Hospital Sketches* in 1863, she had followed that book with *The Rose Family*, a short work similar to *Flower Fables*. In addition, she had just published her new collection of fantasy tales, *Morning-Glories*, for Fuller. With all of her other literary commitments, fairy tales, Alcott must have thought, would take less time to compose. Plus, it was a genre she felt comfortable writing. However, she confessed to her journal, Niles told Bronson that he "wants a *girls' story*" (165). Her emphasis clearly denotes her disappointment or reluctance. Conferring with her mother and sisters, Anna and May, Alcott decided to explore her own family's experiences as a source for her novel: "So I plod away, though I don't enjoy this sort of thing. Never liked girls, or knew many, except my sisters, but our queer plays and experiences may prove interesting, though I doubt it" (166). In later years, Alcott would reread this journal entry and find amusement in this lack of confidence. "Good joke" she would insert (166). In a little over two months, during the late spring and early summer of 1868, she completed her book for girls at the small half-moon desk Bronson Alcott had built in her upstairs bedroom at Orchard House—all the while still writing for *The Youth's Companion* and *Merry's Museum*. However, Frank Leslie, she noted, "clamors for more [thrillers], but must wait" (166).

When Alcott read page proofs in late August, she felt that *Little Women* "reads better than I expected. Not a bit sensational, but simple and true, for we really lived most of it, and if it succeeds that will be the reason of it" (*Journals* 166). Roberts Brothers offered her $1,000 for the copyright, a typical gesture in nineteenth-century publishing. They would pay her a sizable fee—the same amount of money she had earned the previous year by writing twenty-five stories and *Morning-Glories*—and they would assume the financial risk. Who knew if such a girls' book would sell? However, at the same time Roberts Brothers made their offer, they "advised me to keep the copyright"—something she had not done with her previous four books. Three years before her death in 1888, Alcott inserted the following comment in her journal: "An honest publisher and a lucky author, for the copyright made her fortune, and the 'dull book' was the first golden egg of the ugly duckling" (166). *Little Women, or, Meg, Jo, Beth and Amy* was published in October 1868, and before the month's end the first printing sold out. November saw 1,000 more copies purchased, and 4,500 copies were in print by the end of the year (169n18).

Reviews also were, for the most part, positive. "Pleasant notices and letters arrive, and much interest in my little women, who seem to find friends by their truth to life, as I hoped," noted Alcott (*Journals* 167). The *Boston Daily Evening Transcript* wrote, "The book is fresh, sparkling, natural, and full of soul. In characterization it displays uncommon excellence, as compared with ordinary books for girls" (Clark, *Contemporary Reviews* 61). *Little Women* "is a girls' book of quite another sort," declared the *Springfield Daily Republican*, explaining that the March sisters "are not children but . . . are girls with the instincts of womanhood strong and active, but without the simplicity of childhood." Calling these "household adventures . . . wonderfully varied and rich," the reviewer noted that children may not like them, but "they will attract the girl and boy who have an inkling of the world beyond the children's horizon" (63).

With positive reviews and steady sales, Thomas Niles eagerly asked for a sequel. Alcott, buoyed by the acclaim of both readers and critics for her first volume, admitted in her journal that a "little success is so inspiring that I now find my 'Marches' sober, nice people, and as I can launch into the future, my fancy has more play." The one thing she vowed, however, would be the very thing that would disappoint many readers: "I *won't* marry Jo to Laurie to please any one" (*Journals* 167). Alcott worked furiously on the book, almost meeting her goal of writing a chapter a day. On New Year's Day, she sent Roberts Brothers the completed novel with hopes that "it will do as well as the first, which is selling finely, and receives good notices" (171).

Little Women, part 2 appeared in April 1869 and was even more of a success than the first part. Reviews were again extremely positive. Mrs. Henry Ward Beecher, sister-in-law of Harriet Beecher Stowe, declared in *The Mother at Home and Household Magazine* that "it is amusing to see with how much spirit this simple little book is discussed by elderly people who generally look upon young folks' story-books as foolish things." She went on to note that "we have known one grave lady take Jo's refusal of Laurie more to heart than that young gentleman, for he got over it, and our young friend has not yet ceased grumbling" (Clark, *Contemporary Reviews* 77). The *Eclectic Magazine* noted that the sequel "is the very best of books to reach the hearts of the young of any age from six to sixty, though its merits will be most appreciated by those who have reached the contemplative period of life" (76). Initial sales of part 2 surpassed those of the first book. By August, Roberts Brothers had printed 11,000 copies of the novel. Frank Preston Stearns, a friend of the Alcott family, recalled in his 1895 memoir *Sketches from Concord and Appledore*: "First the young people read it; then their fathers and mothers; and then the grandparents read it. Grave merchants and lawyers meeting on their way down town in the morning said to each other, 'Have you read "Little Women"'; and laughed as they said it. The clerks in my office read it, so also did the civil engineer, and the boy in the elevator. It was the rage in '69"

(85). The sales of both parts of *Little Women* were so successful that Roberts Brothers sent Alcott a check for $2,500 on Christmas Day 1869—her royalty for only six months. The hyacinth that had bloomed on New Year's Day in 1868 proved to be a "good omen" indeed, as Alcott and her family would never again worry about poverty or debt. *Little Women* would make Louisa May Alcott wealthy—and famous. By April 1869, the best-selling author confessed: "People begin to come and stare at the Alcotts. Reporters haunt the place to look at the authoress, who dodges into the woods *à la* Hawthorne" (*Journals* 171). The curiosity of the "Jo worshipers," as Alcott often called them, would continue for the remainder of her life, as "the little story" of the March sisters would make her one of the most well-known and most successful authors of the last half of the nineteenth century.

As the golden age of children's literature dawned in the United States, *Little Women*, a work that many scholars view as one of the first realistic novels for young people, soon became a classic. Over the next century and a half, the novel grew into a cherished book for girls and boys alike. Readers as diverse as Carson McCullers, Gloria Steinem, Theodore Roosevelt, Patti Smith, and J. K. Rowling have declared it a favorite. When Little, Brown, who purchased Roberts Brothers in 1898, decided to celebrate the fortieth anniversary of *Little Women* in 1909 with a new edition of the work, the *New York Times Book Review* wrote: "As a rule the classics of youth scarcely live beyond the immediate generation that welcomed their birth. It is a unique distinction of 'Little Women,' however, that it has never grown old, never appeared antiquated to the youngsters of today, who are rather prone, as a rule, to demand somewhat different literary fare from that which satisfied their elders" (22). From the initial publication of the novel in 1868 until Alcott's death in early 1888, Roberts Brothers printed approximately 200,000 copies of *Little Women* (Myerson and Shealy 69–71). Never out of print, Alcott's classic tale of four New England sisters growing up during and after the Civil War has been published in more than thirty countries around the world. Currently, Amazon.com lists numerous separate editions of *Little Women*, from inexpensive abridged copies for young readers to profusely illustrated deluxe editions. While sales of the book worldwide over the last 150 years cannot be accurately established, one safely can estimate that the number is in the millions.

For many readers, the book's main character—the determined, tomboyish, headstrong Jo March—became a character with whom they formed a personal connection, one that would inspire them to pursue their own dreams.

J. K. Rowling, the author of the Harry Potter series (who goes by Jo), once noted the effect that reading *Little Women* as a child had on her: "My favorite literary heroine is Jo March. It is hard to overstate what she meant to a small, plain girl called Jo, who had a hot temper and a burning ambition to be a writer" (BR8). She found herself in Jo March—as did almost countless thousands of readers around the world.

The afterlife of *Little Women*, however, turned Alcott's "girls' book" into something larger as its story became a part of the culture of the United States and new generations discovered their own version of the March sisters. In 1912, *Little Women* debuted on the Great White Way as a successful Broadway play. Each performance began with the novel's now-famous opening line: "Christmas won't be Christmas without any presents." Versions of this play would be performed around the country for years to come. Meg, Jo, Beth, and Amy also found themselves as part of high culture when the first musical adaptation, *Little Women, an Operetta in Three Acts*, appeared in 1940. Almost sixty years later, a new opera, composed by Mark Adamo, opened to positive reviews in 1998. More contemporary audiences met the March sisters on Broadway in 2005's *Little Women: The Musical*. Its advertisements proclaimed: "Six generations have read this story. This one will sing it."

Film, of all the adaptations of *Little Women*, brought the story of the March sisters to even larger numbers of people. Beginning with two silent productions in 1917 and 1919, the celluloid versions of Alcott's classic opened the doors to the March family home, exposing their lives to more viewers than the readers of the novel. After viewing one of the earliest films of *Little Women*, Julian Hawthorne, in 1922, noted, "These audiences, which laughed and were tearful by turns, were composed mainly of persons who either in their childhood or in maturity had read the book; and of the residue who had not read it, few, I imagine failed to get it out of the local lending library immediately afterward" (190). Even in the early years of the motion picture industry Hawthorne is correct in pointing out that many film viewers would come to the movie because they had enjoyed the novel and, like he, they could compare the two. He is also right that the film itself would send more people in search of the novel, thus ensuring a spike in the book's sales.

Films have given Alcott's *Little Women* more of an audience than book sales would ever achieve. Katharine Hepburn's portrayal of Jo in George Cukor's 1933 RKO production made the actress a star and the film itself a classic. In 1949, the novel saw its first film adaptation in Technicolor, assuring it a place in television reruns for the last half of the twentieth century. June Allyson played Jo, with costars Janet Leigh, Margaret O'Brien, and Elizabeth Taylor as her sisters. By the end of the century, a new generation of filmgoers in 1994 experienced the "queer plays and experiences" that Alcott felt so unsure about just three years after the Civil War. Gillian Armstrong, the first female to direct *Little Women*, once again turned the novel into a successful production, one that earned Winona Ryder an Academy Award nomination for Best Actress for her performance as Jo March. In spring 2018, *Little Women* once again came to the small screen over Mother's Day weekend with a multipart television miniseries for PBS's *Masterpiece*. One hundred years after the first American film version, Greta Gerwig's adaptation of the novel, starring Meryl Streep and Emma Watson, appeared nationwide on Christmas Day 2019, to great popular and critical acclaim. The new film, which was nominated for Best Picture, would also bring Oscar nominations for Best Actress to Saoirse Ronan, who played Jo, and Best Supporting Actress to Florence Pugh for her portrayal of Amy.

With movie tie-ins and other spinoffs and merchandise, *Little Women* still remains popular in the national consciousness. Even the US Postal Service honored *Little Women* (1993), giving it its own stamp. In 2005, Geraldine Brooks won the Pulitzer Prize for her novel *March*, a fictional account of Mr. March's wartime experiences. Most recently, in 2018, PBS's "The Great American Read" placed *Little Women* at number eight in its list of one hundred favorite books that Americans still enjoy reading. And each year, since Orchard House opened as a museum in 1912, thousands of admirers from all around the world (the novel is especially beloved in Japan) make a pilgrimage to Alcott's modest family home in Concord, Massachusetts. When Alcott was born in November 1832, Bronson Alcott wrote his father-in-law, Col. Joseph May, that he hoped his new daughter would eventually "deserve a place in the estimation of society" (*Letters of ABA* 20). With the publication of *Little Women*, Alcott certainly achieved that recognition—and more.

One hundred years after Alcott's birth, in November 1932, the first scholarship on her work appeared. An entire issue of the *Elementary English Review*, a periodical aimed at elementary school teachers, devoted its pages to the author of *Little Women* (Alberghene and Clark xxi). However, treatment of Alcott as a serious writer of fiction still was largely ignored by literary scholars in the twentieth century until the 1940s, when more articles slowly began to appear in academic journals. Largely spearheaded by the scholarship of

Madeleine B. Stern, this mainly biographical and historical focus gradually began to turn the tide against a view of Louisa May as "the children's friend," a title bestowed upon her by Alcott's first biographer, Ednah Dow Cheney. Nevertheless, most of the academy still saw the writer merely as an author of children's literature—a field not worthy of serious scholarship.

However, the emergence of feminism in the 1960s led to a new exploration of women's fiction, which began to bring more interest in Alcott. With the 1975 publication of Stern's first collection of Alcott's sensational stories, *Behind a Mask*, scholars began to see a rich, unexplored area of the author's canon, and it helped spark a new interest in her work. By the 1990s, PhD dissertations and critical articles in scholarly literary journals appeared more frequently, especially with the growth of children's literature as a serious academic pursuit. Over the past fifty years, the majority of literary criticism on *Little Women* has had a decidedly feminist perspective, as evidenced by the publication in 1999 of *Little Women and the Feminist Imagination*, a superb collection of personal essays and critical articles, a work that both surveyed the past and pointed to the future of Alcott studies.

Focus on Alcott and on *Little Women* has only increased in the twenty-first century. Now, as the classic novel recently celebrated its sesquicentennial, this new collection of essays will illustrate the enduring quality and significance of Alcott's "little story." It will demonstrate that this memorable novel is far from the "simplest, most naïve thing imaginable," which Julian Hawthorne declared it to be one hundred years ago (190). *Little Women at 150* contains eight original essays by scholars whose research and writings over the past twenty years have helped elevate Alcott's reputation in the academic community. Utilizing various critical approaches, the essays are not focused on a particular topic or theme. Instead, they are richly eclectic, revealing the complexity and sophistication of Alcott's most famous work. What did Louisa May Alcott create that transformed *Little Women*, a novel about an impoverished family, into one of the classic imaginative works of children's literature? Is *Little Women* still relevant in the twenty-first century? What is the reason for the novel's enduring popularity? Did Alcott's earlier fiction influence her most famous work? What was the effect of *Little Women* on readers and writers in other countries? Why does the character of Jo March resonate so much with readers? Does the novel still have important ideas to convey to young readers on the verge of adulthood? *Little Women at 150* goes far to answer these questions and others.

In the lead essay, the Pulitzer Prize-winning author John Matteson, in a broad examination of the novel's major theme, explores *Little Women*'s social vision, which he links to the ideas expressed by the Puritan John Winthrop in his 1630 sermon "A Model of Christian Charity," where all members of society have a particular purpose or role to contribute to the whole community. Matteson contrasts this vision with that of the Marxist author Friedrich Engels, who, in *The Origin of Family, Private Property and the State* (1884), writes that the housewife—because she is a woman—is not allowed to take part in the transactional economy. With this framework, Matteson examines the social position of the March family, that of the "shabby genteel," where they "may both rise from this stratum or fall further down" but still occupy a position "where one is expected to practice many of the virtues of a higher class." On the other hand, they are also expected to help the desperately poor, like the impoverished German immigrants, the Hummels. Matteson argues that Mrs. March, a victim of the society described by Engels, "uses charity to reassert her individual and social worth," an idea that is passed on to her daughters. But Winthrop's vision of the "economy of charity" alone will not make for a better society, as "entrepreneurship and material production" are also essential. *Little Women*'s social vision, Matteson explains, illustrates "a system of sacrifice for the needy, emanating from the home, [which] has its role to play in counterbalancing and strengthening the transactional economy." And, in the end, it is Amy and Jo, along with their husbands, who demonstrate how this is achieved, especially Jo and Friedrich Bhaer, who broaden the concept of family.

Next, Roberta Seelinger Trites narrows the social vision to a more individual one as she looks at the use of *The Pilgrim's Progress* in *Little Women*. While several critical articles have explored the use of Bunyan's famous allegory in Alcott's novel, Trites connects the Puritan work with the essays of Ralph Waldo Emerson. Noting that Alcott's first novel, *Moods* (1864), was criticized by reviewers for being a transcendentalist work, she suggests that Alcott was more subversive in her story of the March sisters. Trites argues that Alcott employs *The Pilgrim's Progress* "to articulate a number of very Emersonian principles. In that sense, *The Pilgrim's Progress* serves as an intertextual palimpsest painted over various transcendental texts in *Little Women* . . . to hide her Transcendental agenda." As Alcott herself admits in her journal after reading the proofs for part 1 of the novel, the plot is "not a bit sensational, but simple and true, for we really lived most of it" (*Journals* 166).

Thus, fictionalizing her own life experiences and those of her family "rather than 'philosophiz[ing]' to readers," Alcott, Trites posits, uses a work that her reading audience, even the young ones, would know well, "an alternative text to Emerson's essays that superficially demonstrated many of the same values but that was more accessible to juvenile readers: John Bunyan's *The Pilgrim's Progress*." By doing so, Alcott, in *Little Women*, "creates a philosophical space in which her female characters can articulate ideas about language, nature, and self—and without fear of censure."

Narrowing the focus to the individual, Sandra Harbert Petrulionis, in an essay that critiques Alcott's own attitudes about social class, examines Hannah Mullet, one of *Little Women*'s most overlooked characters. Alcott's narrator, she argues, "renders Hannah Mullet utterly unmemorable, to the extent that most readers, and likely a majority of Alcott scholars, would be hard pressed to recall her full name." Exploring a character who has been almost untouched in Alcott scholarship, Petrulionis places the March family housekeeper and cook "in the historical context of mid-nineteenth-century domestic servitude" while also looking closely at the significance of the major scenes of Hannah's appearance in the novel. In her investigation, Petrulionis argues that Hannah "must be viewed as an essential complement to Marmee. Without her bifurcated role as both family intimate and maid-of-all-work, *Little Women*'s beloved mother-of-all-wisdom could not exist."

Turning to another unexplored area of *Little Women* scholarship, Beverly Lyon Clark addresses "the gendering of mobility" in Alcott's novel by examining how illustrators of the novel over the last century and a half help transform meaning to its readers. Here, Clark examines a number of illustrators of *Little Women*, "specifically the gendering of transportation, mechanical and otherwise, as interpreted by [these] illustrators." She also contrasts these illustrations of mobility with those depicting stasis, most notably the house. Among the many artists who have illustrated *Little Women* over the last 150 years, Clark looks at the work of Frank Merrill (1880), Elinore Blaisdell (1946), Reisie Lonette (1950), Mark English (1967), Tasha Tudor (1969), and Hodges Soileau (1985).

Continuing the focus on illustrators while also examining the role of the individual in the wider society, Anne K. Phillips, in her essay, takes readers on a deep dive into the final chapters of *Little Women* and explores how Louisa May Alcott uses "purposeful word selection, contradiction, triangulation, and omission to provoke amusement while also subverting conventional expectations," all the while "offer[ing] meaningful observations about the relationship of an individual to herself, her family, and her community." Phillips also examines how several selected artists depict scenes in the final chapters of the novel, and she interprets what their illustrations suggest. One of the major complaints about *Little Women*, in 1868–69 and now, has been the marriages in the novel, especially Jo March and Friedrich Bhaer's. Alcott's final choices, Phillips argues, show ambivalence about the eventual maturation and marriage of her characters while at the same time "suggest[ting] the ways in which she was rethinking what it means to become a wife and mother and offering a new way of talking about those roles." Paying special attention to Jo and Friedrich's relationship as well as that of Jo and Laurie, Phillips argues that Alcott both "satisf[ies] and thwart[s] reader expectations while also upholding ideals of individualism, liberty, interdependence, and community."

Marriage in the novel also forms the center of Christine Doyle's essay. Here, Doyle, returning the reader once again to the transcendentalist influence on Alcott, explores how Margaret Fuller's "The Great Lawsuit" may have influenced Alcott's writing of *Little Women*, especially 1869's part 2. She notes that *Little Women* "concerns itself with the development of American girls into women in practical ways as Fuller's essay does in theoretical ones." Detailing Fuller's various types of marriage equality, Doyle demonstrates how these are depicted in Alcott's novel, beginning with the marriage of Mr. and Mrs. March and continuing with each of the March sisters' marriages. Fuller's essay "provides a rather specific primer" not only for Jo's marriage, Doyle argues, but also for her "progress toward and preparation for it." And it is Jo and Friedrich's marriage that fulfills Fuller's depiction of "the highest level of equality."

Moving away from specific focus on Alcott's novel to a broader examination of its impact on readers on the opposite side of the globe, *Little Women at 150*'s penultimate essay, by Joel Myerson, examines how Alcott's most famous book influenced a late nineteenth-century writer in Australia. He explores what Beverly Lyon Clark calls a "striking trend a century ago," the publication of books for young readers that she terms "spinoffs, conscious responses to *Little Women*—not books by authors who created their own family stories about the Katy who Did or the Anne who went to Green Gables (although the novel did indeed influence these authors) but rather reworkings of specific Alcott characters and incidents" (*Afterlife* 59). Myerson analyzes, for the first time, one of those "spinoffs" in depth: *Seven Little Australians* by Ethel

Turner. Little known to readers in the United States, *Seven Little Australians*, originally published in 1894, remains one of Australia's most popular works, a novel that has sold over two million copies in the last 125 years. Myerson compares and contrasts *Seven Little Australians* and *Little Women* and the lives of Ethel Turner and Louisa May Alcott—"one a colonial writer confronting colonialism and the other a postcolonial writer reinforcing personal values after the Civil War." In his examination, Myerson "suggest[s] reasons why they ultimately had different approaches to their subjects."

Closing out the collection, Gregory Eiselein goes beyond *Little Women* to make the case that Louisa May Alcott, 150 years after the publication of her classic novel, should be studied and taught as "a major author." Alcott, a writer with a large and varied body of work that is both important to literary studies and artistically admirable, is now a canonical author, he argues, one with a significant collection of scholarly criticism about her fiction and nonfiction. While using *Little Women* as the touchstone for his argument, Eiselein explores Alcott's output in various genres and examines how her reputation has changed and developed over the years, especially in the last quarter of a century. One of the most significant parts of his essay lies in his discussion of how Alcott learned from the novels of Charles Dickens "how to use contraries as her chief stylistic and structural principle, how to combine or yoke together apparent opposites for sentimental, comic, dramatic, or intellectual effect." Looking forward to the future of Alcott studies, especially in the classroom, Eiselein notes that *Little Women*, along with her other literary works, "make[s] a compelling case for the empowerment of women, youth, the marginalized and those who live on modest means."

Little Women at 150 in many ways looks backward and forward in time, not only to the influence of the novel upon readers and writers but also to the future. The scholars here in this volume all suggest, in their various ways, the continuing importance and significance of *Little Women*. When Joel Myerson and I, with the assistance of Madeleine B. Stern, began work on editing Alcott's letters and journals in the mid-1980s, the books and scholarship on *Little Women* and Alcott could fit easily onto one small shelf. But that has changed dramatically over the thirty-five years since. Scholarship on *Little Women* and Alcott's other works only increases year by year. Her influence on popular culture, as Beverly Lyon Clark points out in *The Afterlife of "Little Women,"* still enduringly exists. Anne Boyd Rioux, in *Meg, Jo, Beth, Amy: The Story of "Little Women" and Why It Still Matters* (2018), notes that Alcott's classic novel "unearths the tensions between family and self, sisterhood and separation, growing up and failing to find one's way" (220). Louisa May Alcott herself knew all of those tensions well and embedded them within her "little story." In December 1854, when Alcott placed a copy of *Flower Fables* into her mother's stocking as a gift, she confessed to her "Marmee" that "I hope to pass in time from fairies and fables to men and realities" (*Selected Letters* 11). With the publication of *Little Women* 150 years ago, Alcott realized her hopes—perhaps more than she ever knew. In 1871, Alcott wrote to John Seely Hart, a professor of rhetoric at Princeton University who was preparing *A Manual of American Literature* (1873), which would include a profile on the author: "Over a hundred letters from boys & girls, & many from teachers & parents assure me that my little books are read & valued in a way I never dreamed of seeing them. This success is more agreeable to me than money or reputation" (161). *Little Women at 150*, while championing Alcott's success, helps to reveal the layered complexity and significance of one of the United States' most well-known novels.

Works Cited

Alberghene, Janice M., and Beverly Lyon Clark. "Introduction." *"Little Women" and the Feminist Imagination: Criticism, Controversy, Personal Essays*, edited by Janice M. Alberghene and Beverly Lyon Clark, Garland, 1999, pp. xv–liv.

Alcott, A. Bronson. *The Journals of Bronson Alcott*, edited by Odell Shepard, Little, Brown, 1938.

Alcott, A. Bronson. *The Letters of A. Bronson Alcott*, edited by Richard L. Herrnstadt, Iowa State UP, 1969.

Alcott, Louisa May. *Jo's Boys, and How They Turned Out*. Roberts Brothers, 1886.

Alcott, Louisa May. *The Journals of Louisa May Alcott*, edited by Joel Myerson, Daniel Shealy, and Madeleine B. Stern, Little, Brown, 1989; U of Georgia P, 1997.

Alcott, Louisa May. *Moods*, edited by Sarah Elbert, Rutgers UP, 1991. First published 1864.

Alcott, Louisa May. *The Selected Letters of Louisa May Alcott*, edited by Joel Myerson, Daniel Shealy, and Madeleine B. Stern, Little, Brown, 1987; U of Georgia P, 1995.

Bunyan, John. *The Pilgrim's Progress*, edited by W. R. Owens, Oxford UP, 2003.

Clark, Beverly Lyon. *The Afterlife of "Little Women."* Johns Hopkins UP, 2014.

Clark, Beverly Lyon, editor. *Louisa May Alcott: The Contemporary Reviews*. Cambridge UP, 2004.

Hawthorne, Julian. "The Woman Who Wrote *Little Women*" (1922). Rpt. in *Alcott in Her Own Time*, edited by Daniel Shealy, U of Iowa P, 2005, pp. 189–204.

Myerson, Joel, and Daniel Shealy. "The Sales of Louisa May Alcott's Books." *Harvard Library Bulletin*, n.s., vol. 1, no. 1, 1990, pp. 47–86.

Review of *Little Women*, by Louisa May Alcott. *New York Times Book Review*, 8 Aug. 1908, p. 22.

Rioux, Anne Boyd. *Meg, Jo, Beth, Amy: The Story of "Little Women" and Why It Still Matters*. W. W. Norton, 2018.

Rowling, J. K. "J. K. Rowling: By the Book." *New York Times Sunday Book Review*, 14 Oct. 2012, p. BR8.

Stearns, Frank Preston. *Sketches from Concord and Appledore* (1895). Rpt. in *Alcott in Her Own Time*, edited by Daniel Shealy, U of Iowa P, 2005, pp. 78–88.

Class, Charity, and Coming of Age in Little Women

John Matteson

It is fitting and natural to read *Little Women* as a work with strong elements of spiritual idealism, one that urges the reader to embrace values of self-restraint and generosity at the expense of material self-indulgence. Nevertheless, the novel begins with three successive statements of material want. Meg, aspiring to both fashion and fortune, calls her family's poverty "dreadful" (*Little Women* 11). For Amy, the feeling of having "nothing at all" in the way of worldly products and pleasures is a source of deep injury and resentment. And in the unforgettable line that begins the story, Jo observes, "Christmas won't be Christmas without any presents" (11). It is an instructive sentence for those who, in their condemnations of our own time, routinely cite the materialism of our current Christmases as a specifically modern symptom of social malaise. Jo March, a well-instructed minister's daughter, is no stranger to high-minded thoughts. Nevertheless, there is no fooling her; peace on earth and goodwill toward men have always been easier to observe when there is a feast on one's table and a few treats in one's stocking. Mr. March and his family may be spirits in the material world, but, even on the holiest of days, that world is very much with them.

It is obviously essential to remember Beth's contented murmur that she and her sisters have their parents and one another. The love and community that exist within families form the great moral touchstone of *Little Women*, and Alcott means to suggest that such human ties are at least a partial antidote to the world's temptations. Indeed, one may reasonably argue that she begins her novel with a tableau of wants and deprivations precisely so that she can illustrate how such desires can be overcome by a loving mother and a charitable spirit. Nevertheless, money still counts for a good deal in the novel, and the relative positions of its characters on the economic ladder profoundly shape the relations that develop among them. The consciousness of economic class and its discontents are powerfully present in *Little Women*. More often than not, however, Alcott does not represent the social hierarchy as a systemic evil, inspiring scorn on one side and resentment on the other. To the contrary, wealth—even very modest wealth—is figured as an opportunity for philanthropy. It creates a space for feelings of charity on the part of the givers and gratitude in the hearts of the receivers. Material inequality becomes the grounds for a spiritual symbiosis. Moreover, the degree and willingness of one's generosity becomes a dependable measure of the character's evolving maturity and ability to function in the larger world. Tacitly, the novel's social vision hearkens back to the founding moments of colonial America and the tenets of Puritan charity, wherein the classes were seen, not as forming a system of antagonism and struggle but rather as a mutually beneficial structure, in which every participant had her or his function to perform, thereby giving greater glory to God.

This is the vision that was famously articulated by John Winthrop in his famous sermon aboard the *Arbella*: "A Model of Christian Charity." In *Little Women*, Winthrop's principles are given practical form. Distinctions between rich and poor in the novel are not, by themselves, invidious. They are, instead, the structures that enable Alcott's imagined society to operate as a model of universal goodwill. As in Winthrop's homily, they present a vision of an ideal America.

John Winthrop and the Body of Benevolence

To understand what is truly at stake, both culturally and personally, for Marmee and her daughters in their charitable endeavors, it is useful to refer to two other texts, one that the Alcotts likely knew and one that set forth the condition of Western families at the same time that Louisa was living it. The two texts, which have very little in common, are Winthrop's sermon and Friedrich Engels's *The Origin of Family, Private Property, and the State*. Winthrop offered his paradigmatic statement of his social theory in a lay sermon, delivered as he sailed to America in 1630 aboard the *Arbella*. The sermon remains a foundational statement of the social ethos that the Puritans aspired to establish in the New World. As much as the Declaration of Independence set forth the political ideal toward which America has long striven, "A Model of Christian Charity" has offered a moral yardstick for measuring the success (and failure) of America as a spiritual and social ideal.

In the distinction between rich and poor, Winthrop thought he observed the hand of divine benevolence. In his view, class distinctions were not an inequity but rather an opportunity to express God's love and to fulfill the wisdom of His design. The social classes, he argued, had been instituted by God so "that every man might have need of others, and from hence they might be all knit more nearly together in the bonds of brotherly affection" (Winthrop 215).

It seemed clear to Winthrop that the order within society did not rest solely on different allotments of money but also on the kinds of virtues typically practiced within each social order. The wealthy were endowed with mercy, temperance, and justice, whereas the poor were distinguished by their patience, reverence, and obedience. The two classes differed in their strengths, not the better to help themselves but that they might better serve each other, each supplying the values that the other lacked. Winthrop addressed the greater portion of his remarks to the obligations borne by the wealthy. God commanded that they should "give out of [their] abundance." Indeed, when a brother in the Christian faith was in such deep waters that he could be helped no other way, "We must help him beyond our ability, rather than tempt God" (Winthrop 216).

Quite naturally, Winthrop's ponderings on the interdependencies of society led him to invoke metaphors of a physical body. In their specialized functions, deficiencies, and requirements, the individual members of a society all formed a single body, united by the loving spirit of Christ. The spirit of love gathered men and women together like scattered bones and knitted them together in a single form: the metaphorical body of the Redeemer. To be a part of that body was to experience deep delight. It meant entering into a state in which one sees one's reflection in one's neighbor and discovers that he can love that neighbor in no other way than the way he loves himself.

Essential to that love is a feeling of *connectedness*: nobody (and no body) can function healthily if she "wants [her] proper ligament" (Winthrop 220).

For Alcott in *Little Women*, the problem of ligature is fundamental: how are people of goodwill to bind with one another? It is common and understandable to read *Little Women* as the great American hymn to the nuclear family. Yet Alcott's own experience of family had encouraged her to think of family in less literal, more expansive terms than mere blood relations. At her father's failed commune at Fruitlands in 1843, ten-year-old Louisa was ushered into what he called a consociate family: a large group of people united not by heredity but by shared ideals and a transcendent regard for one another's humanity. When she came to write *Little Women*, she retained the idea that ties within a traditional family were essential, but not sufficient. One had to seek a larger body of relations than could be contained within one's own four walls.

Friedrich Engels and the Imprisoning Home

Engels's depiction of the bourgeois family is, in its emotional tenor, the opposite of the world of *Little Women*, in which Jo is able to exclaim in the final chapter, "I do think that families are the most beautiful things in all the world!" (*Little Women* 375). Like Winthrop, Engels saw societies as hierarchies. Unlike the Puritan, he believed that these hierarchies' features were determined, not by the benevolent will of God but by morally indifferent principles of economics and power. Neither sacred nor resting on a foundation of altruism, the family, in its core meaning and function, "is not that compound of sentimentality and domestic stri[ving] which forms the ideal of the present day" (Engels 121). Rather, its meaning related back to its Latin origins, in which famulus meant "domestic slave" and familia stood for the total number of slaves belonging to a single master (125).

Engels regarded the emergence of the bourgeois family as a sign of nascent civilization; indeed, he called the family "the cellular form of civilized society" (Engels 129). Nevertheless, at the same time that monogamous marriage signaled a great step forward for the species, the gains in stability and prosperity that it enabled had demanded the frustration of female hopes and ambitions. Engels observed that, within the modern bourgeois family, the attentions of the wife were perpetually turned inward and away from the sphere of social action. He wrote that, with the division of labor between domestic work and paid employment outside the home, "household management lost its public character. It no longer concerned society. It became a private service; the wife became . . . excluded from all participation in social production" (137). To carry on the domestic duties of a wife, the woman was driven out of the economy.

Louisa May Alcott's mother, Abba, was acutely aware of the condition of imprisonment that awaited an unwary wife. Ironically, it was never made clearer to her than during the supposedly utopian experiment at Fruitlands. As her husband tried to build the ultimately just society, Abba was asked whether the commune employed any beasts of burden. "Only one woman," came the rueful reply (Matteson 141). If anything, Abba might have preferred to have been driven even farther out of the economy. Bronson Alcott's inability to support the family forced Abba, like it or not, to take up a position in the workforce. However, it is highly significant that, when Abba sought employment during the Alcotts' worst days of poverty in 1850s Boston, she chose to find it in what was then called an "intelligence office"—the period's name for an employment agency. There she found jobs for people less fortunate than herself. Abba's employment was a kind of compensated charitable work; even when circumstances compelled her to work for pay, she preserved some small degree of aristocratic grace by making her work as philanthropic as possible.

The real-life Marmee was in her grave before Engels wrote *The Origin of the Family*. Nevertheless, she had been far more aware of and receptive to economic radicalism than one might naïvely image. While she was working in her intelligence office, just two years after the appearance of *The Communist Manifesto*, Abba firmly denounced the abuses of America's free-market economy. Ferociously, she condemned the wage slavery that stood in wait for the poor immigrants who were flocking to Boston. The industrial North was, in her view, maintaining a "whole system of servitude" that felt hardly better than Southern slavery. "My life," she told her brother Samuel, "is one of daily protest against the oppressions and abuses of Society." Sounding very much like Engels himself, she told her journal, "Incompetent wages for labor performed, is the cruel tyranny of capitalist power over the laborers' necessities. The capitalist speculates on their bones and sinews. Will not this cause Poverty—Crime—Despair?" (Matteson 212).

Louisa May Alcott went for walks in the woods with Thoreau. Emerson encouraged her writing and opened his library to her. And she was, of course, her father's daughter. It is therefore tempting to imagine her childhood influences as almost exclusively transcendental. However, it was not so. The legacies of Puritan thought were all around her and so, too, were the winds of full-blown socialism. Throughout her life, the author of *Little Women* had ample occasion to reflect on social and economic theory, and those reflections are seldom far from the surface in her greatest novel.

A Delicate Balance: The Economics of Charity in *Little Women*

Although finer gradations may be observed, the hierarchy of wealth in *Little Women* has three essential stations. At one pole stand the ease and aristocratic comfort enjoyed by personages like Aunt March and Mr. Laurence. At the other extremity lies the condition of serious need represented by the Hummels in part 1 and, offstage, by the unseen freedmen of part 2. Between them lies the liminal, uncertain ground of the shabby genteel, occupied by the nuclear March family. This middle tier is an uneasy space, the one where future prospects are least settled and one's identity is most up for grabs. One may both rise from this stratum or fall further down. It is a place where one is expected to practice many of the virtues of a higher class. One is required to be well read and respectably mannered. One is expected to be visible in polite society and, on such occasions, to maintain scrupulously the appearance of prosperity. Yet those appearances cover up a reality of bread-and-milk breakfasts and threadbare attire. One's claim to respectability is firmly asserted, but it is secretly precarious.

The March siblings have no trouble in relating intellectually to the upper orders. (Indeed, their childhoods and adolescences are spectacularly literary: *Little Women* quotes or alludes to the work of at least sixty other authors.) The sisters, especially Jo, have more problems in the department of manners. But the real crisis lies in appearances. Meg's disastrous decision to have her hair curled by Jo, instead of a costly professional; the impropriety of Jo's soiled gloves; and the scorch mark on the back of a party dress serve as more than fodder for Alcott's sense of humor. They are subjects of embarrassment and outright shame. And the stakes are potentially high. Even though Marmee assures her girls that they should not marry for money, a fortunate match is the clearest way out of poverty for the Marches, and everyone knows it.

Yet at the same time that the Marches are pressed to conform to the outward graces of the upper classes, their obligations also extend downward; they are morally, if not socially, compelled to share what little they have with the more desperately poor. Readers of *Little Women* find it hard to forget one of the novel's earliest scenes: without complaint, the girls acquiesce to Marmee's hint that they should give up their much-anticipated Christmas breakfast and feed it to the poverty-stricken Hummels. The moment is founded in Christian imagery: Mrs. Hummel, "a poor woman with a little new-born baby," calls to mind at once the image of Mary in the stable (*Little Women* 21). Alcott's reversal is a charming one: whereas the Holy Family represents the origins of all Christian giving, the destitute Germans of Alcott's story receive the March girls' benevolence. A circle of goodwill has been completed.

Yet it is deceptively easy to overlook a few unsettling notes in this set piece of self-surrender. The first of these lies in the specifics of the dialogue in which Mrs. March calls upon her daughters to offer up their breakfast. Her request is greeted with an interval of surprised silence. Although Alcott hastens to add that the four daughters hesitate for "only a minute," a minute is more than long enough for a silence to become uncomfortable. Then, when the girls, led by Jo, agree, Marmee's appreciation feels understated. She responds, not with abundant praise but with a rather cool statement of expectations met, but not exceeded: "I thought you'd do it," is the only recognition of what the girls regard as a considerable sacrifice. The phrase is accompanied by a facial expression that Alcott renders conditional and equivocal: Marmee smiles "as if satisfied." (*Little Women* 21). If one trips slightly over the "as if," the awkwardness is understandable. Is Marmee actually *not* satisfied? Why does Alcott's rendering of the moment shade Marmee away from being a joyous Lady Bountiful and somewhat toward the role of a moral taskmistress? Perhaps the reason is that the work that she expects from her children is as much for their benefit as it is for the Hummels'. Like Alcott's own mother, on whom her character is closely modeled, Marmee knows something about how far one can fall in life when one loses one's moral sense of oneself. She knows that, lacking social advantages, her daughters will need all the moral backbone they can muster to make their ways through life. And she is determined to give it to them.

A telling dissonance awaits in the paragraph in which the girls make their way to the poor family's hovel. Alcott writes, "Fortunately it was early, and they went through back streets, so few people saw them, and no one laughed at the funny party" (*Little Women* 21). Evidently, there is something amiss in the social compact of charity. On the one hand, the March sisters fear ridicule for the poor quality of their best clothing and are perpetually trying to conceal its deficiencies. Yet, as we also discover, they are also potentially the objects of unkind merriment because of their charitable deeds. To help a poor family, one sneaks through alleys in the first hours of daylight, as one might do if one's mission were somehow tawdry or shameful. Curiously, one is supposed to perform good works, and yet one dreads what might happen if one is seen doing them. There is a peculiar embarrassment to helping Marmee perform her merciful errands.

The Hummels themselves are denied constructive agency. Alcott's text never presumes to suggest that any member of the Hummel family might feel the urge to reciprocate the March family's kindness, might be inspired to perform some small good work of her or his own, or might someday rise from her or his helplessness. Perhaps even more interestingly, Alcott does not spend any time at all exploring the reasons that have caused the single-parent Hummels to fail, while her other maternally led family, the Marches, has more than managed to maintain itself. Positioned at the very bottom of the charitable chain, the Hummels are inert and abject: their only function is to express gratitude in their "funny, broken English" (*Little Women* 22). Yet this function, insignificant and passive though it may seem, plays a critical role in the structure of charity in the novel, for charity must have an object. Essential to the Marches' self-regard is their capacity to do for others; in their dire need, the Hummels give the Marches emotional relief from their own creeping sense of deprivation. They also tacitly affirm the Marches' Americanness; the recipients of charity in the novel are frequently figured as either political or ethnic foreigners, and by giving to them, one quietly reinforces one's status on the correct side of the socioeconomic line.

One may sense a note of grim determination in Marmee's charity; it is something she must do in order to preserve her dignity. As long as she can give, she is not poor. Once the sisters have been able to give away their breakfast, we hear no more of Amy's need for Faber pencils or of Jo's pining for a copy of *Undine and Sintram*. Reminded of their comparative good fortune and of the sweet feeling that comes from loving one's neighbor better than oneself, the March sisters again find life bearable. Their opportunity to do good transforms them into the "four merrie[st] people" in town (*Little Women* 22). The feeling of having done good is sincere and beautiful. It is also indispensable to the sisters' happiness.

But, as Alcott realized, the awakening of one's charitable conscience is not a complete recompense for a hungry Christmas morning, and kindness grows tiresome when it only flows downstream from oneself. The episode is incomplete without a matching good work from on high. The March girls are reduced to a slim repast of bread and milk at breakfast, but their supper table is filled with ice cream, cake, and bonbons. The delicacies come, of course, from the munificent Mr. Laurence, who, having gotten wind of the breakfast party at the Hummels', now affirms his link in the charitable chain. Although Mr. Laurence's gift is offered as a reward for the March sisters' virtuous self-denial, it is essential to observe that none of the good works performed in the chapter are presented as obligatory. Characters give without any expectation of specific reward. They partake instead in the shared confidence that the local society will behave as a broader network of kindness, dependent not on quid pro quo exchanges of value but on the shared understanding that giving is good.

It is a potentially fragile faith, as evidenced by the fact that the March sisters fear that someone will observe and laugh at their sacrifices for the Hummels. It is made all the more fragile by the fact that some, even in the Marches' extended family, do not feel bound by the rules of the game. Prominent in this regard is Mr. March's sour-faced relation, Aunt March. *Little Women*, especially since it is a novel for what we now call young adults, is noteworthy in its lack of villains. In its pages, no Injun Joe, Long John Silver, or Lord Voldemort leaps forth to strike terror into juvenile hearts. More concerned with the demons and ogres that live in the dark corners of our hearts, Alcott wanted her characters to battle their human failings rather than personified foes. In the benign world of the novel, Aunt March probably comes as close as anyone to being an antagonist, and, though she is a decidedly mild and comedic one, her petty evils cast much light on Alcott's thoughts on the nexus between love and money.

Aunt March's about-face in the novel's closing pages is, for Alcott, a handy deus ex machina. By placing Plumfield in the hands of Jo, Alcott purchases for her heroine both a measure of worldly security and the means for commencing her own cycle of philanthropy by founding her school for boys. As a plot device, however, Aunt March's death, along with her sudden burst of posthumous generosity toward Jo, whom she never seemed to like all that much, feels contrived and somehow beneath Alcott's skill as an author.

Unlike Mr. Laurence's gifts, which emerge from a perception of the March family's goodness and a selfless desire to reward it, Aunt March's largesse in willing Plumfield to Jo seems to be an expression of whim, disconnected from the system of reciprocal charity on which the novel otherwise runs. And because they do not flow from a desire to perpetuate a cycle of generosity, Aunt March's acts of munificence, which are always either random or, on the other hand, overly calculated, do not express love, but merely power. Moreover, she does not hesitate to use her wealth as an instrument of cruelty, as when she uses her position to judge from on high the foibles of her financially inept nephew and when, most memorably, she threatens Meg with disinheritance in an effort to dissuade her from marrying John Brooke. In this latter instance, there is a kind of reciprocity: if Meg refuses John, a lavish payoff awaits her. But it is the reciprocity of a corrupt bargain.

Alcott attributes Meg's rejection of Aunt March's ultimatum to the "spice of perversity in us, especially when we are young, and in love" (*Little Women* 181). But Meg's reaction is more than mere contrariness. It is the reaction of a young woman rightly aghast at the idea that her choices in love should be the subject of a deal. Alcott uses the episode to illustrate the fallacies of basing human relations on mere economic exchange. Economic marketplaces function on a system of punishment and reward. We perform tasks in exchange for money, and, though we may complain about the adequacy of the compensation, few complain about the basic principle of quid pro quo. Aunt March, however, engages in emotional brokerage; she presumes to buy and sell affections. She deems it within her power and her prerogatives to make marionettes of the hearts she attaches to her purse strings. As she does so, the reader knows at once that she has crossed an inviolable line. By having the older woman repeatedly butcher Meg's suitor's name, Alcott invites us to laugh at the scene. The joke, however, falls flat. It fails to amuse because the chapter is dominated by our awareness that Aunt March has stepped beyond the circle. She has reduced family relations, an object of sanctity in the novel, to the cynical level of a negotiation. In the moral universe of *Little Women*, few sins are more reprehensible than this.

But we return to the subject of charity outside the family in *Little Women*, recollecting for a while the interpretive lens of Engels that has been previously proposed. In *Little Women*, Alcott could not bring herself to show Marmee working for wages. Mrs. March is, in this sense, a victim of the social trap identified by Engels: the strictures imposed on the bourgeois housewife on account of her sex exclude Marmee from the transactional economic life of the community beyond the home. And yet Marmee does work vigorously outside the home, accepting no compensation as she brings comfort to the poor. Not contented to become the kind of domestic slave whom Engels somewhat hyperbolically describes, Marmee uses charity to reassert her individual and social worth. In so doing, she tacitly points to a flaw in Engels's theory of domestic enslavement. Presuming that the only values in society worth considering are those of production and transaction, Engels fails to recognize the value of work that is not performed for financial gain. As Marmee's example illustrates, this kind of work demands to be considered. It brings relief to the recipient and happiness to the donor. At least potentially, it also benefits the economy, giving to the indigent the means that they might use to better their lives. The economy of charity, as envisioned by Winthrop, is not sufficient in itself to establish a successful society: civilizations depend in large part upon the stereotypically masculine tasks of entrepreneurship and material production. Yet, as Alcott's social vision in *Little Women* reveals, a system of sacrifice for the needy, emanating from the home, has its role to play in counterbalancing and strengthening the transactional economy.

Charity, Economics, and the Road to Maturity: The March Sisters

The central problem of *Little Women* is the transition from girlhood to adulthood, and one of the features of *Little Women* that distinguishes it from the most influential American bildungsromans that followed it is the success with which its heroines negotiate the passage. Huckleberry Finn runs away toward an uncertain future in the Territory because the horrors and hypocrisies he has seen are finally too much for him; Holden Caulfield is institutionalized. By contrast, the surviving March sisters emerge from the story well equipped to navigate the grown-up world, and their ability to do so relates directly to their growing ability to practice charity.

This being said, it is an obvious error to regard the novel as a simplistic hymn to the efficacy of good works. Alcott herself had seen ample instances of good deeds that were severely and unjustly punished. The history of her family had been a virtual litany of such situations. In the late 1830s, her father had resisted warnings not to enroll a black child in his school—and the school had foundered when the white families fled en masse. Fruitlands, the Alcotts' supreme attempt at virtuous living, took only seven months to succumb to cold, hunger, and despair. Louisa's younger sister Lizzie delivered food to a penniless family in Walpole, New Hampshire, and contracted the scarlet fever whose complications eventually killed her. As for Louisa herself, her most striking act of self-sacrifice in a noble cause—her service as an army nurse in the Civil War—had also led to a life-threatening illness, contracted in her hospital. As Louisa hovered between life and death, stricken by typhoid pneumonia, her mother proclaimed that she had had enough of doing good works and the bitter rewards that had come with them: "We have been cruelly dealt with by [the world], and owe it no more sacrifices of flesh and blood. If we have sinned greatly against the Lord and these are the compensations he takes, he is welcome and I am sure satisfied if the amount of personal suffering and misery is the true test of the penalty" (Matteson 287). Yet no matter how much Louisa's belief in loving self-sacrifice may have been challenged, that faith was never dislodged. Throughout her fiction, the capacity to do cheerfully for others what they cannot accomplish for themselves remains the most reliable measure of a character's maturity.

In this regard, Meg's capacity is the least developed, and her mature life is, correspondingly, the most frustrated. Meg is easily the most domestic of the surviving little women, and the sphere of her generosity is more or less defined by John, Demi, and Daisy. Meg's professed "great wish is to be to [her] husband and children" what Marmee has been to hers (*Little Women* 308). Alcott chooses not to imagine for Meg an existence beyond the one in which a crisis arises when the jelly refuses to gel.

In judging Meg's limitations, one must be cautious: to what extent is it merely a modern prejudice that may lead a twenty-first-century reader to discredit the happiness that Meg finds in the small but reassuring space of hearth and home? We know that, in real life, Louisa sometimes envied the station in life that her sister Anna, Meg's alter ego, achieved. The pleasures of writing and publication sometimes looked pale in comparison to the satisfactions of Anna, snugly nestled with her husband and young sons. "She is a happy woman!" Louisa told her journal. "I sell *my* children, and although they feed me, they don't love me as hers do" (*Journals* 163). When, in *Little Women*, Alcott calls Meg happy, which she does with an insistence that rises almost to stridency, she is not deviating from her assessment of her actual sister.

Nevertheless, although Alcott declares with raw determination that Meg is happy, even she seems to lose interest in Meg in part 2 of the novel. Accorded a paltry number of chapters after her marriage to John, Meg becomes a background figure. The thinness of her existence becomes especially evident for someone who has, as I have, selected illustrations for an annotated edition of the novel. For Amy in part 2, the pertinent images range from the French royal family and the empress of Hawai'i to Goethe's house and the promenades of Nice; the question for an editor is which pictorial splendors one dares to leave out. On the other hand, one struggles to keep the margins of Meg's pages from remaining a host of frustrating blanks. Meg is, as Alcott tells us, "safe from the restless fret and fever of the world." However, the reader well knows that Marmee raised her daughters for something more than safety. Meg's development feels truncated, and it feels so in large part because her charity both begins and ends at home. She is the image par excellence of the entrapment that Engels outlines in *The Origin of the Family*.

As Meg's trajectory suggests, the failure to engage charitably with the larger world imposes a cost upon one's inner growth. Conversely, however, taking an active part in the chain of charity guarantees no happy ending in the universe of *Little Women*. Beth, the one March sister who is fated never to reach adulthood, is literally destroyed by her efforts at charity. In assigning this outcome to Beth's story, Alcott intended no irony; rather, Beth's decline and death form one of the threads of her plot that run closest to the Alcotts' real-life story. Although there are moral lessons aplenty to be drawn from Beth's demise, surely Alcott was not cautioning her readers against kindness. It seems that, to understand Beth's lessons correctly, we need first to free ourselves from the assumption that Alcott saw Beth's end as a wholly negative outcome. I freely acknowledge that Beth's departure vies with Harriet Beecher Stowe's dispatching of Little Eva as the most memorably tear-jerking moment in nineteenth-century US literature, but bear with me.

While we may reflexively regard death as a negative outcome, no matter what the circumstances, there is ample evidence that Alcott did not share this assumption. From the death of John in *Hospital Sketches* to the passing of David Sterling in *Work* and in other writings besides, Alcott chose not to represent the death of a virtuous person as an occasion for unmitigated grief. Believing as she did in the glorious reality of a life to come, Alcott often saw death, not as a tragedy but as a transfiguration—the natural next step of an elevated soul toward an upward destiny. In the wake of Lizzie Alcott's death, Louisa was, of course, devastated. Nevertheless, she remained capable of seeing her sister's passing as a positive event. In her journal, Alcott called Lizzie's death "a liberator for her, a teacher for us." A month later, she observed that her sister was "nearer and dearer than before; and I am glad to know she is safe from pain and age in some world where her innocent soul must be happy." Louisa had never considered death terrible, but now she found it "beautiful . . . friendly and wonderful" *Journals* 89). Alcott imparts this same attitude into the death scene of the fictional Beth, for whom death comes as "a benignant angel," whose ministrations make the patient "well at last" (*Little Women* 328). And, to this author's knowledge, never did Alcott blame Lizzie's charitable services to the poor family in Walpole for her sister's untimely death.

It seems to have been clear, to Alcott at least, that the real tragedy of Lizzie and Beth was not that they engaged in too great a charitable relation with the world, but that they *were not sufficiently attached* to the larger world to want to remain here. Gifted with a naturally charitable spirit, Lizzie/Beth finds no adequate way to translate that spirit into action beyond the domestic sphere. As the real-life Lizzie languished, several months before her death, a worried Louisa wrote, "I fear she may slip away; for she never seemed to care much for this world beyond home" (*Journals* 85). Beth March shares this inability to situate herself successfully in the world. For some readers, the true moment when Beth's tragedy becomes apparent is not in her death scene, but rather in a confession she makes to Jo some chapters earlier: "I'm not like the rest of you; I never made any plans about what I'd do when I grew up; . . . I couldn't seem to imagine myself anything but stupid little Beth, trotting about at home, of no use anywhere but there" (*Little Women* 294–95). Whether Beth is being fair to herself in so harshly deprecating her position as the Angel in the House may be debated. What matters more crucially is that she believes herself when she does so. With neither the economy of production or the economy of charity satisfactorily open to her, she has no path before her in the novel.

The two sisters who achieve the fullest measure of adulthood in *Little Women*, Jo and Amy, arrive at their maturity through a combination of good works and productivity. Of the two metamorphoses, Amy's is arguably the more striking. She begins the novel as the most childish of the March sisters, both in years and in her sense of her economic self. When we meet her, she is nothing other than a consumer. In a limited sense, Amy appears early in the novel to be a true female offspring of *Homo economicus*: she is almost obsessively engaged in the market economy of the school playground, the site of robust commodities markets in pencils, paper dolls, and pickled limes. But these exchanges only gratify her selfishness, which Alcott establishes as her defining character flaw. Amy's will, which she writes in melodramatic response to Beth's illness, might be expected to be a document of generosity. Instead, it is a comic device, masterfully deployed by Alcott to lampoon the character's self-absorption.

Nevertheless, although it takes time, Amy learns better than any of her siblings how her society functions as a body of charitable relations. Her metamorphosis becomes apparent toward the end of the "Calls" chapter, during her conversation with Jo, Aunt March, and Aunt Carrol—the discussion on the basis of which the aunts decide that Amy will go to Europe and Jo will stay home. Jo unwittingly forfeits her chance to travel by replying brusquely to her aunt's questions and by admitting her failure to learn French, but other factors are also at work. In the scene, Jo vents her resentment regarding the upcoming fair that the wealthy Mrs. Chester has organized to benefit the freedmen. She detects an unbearable hauteur in the Chesters' invitation to join in the event: she hates to be patronized and bristles at the "great favor" the Chesters are performing in asking her to help (*Little Women* 236). Amy, who as a child regarded the world of the wealthy "with an injured sniff," sees no such condescension in the invitation (11). She realizes that in working at the fair she is helping not only the Chesters but the deserving poor. As she sums up the situation, "Patronage don't trouble me when it is well meant" (236).

Then as now, Americans lived their lives in an attempt to balance two contradictory desires. Our culture exhorts us to distinguish ourselves, to rise above the mass and set ourselves apart by our individual achievements. Yet at the same time we crave community and belonging, and we spend much of our lives looking for the secret to having it both ways. Jo's error in Aunt March's parlor is her moving too far in the direction of self-reliance. She declares, "I don't like favors: they oppress and make me feel like a slave; I'd rather do everything for myself, and be perfectly independent" (*Little Women* 236). Her little speech is probably the most crystalline statement of Jo's character in the novel. However, although she intends her miniature manifesto as a positive statement about herself, what she describes is, in the universe of *Little Women*, a damning flaw. Somewhat unfairly, it identifies her, not as an admirably bold adventurer but as a "haughty, uninteresting creature" (237). The ideal goal in the novel is not to achieve Emersonian self-reliance but rather Winthropian interdependence: doing for others and then receiving from different others with an identical spirit of grace and gratitude.

"[No] Greater Happiness than This": A Philanthropic Ending

Reviewing *Little Women*, the critic for *Putnam's Magazine* observed that Alcott's work differed from previous "juvenile books" in that it declined to define duty as "doing what you don't want to" (Clark 67). The reviewer chose not to identify what definition of duty Alcott had substituted for the assumed one. If he had, however, it might have been something like "doing what is best for all, because you have discovered that that course of action is best for you as well." To truly perceive one's interconnection with the social whole is the foundation of duty in *Little Women*, and this idea was in Alcott's mind long before she wrote her greatest novel. And that belief began with her broadly encompassing concept of family.

Alcott was raised on the belief that the family is the essential building block of charity. Her father's schools in Boston, which always included a highly accomplished female assistant like Elizabeth Palmer Peabody or Margaret Fuller, were consciously modeled on the two-parent family. At Fruitlands, the commune members regarded one another as a "consociate family." In Bronson Alcott's ideal vision, a family was a unit that worked together for the larger benefit of society; the love and support shared by all within the structure would eventually and naturally throw its beneficence outward, both through good works and through the shining influence of its own example. In the closing chapters of *Little Women*, two couples—Amy and Laurie, and Jo and Professor Bhaer—ascend in the direction of this ideal philanthropy. The Laurences have vowed to use their wealth to subsidize struggling female artists, and the Bhaers have founded their school for boys at Plumfield. Of the two projects, the one nearer to Alcott's idea of the summum bonum is Plumfield, for it, like Fruitlands, is modeled on the family.

Significantly, the arrivals of both Amy and Jo at this pinnacle of humane development are stories of voyage and return. Both women have become prepared for their lives of generosity only after they have ventured forth on their own to test their abilities in the larger world: Amy with her pursuit of an artistic career in Europe and Jo with her brush with literary fame in New York. Self-reliance in *Little Women*, though it comes under critical scrutiny, is by no means dead or entirely discredited. To the contrary, Alcott implies that a person of talent should seize the opportunity to discover just how far her talents can take her, not only because of the successes that might ensue but also because of the wisdom that comes with discovering one's limitations.

Amy, having given her best efforts to developing as a painter, realizes amid the glories of Rome that "talent isn't genius, and no amount of energy can make it so" (*Little Women* 317). For Amy in her younger incarnation, this realization would have been the stuff of tragedy. For the mature young woman, it is a simple coming to terms with reality. Having won both Laurie's hand and his fortune, she resolves that, if she herself is not a vessel of genius, she can find women of stronger ability, "put out my hand and help them, as I was helped" (357). And in this resolve, she finds her apotheosis.

Jo nearly falls short of this kind of self-realization. Left stunned and directionless by the loss of Beth, her works of pulp fiction denounced by Professor Bhaer, she nearly retreats into something resembling the domestic dead end that has claimed her older sister. It should be noted here that Jo has done more than any of her siblings to contribute to what Engels called "social production." In her stories for the penny press, she has created an object of commerce for which people have been willing to pay. "If there is a demand for it," Jo observes, "I don't see any harm in supplying it" (*Little Women* 280). However, as Professor Bhaer sternly observes, the amoral logic of the marketplace is an inadequate test of value. The public also demands whiskey, he reminds her, but respectable people feel no compulsion to sell it. Engels, too, disapproved the abuse of alcohol, and he indicted the social conditions that drove the proletariat to drink. Yet Alcott was possibly even more assertive than Engels in pointing out that some kinds of social production do not generate wealth. They generate, to use John Ruskin's term, "illth" (Ruskin 105). Where the goods produced were ones of negative utility, Alcott preferred no production at all.

Jo almost talks herself into believing that the "something splendid" for which she has always prepared herself is "to devote her life to father and mother, trying to make home as happy to them as they had to her" (*Little Women* 339). If such were the end of Jo's story, one might be moved to tears over her defeat. The "splendid" act of helping one's parents is certainly noble in its fashion. Yet for Jo it would have signaled a Beth-like retreat from the world and an abdication, not only of her powers of socioeconomic production but also of her function in the figurative body of charity in which John Winthrop discerned the body of Christ. But the spirit of both producing and giving outside the home does not die inside Jo. We discover in the final chapter that her idea for Plumfield was present all along: it is no new idea of hers, but rather "a long-cherished plan," waiting only for the opportunity to bring it to life (374). The nuance is important, for through it Alcott counsels us that, in a good person, the charitable spirit is not something that arises only once we have money and need to think of something to do with it. It emerges, instead, from a *preexisting* desire to give that waits to be awakened by circumstance, like a dormant seed in the spring rain.

Current readers tend often to conclude that Jo's founding of Plumfield is itself an unacceptable retreat. They lament her abandonment of her writing career, brought on by the masculine judgments of her husband. Tending to forget Laurie's foundation for the support of artistic women, they decry the fact that Plumfield, in its earliest incarnation, caters only to the needs of boys. Such a reading misses the very point of Alcott's moral vision: we rightly measure our achievements, not by the extent to which they fulfill our selfish ambitions but by the benefit, both material and spiritual, that we bring to others. And, of course, those who condemn Jo's seeming surrender tend to be those who have not read the entire *Little Women* trilogy. By the time described in the last volume, *Jo's Boys*, Plumfield has grown from a boys' school to a fully coeducational, sexually egalitarian college, where young women study to become doctors and proudly thump the boys on the tennis courts. As for Jo herself, her middle age has been enriched by the success of a novel that, very much like *Little Women*, has unexpectedly "sailed into the public favor, and [come] home heavily laden with a . . . cargo of gold and glory" (*Jo's Boys* 46). Jo's redemption is finally material as well as spiritual.

The Alcott family aspired to utopia. In a world of war, disease, and unpaid debts, they found their hoped-for heaven of good works impossible to achieve. Yet in her writings, Louisa May Alcott was free to imagine a utopia of the heart in which material productivity could freely combine with the blessings of charity to realize the ideals of a great societal family. Her father's Temple School, the commune at Fruitlands, and the Union Hotel Hospital where Nurse Alcott worked herself almost to death to create a space for grace and healing in the midst of pain and horror—all these are long gone. But the little glimpse of moral paradise in Alcott's novels remains, and it always rewards the weary visitor.

Works Cited

Alcott, Louisa May. *Jo's Boys, and How They Turned Out.* Boston: Roberts Brothers, 1886.
Alcott, Louisa May. *The Journals of Louisa May Alcott,* edited by Joel Myerson, Daniel Shealy, and Madeleine B. Stern, Little, Brown, 1989; U of Georgia P, 1997.
Alcott, Louisa May. *Little Women, or, Meg, Jo, Beth and Amy,* edited by Anne K. Phillips and Gregory Eiselein, Norton Critical Edition, W. W. Norton, 2004.

Clark, Beverly Lyon, editor. *Louisa May Alcott: The Contemporary Reviews*. Cambridge UP, 2004.

Engels, Friedrich. *The Origin of Family, Private Property, and the State*. International Publishers, 1972.

Matteson, John. *Eden's Outcasts: The Story of Louisa May Alcott and Her Father*. W. W. Norton, 2007.

Ruskin, John. *Unto This Last: Four Essays on the First Principles of Political Economy*. Wiley, 1886.

Winthrop, John. "A Model of Christian Charity." *The Norton Anthology of American Literature*. 5th ed., W. W. Norton, 1: 215, 1998.

Louisa May Alcott's Emersonian Use of *The Pilgrim's Progress*
Little Women as Palimpsest

Roberta Seelinger Trites

In an incident of literary history that is now infamous among Alcott scholars, Henry James criticized Louisa May Alcott's first novel, *Moods* (1864), for being neither as philosophical as it purports to be nor as experienced a reflection on human nature as it could be: "Has Miss Alcott proposed to herself to give her story a philosophical bearing? We can hardly suppose it" (qtd. in Clark 35). He continues: "The two most striking facts with regard to 'Moods' are the author's ignorance of human nature, and her self-confidence in spite of this ignorance" (qtd. in Clark 38).[1] James would have known that Alcott's sense of philosophy was influenced by her well-known relationships to many transcendentalists: Ralph Waldo Emerson was her neighbor; her father, Bronson Alcott, was a close friend of Emerson; and Henry David Thoreau was Alcott's schoolteacher for a short time during her childhood (Urbanski 324). Margaret Fuller was a frequent visitor to the Alcotts' home in Louisa's childhood. Alcott's novel *Moods* signals its connection to transcendentalism early in the text, for it employs as its epigraph a quotation from Emerson's "Experience" (1844): "Life is a train of moods like a string of beads; and as we pass through them they prove to be many colored lenses, which paint the world their own hue, and each shows us only what lies in its own focus."[2]

Moods, however, also includes some intertextual references to John Bunyan's *The Pilgrim's Progress* (1678) along with its references to Emerson. Indeed, *The Pilgrim's Progress*, rather than Emerson, supplies the epigraph for Alcott's next major novel, *Little Women* (1868, 1869). Given the differences between Emerson's and Bunyan's religious philosophies, these epigraphic choices seem, at first glance, to be almost antithetical. Closer investigation, however, reveals that in *Little Women*, Alcott uses *The Pilgrim's Progress* to articulate a number of very Emersonian principles. In that sense, then, *The Pilgrim's Progress* serves as an intertextual palimpsest painted over various transcendentalist texts in *Little Women*.

Sandra M. Gilbert and Susan Gubar define the palimpsest as a typical strategy for women writing in the nineteenth century. A palimpsest is a text "whose surface designs conceal or obscure deeper, less accessible (and less socially acceptable) levels of meaning" (73). Thus, Alcott appears to have used *The Pilgrim's Progress* to hide her transcendental agenda, lest she again be accused of being too "philosophical."

Alcott's feat in putting the Puritan text *The Pilgrim's Progress* to transcendental uses becomes clear from studying her biography and her first two novels: *Moods* and *Little Women*. In the following sections, then, I will demonstrate the relationship between Alcott's relationship to transcendentalism, specifically as it was articulated by Emerson, and her relationship to *The Pilgrim's Progress*. Ultimately, in painting the puritanical allegory *The Pilgrim's Progress* over Emersonian philosophy, Alcott creates a philosophical space in which her female characters can articulate ideas about language, nature, and self—and without fear of censure.

Alcott and Emerson

Alcott herself was no avid fan of philosophy. She claimed that she did not understand her father's transcendentalism, and she did not seem to have much respect for philosophers in general because she thought reformers did more for the world than philosophers (*Selected Letters* 251).[3] Moreover, the transcendentalists, notably Emerson, were reluctant to advocate women's suffrage, and Alcott would have understood the intellectual tensions she witnessed that occurred between Emerson and Fuller and between her father and Elizabeth Peabody (Crouse 259–79; Matteson 74–80).

Emerson is thus a notable exception to Alcott's open disdain for philosophers. As her neighbor, her mentor, and her father's closest friend and benefactor, Emerson's life was intertwined with the Alcotts from the days of Louisa's childhood, and she provides ample evidence of his influence in her journals and letters.[4] The year she turned twenty, she "made a resolution to read fewer novels, and those only of the best"; she then listed "Emerson's poems" among the list of "books I like" (*Journals* 67–68). In a letter, she counseled a friend to "read Ralph Waldo Emerson, and see what good prose is" and then called his poetry "the best . . . we have" (*Selected Letters* 231). Later in her life she wrote: "Never a student, but a great reader. . . . My library consists of Goethe, Emerson, Shakespeare, Carlyle, Margaret Fuller, and George Sand" (296).

Although she claimed that Goethe became her chief idol after Ralph Waldo Emerson gave her *Wilhelm Meister* in 1847, in 1860 she proclaimed that Emerson himself was "the god of my idolatry, and has been for years" (*Journals* 60, 99). When he died in 1882, she referred to him as "my minister & friend" (*Selected Letters* 302) and described him as:

> our best & greatest American. . . . The nearest & dearest friend father has ever had, & the man who has helped me most by his life, his books, his society. I can never tell all he has been to me from the time I sang Mignon's song under his window, a little girl, & wrote letters a la Bettine to him, my Goethe, at 15, up through my hard years when his essays on Self Reliance, Character, Compensation, Love & Friendship helped me to understand myself & life & God & Nature. (*Journals* 234)

That Louisa Alcott learned about "life & God & Nature" from Emerson while simultaneously revering him is clear.

When Alcott was twelve, she recorded in her journal a description of her religious conversion that echoes Emerson's understanding of the relationship between nature and divinity. Although Alcott would have had more conversations about religion with her father than with Emerson, by 1845, the friendship between Emerson and Bronson had created such an interdependency between their philosophies that it seems quite likely that Louisa would have also read and internalized transcendentalist ideas as they were expressed in Emerson's *Nature* (1835).[5]

> I had an early run in the woods before the dew was off the grass....
>
> It seemed like going through a dark life or grave into heaven beyond. A very strange and solemn feeling came over me as I stood there, with no sound but the rustle of the pines, no one near me, and the sun so glorious, as for me alone. It seemed as if I *felt* God as I never did before, and I prayed in my heart that I might keep that happy sense of nearness in my life. (*Journals* 57)

As Emerson puts it in *Nature*: "The happiest man is he who learns from nature the lesson of worship" (1: 37). Alcott also described Emerson's religious philosophy in terms of pantheism:

> He is called a Pantheist or believer in Nature instead of God. He was truly *Christian* & saw God *in* Nature.... finding strength & comfort in the sane, sweet influences of the great Mother as well as the Father of all. I too believe this, & when tired, sad, or tempted find my best comfort in the woods, the sky, the healing solitude that lets my poor weary soul find the rest, the fresh hope, or the patience which only God can give us. (*Selected Letters* 277)

Emerson's belief in the divinity within the "each and all" gave Alcott an understanding of God that she found comforting and accessible—and one that had a female face in the form of Nature as "Mother." Alcott frequently articulates this understanding in her early novels. For example, the protagonist of *Moods*, Sylvia Yule, observes a character named Adam resting by a riverside and charming birds into eating out of his hands: "It was a pretty picture for the girl to see; the man, an image of power, in his hand the feathered atom, that, with unerring instinct, divined and trusted the superior nature which had not yet lost its passport to the world of innocent delights that Nature gives to those who love her best" (55). Appreciating nature for its transcendent possibilities provided some of Alcott's early characters with an improved sense of moral intuition.

Alcott and *The Pilgrim's Progress*

When Alcott was twenty-six, she wrote about owing "much of my education" to Emerson (*Journals* 95). Alcott's love of *The Pilgrim's Progress*, however, preceded her love of Emerson. When she was eleven and her family was participating in Fruitlands, a loosely transcendentalist commune that failed within a year, she wrote in her diary, "I did my lessons, and walked in the afternoon. Father read to us in dear Pilgrim's Progress" (47). In her Christmas entry that same month, she transcribed into her journal five poems from *The Pilgrim's Progress*. Years later, when she was editing her own journals, Alcott added: "The appropriateness of the song at this time was much greater than the child saw. She never forgot this experience" (50). The "experience" that Alcott would never forget was the failure of Fruitlands. At the age of eleven, Alcott witnessed her father's severe depression as his ideals began to falter.[6] He never again held a full-time job and was supported by his wife, his daughters, and friends such as Emerson for the rest of his life.

To help the Alcott family, Emerson eventually and quietly secured a sinecure for Bronson as the superintendent of the Concord Public Schools. At the end of the school year festival in 1861, "One school to whom Father had read Pilgrim's Progress told the story, one child after the other popping up to say his or her part; and at the end a little tot walked forward, saying with a pretty air of wonder,—'And behold it was all a dream'" (*Journals* 104).[7] When the town's schoolchildren then presented Bronson with copies of *The Pilgrim's Progress* and some poetry, "Father was much touched and surprised, and blushed and stammered like a boy, hugging the fine books while the children cheered till the roof rung" (104). Alcott reported this event, with its confluence of Emerson and *The Pilgrim's Progress*, in the same journal entry in which she also describes her first serious revision of *Moods* (103–4). As early as 1861, then, Emerson and *The Pilgrim's Progress* mingled in her mind during her composition of *Moods*.

A Christian allegory written by Bunyan while he was imprisoned for his religious convictions, *The Pilgrim's Progress* traces, in book 1, a character named Christian on his path to the Celestial City and eternal salvation. Following standard allegorical form, the characters and settings are personifications of various traits or tribulations they encounter. Before Christian leaves his hometown, the City of Destruction, Evangelist gives the pilgrim a roll of paper on which is written "Fly from the Wrath to Come" (11). Christian's wife and children refuse to accompany him at this time, but neighbors vow to follow him and drag him home. Christian convinces them to accompany him, but they fall into the Slough of Despond, and Christian, too, begins to "sink in the Mire" (16). A character named Help shows him the way out of the Slough, and they travel together; Christian also travels with a dear friend named Faithful and another named Hopeful. On the journey, Christian travels through the Hill of Difficulty to the House Beautiful, the Valley of the Shadow of Death, and Vanity Fair. When he is imprisoned in the Doubting Castle, the key called "Promise" helps him escape. In the final scene, he reaches the Celestial City with the help of his friend Hopeful.

In book 2, his wife, Christiana, journeys with their four sons, and they are also accompanied by her friend Mercy. They travel through many of the same places Christian has been, and their guide is named Greatheart, who also appears in book 1. The four sons get married as part of their pilgrimage, and eventually the whole band reaches the River of Death in Beulah. Christiana and various pilgrims are welcomed to the Celestial City, but the sons and their wives and children remain on the side of the living to continue spreading the gospel.

Theologically, *The Pilgrim's Progress* demonstrates the importance of grace in the individual's path to salvation (Hinson 257, 258). Moreover, the focus on Christiana's pilgrimage in the second half of the allegory emphasizes Bunyan's belief in the importance to both males and females of following the path to spiritual redemption (Phillips 216). Although Bunyan was committed, like Emerson, to the idea that each individual must effect his or her own relationship with God, Bunyan's theology was far more influenced by Calvinism than Emerson's. While Bunyan believed that faith in Christ's divinity offers the pilgrim the only path to God's grace, Emerson asserts in "The Divinity School Address" that Christ was a "true man," that is, not a god, and that historical Christianity "is not the doctrine of the soul but an exaggeration of the personal, the positive, the ritual" (1: 82). Emerson condemns the conversion experience: "To aim to convert a man by miracles, is a profanation of the soul" (1: 83). True conversion comes from understanding the divinity within: "The time is coming when all men will see, that the gift of God to the soul is not a vaunting, overpowering, excluding sanctity, but a sweet, natural goodness, a goodness like thine and mine, and that so invites thine and mine to be and to grow" (1: 83). Emerson's emphasis on the importance of moral intuition over church doctrine shares with Bunyan a theology that allows women to have an independent relationship with God that is not necessarily dependent on the intervention of a patriarchal church structure. Nevertheless, Bunyan would have found Emerson's denial of Christ's divinity and his downplaying of scripture to be apostasy.

As it happens, Emerson appears to have had little admiration for Bunyan other than for his skills in writing allegory and for his ethics despite adversity. In *Early Lectures*, Emerson praises Sir Walter Scott's allegorical style using Bunyan's name as a synonym for allegorical structures (260–61). Emerson also praises Bunyan as one of the "ethical writers" who satisfy "the English mind . . . thirsty for this [ethical] truth" (361). Emerson, however, had little else to say about Bunyan, although he, like most other American intellects of the time, certainly knew the allegory well.

The Pilgrim's Progress was strong in its sales in the United States since three years after its initial publication in 1678, and Luther Mott lists the book as one of eight best sellers in the United States in the seventeenth century (19, 303). During the 1820s, the American Tract Society and the American Sunday School Union began a wholesale effort to make the allegory available to as many readers as possible, and by the 1850s traveling panoramas and murals illustrating *The Pilgrim's Progress* toured a variety of cities on the east coast (MacDonald, "Case" 29). A new round of sales seems to have been inspired by the ending of the Civil War when cheap editions were issued (29). Even more important, *The Pilgrim's Progress* was revised into a new edition for children in 1866, indicating how available Bunyan's tale was to Alcott's juvenile reading audience by the time book 1 of *Little Women* was published in 1868. In addition, Routledge first published Mary Godolphin's *The Pilgrim's Progress in Words of One Syllable* in 1869, coinciding with the year book 2 of *Little Women* was published.

Alcott and *Moods*

Before the Civil War had even ended, however, Alcott published the novel she had been working on for at least four years, *Moods*. Clearly influenced by transcendentalism, and especially Emerson, *Moods* explores the concept of a woman's spirituality in terms of an individual pilgrimage. In the 1864 version of that novel, Sylvia Yule is a young woman involved in a love triangle with an older and emotionally stable man, Geoffrey Moor, and a younger, more idealistic and temperamental man, Adam Warwick, who is clearly modeled on Henry David Thoreau (S. Elbert xxx). Believing that Adam, the man she loves more passionately, is already committed to another marriage, Sylvia agrees to a companionate marriage with an Emersonian figure, Geoffrey. When Adam returns unmarried and expecting to wed Sylvia himself, she laments the youthful impulsiveness that has led her to marry for stability. Geoffrey, sensing something is missing in their relationship, confronts Sylvia, who admits to loving Adam. All three of the lovers involved in the triangle consult the wisest person in the book, Faith Dane, who was inspired by Margaret Fuller (Seelye 144). Based on Faith Dane's advice, Geoffrey gives Sylvia her freedom. He then heads to Europe to fight for Italy's freedom—and because Sylvia feels she cannot marry Adam at this point, he, too, goes to fight for Italy. Eventually, Adam and Geoffrey sail back to the States in a boat that sinks "in sight of shore," evoking Fuller's death (205). Adam sacrifices his life to save Geoffrey from drowning—who then hastens to his wife's side, only to find her dying, although they are reconciled in the moments before her death.

In choosing for the novel's epigraph Emerson's quotation from "Experience," Alcott privileges one of his most troubled essays.[8] Emerson therein describes life as a journey in which we are sometimes connected to and sometimes disconnected from the significance of our experiences.

Alcott uses the Emersonian concept of "self-reliance" to imply that both men and women can attain emotional stability and maturity. Although *Moods* twice describes Adam as self-reliant (38, 158) and Sylvia, in her immaturity, as "not yet self-reliant" (84), the character Faith Dane is granted that most Emersonian of compliments: she is "a self-reliant soul" (144). This idea of self-reliance leads Helen Deese to analyze *Moods* in terms of transcendentalism ("Louisa" 447), and Sarah Elbert also acknowledges as much (xvi). That said, Bunyan's influence undergirds the way individuals experience their pilgrimage so that they can earn their own redemptions in *Moods*. As Alcott's character Adam puts it, the most enviable people are those who "work out their own salvation" (69). Later, he tells Sylvia, "like that other wandering Christian, I cried out, submitted, and was the meeker for it" (127). The text describes Adam in terms of the relationship between moral intuition and self-reliance: "For to those who harbor the strong virtues with patient zeal, no lasting ill can come, no affliction can wholly crush, no temptation wholly vanquish" (131); he is "a strong soul, with the wisdom of a deep experience, genial with the virtues of an upright life, devout with that humble yet valiant piety which comes through hard-won victories over 'the world, the flesh, and the devil'" (203). With their focus on the relationship between virtue, independence, and a strong soul, both passages evoke Emerson, just as both also evoke Bunyan with their concern about temptation and the devil.

Sarah Elbert identifies exactly how Alcott's first novel relies on *The Pilgrim's Progress* (xxxv). When Alcott alludes to *The Pilgrim's Progress* in *Moods*, she does so to evoke either the metaphor of pilgrimage or a metaphor of specific allegorical attributes, such as "Poverty" or "Opulence" (82). In *Moods*, Alcott uses *The Pilgrim's Progress* more for its specific object lessons than its philosophy, whereas transcendentalism informs the book on many ideological levels.

For example, before Sylvia dies, she narrates to her husband an apocryphal vision she has dreamed. In her dream, she is standing on a rooftop of a "shadowy city" on the last day of the world, and all she can see is a sea of "human faces," while the letters of the word "Amen" appear in the sky "burning with a ruddy glory":

> I felt no fear, only the deepest awe, for I seemed such an infinitesimal atom of the countless host that I forgot myself. Nearer and nearer came the flood, till its breath blew on my cheeks, and I, too, leaned to meet it, longing to be taken. A great wave rolled up before me, and through its soft glimmer I saw a beautiful, benignant face regarding me. Then I knew that each and all had seen the same, and losing fear in love were glad to go. (289–90)

Sylvia's eschatology has more to do with Emerson than Bunyan. As she employs the phrase from Emerson's eponymous poem "Each and All," she has an epiphany and finally understands that greater peace comes from union with the natural divine than can ever come from human union in marriage. In describing the transcendence of God over human constructs, Emerson writes in "Experience," "Marriage (in what is called the spiritual world) is impossible, because of the inequality between every subject and every object.... Never can love make consciousness and ascription equal in force. There will be the same gulf between every me and thee, as between the original and the picture" (3: 44). While Emerson's tone regarding marriage is bleaker than Alcott's at the end of the 1864 version of *Moods*, both are commenting on the ultimate lack of fulfillment to be found in the patriarchal conventions of marriage.

The book concludes with Emersonian passages that also allude briefly to *The Pilgrim's Progress*. Sylvia's father asks her what she has learned, and she answers that "if the chief desire of the heart is for the right," anyone can learn "to bring good out of evil," so "who could doubt that *she* had learned the lesson, when from the ruins of the perishable body the imperishable soul rose steadfast and serene, proving that after the long bewilderment of life and love it had attained the eternal peace" (215–16). Sylvia, now a woman and no longer the impetuous, mood-driven girl of her youth, has understood that most basic tenet of transcendentalism: moral intuition is the inner force— the very soul of each individual—that leads him or her to understand the transcendent divinity of the each and all. She has learned this through a metaphorical journey: her dying is a "little journey," for her life has been a "short pilgrimage" (216), and like Christiana, she finds "eternal peace" (216).

Alcott wrote of her character Sylvia to the friend who helped her find a publisher for *Moods*, Caroline Dall, "Her life was meant to be a failure in all respects but one, for she was unstable by nature . . . ; but the *desire* to go right, & the *effort* to do so never failed, & in the end, despite her sorrowful experiences, she sees, acknowledges & accepts the lesson which life & love have taught her through her moods" (qtd. in Deese, "Louisa" 452). Apparently, then, what Alcott took away from Emerson's "Experience" is its emphasis on life as a series of moods and experiences through which the individual passes sometimes unaware of the implications of those moods, its metaphor for life as a journey, its insistence that we learn best by experience (as opposed to formal study), and its implication that the ability to simultaneously understand the duality of language and Nature leads to what few moments of transcendence anyone enjoys. What she took away from *The Pilgrim's Progress* was its sense of structure—the pilgrimage as metaphor and moral virtue as allegorically depicted. Significantly, Alcott could see the potentials of both the moral pilgrimage and spiritual transcendence for women as well as men.

The Pilgrim's Progress as Palimpsest in Little Women

Once the reviews of *Moods* began to appear in 1864, Alcott felt the sting of being accused of writing too esoterically.[9] Perhaps that is why in 1868, four years after *Moods* was published, when a publisher she trusted suggested she write about girls, she protested that she "never liked girls or knew many"—and so she wrote about what she knew very well—the sisters in her family—all of whom were guided not only by Emerson's essays but also by a book that virtually every reader in the United States would have known: *The Pilgrim's Progress* (*Journals* 165–66).

The Pilgrim's Progress provides *Little Women* with a tightly controlled structure of pilgrimage as a metaphor for growing up, as Phillips elegantly notes in her essay "The Prophets and the Martyrs" (213).[10] Life, in Bunyan's allegory, occurs as a journey through which the pilgrim learns by experience. Christian's faith guides him in his journey, but what he learns from experience helps his faith grow stronger. *The Pilgrim's Progress* thus provides a vehicle that intertextually informs the plot of Alcott's story for children *Little Women*—and it is a text that would have been far more familiar to juvenile readers than Emerson's essays. The question of whether we learn better from formal study or from experience is an argument Emerson advances in "Experience"—"The great gifts are not got by analysis. Everything good is on the highway" (3: 36). That sentiment might also serve well as an epigraph for *The Pilgrim's Progress*. One of Bunyan's allegorical characters phrases it in roughly equivalent terms: "Nothing teaches like Experience" (246). *The Pilgrim's Progress* advocates the importance of living and growing, even if people do not always understand the import of what they are facing, as does Emerson's "Experience." For both philosophers, all pilgrims' salvation is also their own self-reliant responsibility. In asserting that we learn from experience along an individual path to salvation, *The Pilgrim's Progress* provides Alcott with a means by which she can advance Emersonian ideas about experience without making herself vulnerable to accusations of philosophical ignorance, such as those leveled against her by Henry James.

Nine chapter titles in *Little Women* allude to incidents or ideas in *The Pilgrim's Progress*.[11] Moreover, *The Pilgrim's Progress* shapes many of Alcott's characterizations and the plot itself, as Phillips demonstrates when she connects Mr. March's role to Evangelist's (because he sets his daughters on their pilgrimage) or when Alcott's narrator details how Mrs. March's character evokes Help; Jo even refers to her mother as the Bunyan character "Help" (*Little Women* 18), and in the girls' conversations with their mother, they frequently invoke the word "help" to describe Marmee (Phillips 213, 222).

Later in the novel, John Brooke is identified directly as "Mr. Greatheart" (135), and Mr. Bhaer can be read as Bunyan's character Good-Will, for the text clearly associates him with the traits of that allegorical character. Jo identifies "benevolence" as the source of Bhaer's miraculous "charm" (276)—even his very boots are described as "benevolent" (276), implying that he walks the pilgrim's path of kindness and goodwill. Significantly, in the very next paragraph, Jo equates benevolence with "goodwill," when she discovers "that genuine good-will toward one's fellow-men could beautify and dignify" even a humble man, such as Bhaer (276). Because of him, Jo begins to recognize "that character is a better possession than money, rank, intellect, or beauty; and to feel that if greatness is what a wise man has defined it to be,—'truth, reverence, and good-will'—then her friend Friedrich Bhaer is not only good, but great" (278).[12] In his role as Good-Will, Bhaer directs Jo toward salvation when esoteric conversation during a salon discussion confuses her, engaging what Phillips identifies as the novel's emphasis on both men and women achieving "personal salvation" and "self-knowledge" (216).

Little Women's specific reworkings of Bunyan's allegorical characters occur in the context of many direct references to *The Pilgrim's Progress*. Allusions to Bunyan's story are made as early as the prefatory epigraph in *Little Women*, and in chapter 1, the March sisters decide to "play pilgrim" as a game of moral improvement (17).[13] Although Amy resists playing the game, Meg urges her sister to play because, "the story may help us" (18). Marmee then gives each girl a copy of the New Testament as her guide on Christmas morning, and each girl will subsequently reenact at least one incident from the biblical allegory *The Pilgrim's Progress* in her journey toward maturation.

For example, in "Castles in the Air," the four sisters don big hats and pouches and carry "long staff[s]" (115), while they climb a hill that they identify as the "Delectable Mountain" (117). They tell their friend Laurie that they have been reenacting their childhood game of playing "Pilgrim's Progress . . . going on with it in earnest all winter and summer" (116). Their ensuing conversation involves various definitions of heaven, both on earth and in the afterlife. As their small group contemplates the autumnal sunset, Beth says, "Jo talks about the country where we hope to live some time; the real country, she means, with pigs and chickens, and haymaking. . . . But I wish the beautiful country up there was real and we could ever go to it" (117). Meg reminds her "There is a lovelier country even than that, where we *shall* go, by and by, when we are good enough" (117). Beth then reassures her sisters and Laurie with another reference to *The Pilgrim's Progress*: "If people really want to go, and really try all their lives, I think they will get in [to heaven]; for I don't believe there are any locks on that door, or any guards at the gate. I always imagine it is as it is in the picture, where the Shining Ones stretch out their hands to welcome poor Christian as he comes up from the river"

(117). Jo immediately responds, "Wouldn't it be fun if all the castles in the air which we make could come true, and we could live in them?" (117). Jo wants her castle to be full of horses and books: "some day, I think I shall write books, and get rich and famous" (118). Thus, while Beth longs to live in the natural beauty of the sunset and the heavens, Jo longs for a more concrete home that she can fill with books. Their words are reminiscent of Emerson's wording in "Experience": "Nature and books belong to the eyes that see them. It depends on the mood of the man whether he shall see the sunset or the fine poem" (3: 30). Looking at the same sunset, Beth sees something closer to nature, which she equates with heaven, while Jo sees something more like a fine poem—in her words, books written out of a "magic inkstand" (118). The two characters have used allusions to *The Pilgrim's Progress* to evoke Emersonian thinking about the duality between Nature and language.

After Beth's illness and their father's return from his journey after serving as a chaplain in the Civil War, the family gathers together almost a year from the opening of the novel in a chapter named for a scene in *The Pilgrim's Progress*, "Pleasant Meadows." Their father tells the sisters, "Rather a rough road for you to travel, my little pilgrims, especially the latter part of it. But you have got on bravely; and I think the burdens are in a fair way to tumble off very soon" (175). Beth closes the chapter, commenting, "I read in 'Pilgrim's Progress' today, how, after many troubles, Christian and Hopeful came to a pleasant green meadow, where lilies bloomed all the year round, and there they rested happily, as we do now, before they went on their journey's end," and she sings a hymn sung by the shepherd's boy in part 2 of *The Pilgrim's Progress* (177). The final verse of that chapter is noteworthy:

> Fulness to them a burden is,
> That go on Pilgrimage;
> Here little, and hereafter bliss,
> Is best from age to age. (qtd. in Little Women 177)[14]

The "ful[l]ness" Bunyan describes could be interpreted as either "heaviness" or "fulfillment," but either way, the movements of the pilgrims—the journey and its attendant experiences—lead to salvation, as they do for Beth. While she is dying in "the Valley of the Shadow," she is "the first pilgrim called" and "likewise the fittest"; her family "wait[s] with her on the shore, trying to see the Shining Ones coming to receive her when she crossed the river" (325), just as the Shining Ones receive Christian when he dies in *The Pilgrim's Progress* (154). In an elegy written for Beth, Jo describes her sister's death in terms of being "safe across the river / . . . waiting for me on the shore" and believes that Beth, by the hands of "Hope and faith," will lead her to heaven, too, alluding to how the characters Hopeful and Faithful have journeyed with Christian (326–27).

Emerson does not deal directly with heaven as the site of the afterlife in "Experience," but he does describe the ecstasy of communion with the "First Cause" in language that references life as a journey:

> Underneath the inharmonious and trivial particulars [of life] is a musical perfection, the Ideal journeying always with us, the heaven without rent or seam. Do but observe the mode of our illumination. . . . By persisting to read or to think, this region gives further sign of itself, as it were in flashes of light, in sudden discoveries of its profound beauty and repose, as if the clouds that covered it parted at intervals, and showed the approaching traveler the inland mountains, with the tranquil eternal meadows spread at their base. (3: 41)

Perhaps Bunyan's language of the pilgrim seeking spiritual salvation while traveling through meadows and over mountains influenced Emerson to depict similar imagery of light, beauty, and meadows lying at the foot of mountains from which clouds temporarily part to give us temporary insight into visions of transcendence. Regardless, Alcott seems to be employing the language of both authors when she describes Beth's pilgrimage through life and into death.

Modern readers, however, may well miss some of these details and the psychological complexity embedded in the allusions to *The Pilgrim's Progress* because they are not as aware of the story as Alcott's readers would have been during her lifetime. For example, the humiliation Amy suffers is tame compared to the experience Christian experiences in the Valley of Humiliation when Apollyon confronts him in *The Pilgrim's Progress*—but Jo's confrontation with Apollyon is psychically terrifying and sets the stage for Marmee to articulate some aspects of her own Emerson-inspired morality. One of the darkest and most interesting of Bunyan's allegorical characters, Apollyon is monstrous.[15] Apollyon tries to persuade the pilgrim from his path by both threats and (il)logic, but when Christian invokes Christ's merciful forgiveness, Apollyon breaks "into a grievous rage," and they enter into a battle (*Pilgrim's Progress* 59). The narrator claims, "'Twas the dreadfullest sight that ever I saw"

(61). Apollyon is evil, forceful, proud, merciless, and completely destructive. Jo is acknowledging the destructiveness of pure rage when she describes her temper as her Apollyon, which she does in admitting to herself that she "feel[s] stronger than ever to meet and subdue her Apollyon" (101). When she is enraged, she is incapable of accessing true moral intuition, but as she matures, she is able to consult her moral intuition to subdue her temper.

Without the context of *The Pilgrim's Progress* and without any knowledge of Apollyon's complexity as a character, twenty-first-century readers might well miss the wealth of information they are being given with the references to Apollyon. Jo's displays of anger are not garden-variety temper tantrums; they are moods that are calculated, raging, and destructive: "It seems as if I could do anything when I'm in a passion; I get so savage, I could hurt any one, and enjoy it" (*Little Women* 68). That she knows she must fight these sadistic urges—and gains some insight into how to control her own destructive impulses—is a result of her ability to equate her temper with Apollyon, that is, Satan. Only at this point in the novel can she listen to her parents' moral philosophy, which is supplied by Marmee, who admits to sharing the same fault. Marmee describes her own anger as "weak and wicked" and tells Jo to think of it as "your 'bosom enemy'" (69). Marmee then offers theological advice much like that which is given to Christian throughout *The Pilgrim's Progress*: "Learn to feel the strength and tenderness of your Heavenly Father.... The more you love and trust Him, the nearer you will feel to Him, and the less you will depend on human power and wisdom. His love and care never tire or change, can never be taken from you, but may become the source of life-long peace, happiness, and strength" (70). The image of Jo as someone on a journey, as a pilgrim, drives Marmee's words: the goal is to feel "nearer" to God so as to depend less on humanity. This effort to be nearer to God than to people also evokes Emerson's sense of divinity: "The simplest person, who in his integrity worships God, becomes God" ("Over-Soul" 2: 173).[16] In Marmee's formulation, moral self-reliance leads to transcendence. Both the psychological complexity of Jo's anger and Marmee's theological explanation of Christianity as a transcendent journey rely for their formation on characters and plot points in *The Pilgrim's Progress*—but the philosophy is closer to Emerson's than Bunyan's.

Although Alcott separates the character Faithful from the setting of Vanity Fair, the structure provided by *The Pilgrim's Progress* would have ensured that nineteenth-century readers would understood the fate of Faithful in Vanity

Fair far better than casual twenty-first-century readers might. As Christian and Faithful enter the city Vanity Fair, they are accosted by materialism and apostasy. Faithful is put on trial for being treasonous to the so-called religion of Vanity Fair: "First, they Scourged him, then they Buffeted him, then they Lanced his flesh with Knives; after that they Stoned him with Stones, then prickt him with their Swords, and last of all, they burned him to Ashes at the Stake. Thus came *Faithful* to his end" (95). Faithful transcends Vanity Fair, however, for the narrator describes "that there stood behind the multitude, a Chariot and a couple of Horses, waiting for *Faithful*, who (so soon as his adversaries had dispatched him) was taken up into it, and straightway was carried up through the clouds, with sound of Trumpet, the nearest way to the Cœlestial Gate" (95). Thus, when Alcott refers to Beth as "Little Faithful" for ministering among the poor and contracting scarlet fever, the metaphor is nontrivial. Like Bunyan's Faithful, she will burn for her efforts—initially, she burns with fever: her forehead is "hot" (*Little Women* 143), during "fits" of the fever, she talks deliriously (146), her hand is "hot" (147); her lips are "parched" (150); her face has been "flush" (151). When she dies later, in the chapter "The Valley of the Shadow," Beth is immediately depicted as having transcended the world's pain, just as Bunyan's Faithful has: "With tears, and prayers, and tender hands, mother and sisters made her ready for the long sleep that pain would never mar again—seeing with grateful eyes the beautiful serenity that soon replaced the pathetic patience that had wrung their hearts so long, and feeling with reverent joy, that to their darling death was a benignant angel—not a phantom full of dread" (328). From this painful loss, Jo gains a burden far greater than the rage she has been trying to control: her new cross to bear is the grief of "ceaseless longing" now that all the "light, and warmth, and beauty" have left their home (337). Only with her parents does the "burden [seem] easier to bear" (337). She calls the conversations she has in her father's study "the church of one member" and looks to family and work—not organized religion—to sooth her soul (338).

Jo and her sisters are pilgrims journeying toward salvation, although the divinity they seek relies more on their parents' philosophy and Emersonian concepts of nature than on Christ's intervention in their lives. Alcott consciously relies on Bunyan to evoke Emerson's metaphor of life as a journey of experiences lived on a highway that we never completely comprehend. She also uses *The Pilgrim's Progress* to communicate information about how emotions (or "moods") affect people, about learning from experience, about transcendence, and about faith, which can be found perhaps more easily in nature than in church. Christian, after all, never once attends church, testifying to the importance of the individual's role in serving as his own mediator with God. Thus, Emersonian principles of self-reliance, Nature, transcendent divinity, and experience are being communicated to child readers in Little Women couched neatly in accessible references to the widely accepted The Pilgrim's Progress.

Language and Creating Narrative in Little Women

Not only is Little Women relying on The Pilgrim's Progress to disguise its transcendentalism, but it is also directly involved in advocating for women to value their experiences, especially those that involve understanding the relationship between language and narrative. The characters in Little Women grow, for example, not only because of having lived through various experiences and moods but also because they are able to analyze each of these situations and learn from them, usually with the help of a mentor who validates female experience. Those reflective conversations often involve some sort of story that works as a moral compass—Beth finding out about the granddaughter Mr. Laurence has lost or Jo finding out the story of her mother's lifelong fight with her temper, for example. In allowing the girls to converse about, reflect on, and contemplate the intertextual allegory that is guiding their lives, Alcott emphasizes the importance of language as the tool by which narrative is created. That the March sisters have read The Pilgrim's Progress is not enough; their reflections on, their conversations about, and their analyses of the allegory as story also help them grow. Stories are, of course, composed of words, and they involve a process of dialogue between, at a minimum, an author or teller and a reader or listener.[17] Alcott includes many stories-within-the-story of Little Women because she clearly valued storytelling as a language-based means of human interaction, especially among women.

Emerson's thoughts on language provide an epistemology of language that influenced Alcott. In Nature, Emerson argues in the chapter on "Language" from three premises:

1. Words are signs of natural facts.
2. Particular natural facts are symbols of particular spiritual facts.
3. Nature is the symbol of spirit. (1: 17)

In this passage, Emerson crafts something of a syllogism.[18] The logical conclusion of the first two premises could be interpreted like this: "Words are symbols or signs of spiritual facts." Combined with the third premise, "Nature is the symbol of spirit," Emerson implies that it is therefore with "Words" that language is connected to Nature through the spirit. He insists, "Every natural fact is a symbol of some spiritual fact. Every appearance in nature corresponds to some state of the mind, and that state of the mind can only be described by presenting that natural appearance as its picture" (1: 18).[19] It may be useful here to remember that early in his career, Emerson defines Nature as everything that is not the self: "All that is separate from us, all which Philosophy distinguishes as the NOT ME, that is, both nature and art, all other men and my own body, must be ranked under this name, NATURE" (1: 8). F. O. Matthiessen regards Emerson's understanding of language as a duality: in one sense, Emerson thought of "language as the vehicle for concrete facts, as, by license of analogy, the substantial material that could be handled by rhetoric and built into style," but in another sense, "language was symbol, the bridge that enabled man to pass from concrete appearance to spiritual reality" (32). In this second sense, language is the bridge between nature and the spirit, between the self and the "NOT ME." In "Experience," then, when Emerson makes his crucial distinction between nature and criticism, he seems to be separating nature from language, even though in *Nature*, he has argued that language is the only means by which we understand that which is Nature, in other words, that which is not our own spirit. Alcott apparently understood Emerson more as setting nature apart from civilization and its discourses than defining nature as all that is "NOT ME." In her novels, people find divinity and spiritual calm when they are observing nature, as Sylvia does on the river with Adam or as Jo and Beth do at the seaside. As a result of understanding language as a means of understanding Nature, and in turn divinity, Alcott comments on language in two ways in *Little Women*: in terms of the relationship between experience and language in its written form and in terms of the connections between language, nature, and the spirit.

Little Women depicts the importance not only of learning from experience but also of writing from the language of experience. In the second part of *Little Women*, Friedrich Bhaer advises Jo March "to study simple, true, and lovely characters, wherever she found them, as good training for a writer" (276). Although at this point, the narrator goes on to tell the reader that Jo "coolly turned round and studied" Bhaer (276), his point informs the whole story: Alcott asserts that writers must take their guides from "simple, true, and lovely characters" in their own lives. When Jo first begins to write sensation stories, the narrator makes much of the fact that she does not have the experience to write about her chosen topics: "Her story was as full of desperation and despair as her limited acquaintance with those uncomfortable emotions enabled her to make it" (214). *Little Women* eventually condemns these stories as immoral—but they are also bad stories because they are not based in life as Jo has experienced it. After she publishes a first novel that is similar to Alcott's own *Moods*, Jo's self-assessment about having written transcendental characters into her novel uses contradictory terms about writing from experience: "If my people *are* 'philosophical and metaphysical,' it isn't my fault, for I know nothing about such things, except what I hear father say, sometimes. If I've got some of his wise ideas jumbled up with my romance, so much the better for me" (216). Jo distances herself from any direct knowledge of philosophy, while at the same time admitting that her father's ideas have affected her after all: "Her father liked the metaphysical streak which had unconsciously" been written into the novel (216). *Little Women* even includes humor about what it means to write from experience: although Jo's critics can't tell the difference between what Jo has written from her own experiences and what she's written from her imagination, she knows: "I've got the joke on my side, after all; for the parts that were taken straight out of real life, are denounced as impossible and absurd, and the scenes that I made up out of my own silly head, are pronounced 'charmingly natural, tender, and true'" (217).

Jo later publishes a more successful tale reflecting Alcott's success in writing book 1 of *Little Women*: "Something got into that story that went straight to the hearts of those who read it" (340). That "something" is the fact that she has written about what she knows; her father says, "There is truth in it," meaning, the truth that their family has lived. He tells her, "You have found your style at last," and she continues writing domestic realism (340). Like Alcott, Jo has learned, by experience, to write from her own experiences: "So, taught by love and sorrow, Jo wrote her little stories" (340). The novel's ultimate assessment of her writing talent again references experience in the final chapter: "I haven't given up the hope that I may write a good book yet, but I can wait, and I'm sure it will be all the better for such *experiences* and illustrations as these," she says, pointing to her sons, her students, her husband, and her father (379, emphasis added). That Alcott is validating women's experience as legitimate narrative material is an early act of feminist self-assertion that owes something to what Emerson has taught her about the relationship between experience and language.

Alcott also would have learned these lessons from her own background as an author. Upon first reading the manuscript of *Moods*, her father remarked, "Emerson must see this. Where did you get your metaphysics?" (*Journals* 104). The British, she noted, disapproved because "English people don't understand 'Transcendental Literature' as they call 'Moods,'" so she wrote with disgust, "My next book shall have no *ideas* in it, only facts, & the people shall be as ordinary as possible, then critics will say its [*sic*] all right" (140). Given that her next book was *Little Women*, she seems to have learned well how to code her characters as people drawn from her own life rather than people elucidating specific philosophies. At one point during her many revisions of *Moods*, she paraphrased Emerson's "Self-Reliance" in her journal: "Emerson says 'that what is true for your own private heart is true for others,' so I wrote from my own life & experience & hope it may suit some one & at least do no harm" (*Journals* 133).[20] Although she did not seem to have followed that formula as successfully with *Moods* as she might have wished, she did succeed in doing so with *Little Women*. While proofreading the final copy of *Little Women*, Alcott realized, "It reads better than I expected. Not a bit sensational, but simple and true, for we really lived most of it; and if it succeeds that will be the reason of it" (*Journals* 166). Perhaps Henry James's words were still ringing in her ears, since he wrote as he concluded his 1864 review of *Moods*, "There is no reason why Miss Alcott should not write a very good novel, provided she will be satisfied to describe only that which she has seen" (224).

Not only is *Little Women* direct in its advice to writers, but the novel also emphasizes the importance of reading and writing in providing writers with experience they might not otherwise know. *Little Women* refers to at least eighty other narratives, poems, plays, essays, and authors, ranging from Aesop's *Fables* and *The Odyssey* to *Uncle Tom's Cabin* and seven of Dickens's works. The girls, especially Jo, read constantly, and everyone in the family writes. They write letters and notes to each other; the girls write their own newspaper; Jo, of course, writes her poems and stories. Literacy, especially narrative, creates community in this family.

This emphasis on language, literacy, and narrative carries Emersonian overtones throughout *Little Women*, particularly when Alcott connects language to spirituality. For example, surrounding Beth's knowledge of her death is an ineffable sorrow, one she cannot articulate. From Jo's perspective, "there seemed something sacred in the silence," and she waits for Beth to acknowledge she is dying (291). When Beth does, the language she employs implies the interrelationship of language, nature, and spirituality. The two sisters are at the seaside, where Jo has taken Beth hoping to restore her health, so they rest on the shore, enjoying the natural beauty of the beach: the warm rocks on the shore, the cheerful sandpipers, the coming and going of the tide. Resting thus at peace in nature, Beth finally admits that she knows she is dying without even saying so: "Jo, dear, I'm glad you know it. I've tried to tell you, but I couldn't" (293). Jo grieves, and Beth comforts her: "Like a confiding child, [Beth] asked no questions, but left everything to God and nature, Father and mother of us all, feeling sure that they, and they only could teach and strengthen heart and spirit for this life and the life to come" (294). With this formulation, the text constructs divinity and nature as progenerative partners. Later, wondering how to tell their literal father and mother, Jo reassures Beth, "They will see it without words" (294), tying the import of this spiritual journey to language—or at least, a loss thereof. Beth doesn't "know how to express myself," but she delivers one of the longest speeches she gives in the novel, explaining that she is not as afraid of dying as she is afraid of missing Jo in heaven (294–95). The text notes that this "talking change was the greatest," for Beth has never before had such ready access to language (295). When the girls return home, Jo's intuition is confirmed: "There was no need of any words when they got home, for father and mother saw plainly, now" (295). The absence of Jo's and her parents' language is tied to knowledge, and specifically to knowledge of the divine, while Beth's use of language is tied to her transcendence to heaven. Nevertheless, only while observing nature have Jo and Beth found the language to talk about the spiritual journey the latter must face alone.

When Jo begins writing again after Beth dies—that is, when she immerses herself once more in the use of language to create narrative—the text of *Little Women* compares her writing process to Christian's experience at the arbor where he rests during his climb up the "Hill Difficulty" (Bunyan 41):

> Still another [help] was given her, and she took it—not as a reward, but as a comfort, as Christian took the refreshment afforded by the little arbor where he rested, as he climbed the hill called Difficulty.

> "Why don't you write? that always used to make you happy," said her mother, once, when the desponding fit overshadowed Jo....
>
> An hour afterward her mother peeped in, and there she was scratching away, with her black pinafore on, and an absorbed expression, which caused Mrs. March to smile, and slip away, well pleased with the success of her suggestion. (339)

Returning to her writing feels to Jo like being in an oasis—like a return to nature—because it is a restorative cure for her to return to her first love: using language to craft story.

But the allusion to Christian's arbor on the Hill of Difficulty is richer than the text of *Little Women* indicates because it is while first resting in the arbor on the Hill, a natural haven "made by the Lord of the Hill, for the refreshing of weary Travailers" (Bunyan 42), that Christian loses his precious "Roll," his gospel of the Good Word (44).[21] When Christian recognizes his loss, he is angry with himself for needing to retrace his steps, even though he has enjoyed the pleasure of his commune with nature while resting in the arbor. Losing the roll, however, constitutes a greater loss than the mere waste of time; he has lost the words of eternal assurance, the words that make the promise of salvation real to him. When he recovers the roll, he trembles: "Who can tell how joyful this man was, when he had gotten his Roll again? For this Roll was the Assurance of his life, and acceptance at the desired Haven" (45). Christian's story of resting at the arbor and losing his roll is a story of the language of spiritual salvation lost and then recovered, just as Jo has lost her ability to write but recovers a sense of hope when she again finds the ability to create narrative. Moreover, Christian loses and subsequently regains the language of his salvation because he has rested *pax natura*, in peace with nature.

In using Christian's rest in the arbor as an analogy for Jo's writing, Alcott evokes Emerson's philosophy about the relationship between words, nature, and spirituality, just as the chapter "Beth's Secret" does. If the arbor is the bridge where Christian's language and spirit are reconnected, Jo's writing is the process of immersing herself in language by which she can be returned to spiritual healing. Jo's writing is, in this scene, a resumption of her ability to act and to think independently—self-reliantly—from her parents, without worrying that she must spend so much of her time attending to their grief. In his essay on "Language," Emerson asserts that "Nature is the vehicle of thought" (*Nature* 1: 17); that is, "the whole of nature is a metaphor of the human mind" (1: 21). We cannot think without language, nor would we be able to describe nature without it. Using language to write is Jo's natural haven, her arbor; it is the "vehicle of thought" without which she cannot heal or act self-reliantly (1: 17).

Emerson believes allegory to be a fundamental condition of language: "Good writing and brilliant discourse are perpetual allegories" (*Nature* 1: 20). Individuals in every age are drawn to make comparisons as a way to understand relationships: "Man is an analogist and studies relations in all objects" (1: 19). Perhaps Alcott perceived in *The Pilgrim's Progress* a literal precursor to Emerson's philosophy about the relationship between language and spirit because in Bunyan's allegory, every "natural" state of human emotion or behavior is depicted as a word, allegorically, as a "particular spiritual fact." For instance, in Bunyan's story, pure-heartedness or corruption are communicated directly by the language used to name each character. Moreover, like Bunyan, Emerson also connects purity of language and thought to corruption and sin: "A man's power to connect his thought with its proper symbol, and so to utter it, depends on the simplicity of his character, that is, upon his love of truth, and his desire to communicate it without loss. The corruption of man is followed by the corruption of language" (1: 20).

While it might have been a stretch for Alcott to include this type of philosophy about spirituality and language in a novel written for the juvenile market, it would not have been difficult at all for her readers to understand an equation between simplicity of character and love of truth—say, for example, Faithful's simplicity of character and love of God, which *Little Women* allusively compares to Beth's purity. Emerson believed that language connected the spirit to Nature, and Bunyan's allegorical language provides a simple way for child readers to immediately identify characters' spiritual qualities by a single word. If Emerson believed that the corruption of humans leads to the corruption of language, Bunyan certainly prefigures that concept with characters such as Talkative, Envy, Pickthank, and Superstition, whose illogical language reflects their corrupt nature. Nor would it have been difficult for Alcott's readers to understand the connection between what Emerson says about the corruption of action and of language: Amy, with her many "vocabulary" (*Little Women* 12) errors and "lapse[s] of lingy" (57), is, after all, the allegorical figure whose corruption leads to the fall from grace of both her pride and several pickled limes, cast ingloriously down from the schoolroom window.

Conclusion

Because in writing the first book of *Little Women* Alcott has learned to write from her own experiences rather than "philosophize" to readers, when she needed to write about the relationship between actions, experience, language, and "simplicity of character," she relied on a text popular with the reading public, an alternative text to Emerson's essays that superficially demonstrated many of the same values but that was more accessible to juvenile readers: John Bunyan's *The Pilgrim's Progress*. Alcott's use of the allegory to communicate Emersonian philosophies is not so much a reductive simplification of his philosophies for child readers as it is palimpsestic; that is, Alcott is guided by a version of *The Pilgrim's Progress* that seems to have been written over a manuscript of Emerson's finest principles. Significantly, Alcott fashioned this Emersonian revision of *The Pilgrim's Progress* to depict female characters empowered by a philosophy, transcendentalism, that was not always as kind to early feminist thinking as it might have been.[22] In creating a model in which she encouraged female readers to learn from experience, Nature, and self, especially those who would be writers, Alcott translated transcendentalism into accessible terms that were distinctly feminist—and she disguised that radical revision with a selective and deliberate use of Bunyan's *Pilgrim's Progress*.

Notes

1. Nathaniel Hawthorne's son Julian, Louisa Alcott's next-door neighbor for a time when they were younger, reminisced in his later life that Henry James told her soon after the publication of *Little Women*, "Louisa—m-my dear girl—er—when you hear people—ah—telling you you're a genius you mustn't believe them; er—what I mean is, it isn't true!" (qtd. in Shealy, *Alcott* 203).

2. Alcott, *Moods* 1. Alcott has misquoted Emerson in this epigraph. The exact quotation is as follows: "Life is a train of moods like a string of beads, and, as we pass through them, they prove to be many-colored lenses which paint the world their own hue, and each shows only what lies in its focus" (Emerson, "Experience" 30). Alcott has added the word "us," slightly altering the meaning of the quotation, from being a depiction of "moods" as something like autonomous stages that affect our lives to a more active understanding of moods as something that people generate themselves.

3. For example, in 1868 Alcott referred to the members of Boston's Radical Club as "a curious jumble of fools and philosophers," and in an 1872 letter to her mother, she called the Club "a funny mixture of rabbis and weedy old ladies, 'the oversoul' and oysters" (*Journals* 165, *Selected Letters* 165). Of the Concord School of Philosophy, Alcott wrote privately in 1879, "If they were philanthropists I *should* enjoy it, but speculation seems a waste of time when there is so much real work crying to be done. Why discuss the Unknowable till our

poor are fed & the wicked saved?" (*Journals* 216). For a thorough account of the Concord School of Philosophy, see Ronda.

4. For an insightful account of the historical relationship between Emerson and Alcott, see Shealy, "Friendship."

5. Harriet Reisen asserts that Emerson's *Nature* relies heavily on material found in Bronson Alcott's journals (35).

6. For an emotionally complex account of the tensions the Fruitlands experience created within and for the Alcott family, see Matteson, *Eden's Outcasts* 116–49.

7. For Alcott's retelling of the incident in a letter to her older sister, see also Alcott, *Selected Letters* 62–63. The final line of part 1 of *The Pilgrim's Progress* reads, "So I awoke, and behold it was a Dream" (Bunyan 154).

8. Written while Emerson was grieving his two-year-old son's death, "Experience" has a notably different tone than *Nature*. According to David M. Robinson, "Experience" is Emerson's "greatest essay" ("Emerson" 167). Robinson observes that in its attempt to reconcile Emerson's feelings of "disconnection and disorientation," "Experience" is "widely recognized as a turning point in Emerson's development" (391). Robinson traces the shift from *Nature* to "Experience" as an almost destructive expansion: "The mind's 'great proportions' has now become the steady enlargement of the rapacious subject that takes all things into it" (393). Roger Lundin, on the other hand, analyzes the distinctions between *Nature* and "Experience" in terms that parallel Alcott's use of the two essays: "Where in *Nature* we see the 'world in God' and, thus, in the human spirit, in 'Experience,' an unbridgeable chasm yawns between the ME and the NOT ME" (48).

9. Alcott expressed her frustration that critics misunderstood her artistic goals: "It was meant to show a life affected by *moods*, not a discussion of marriage which I knew little about, except observing that very few were happy ones" (*Journals* 147).

10. As MacDonald also notes, "The quest motif controls the narrative" ("Case" 30); Hunt considers the theme of "the purposefulness of human life" to be the major theme that Alcott borrows from *The Pilgrim's Progress* (259). Additional scholarship focusing on the relationship between *The Pilgrim's Progress* and *Little Women* includes Kerber; MacDonald's *Christian's Children*; and Walters.

11. The nine are "Playing Pilgrims," "Burdens," "Beth Finds the Palace Beautiful," "Amy's Valley of Humiliation," "Jo Meets Apollyon," "Meg Goes to Vanity Fair," "Little Faithful," "Pleasant Meadows," and "The Valley of the Shadow" (*Little Women*).

12. Although it was not published until several years after *Little Women*, Alcott is quoting from Emerson's essay "Greatness" (1878), published in *Letters and Social Aims*, wherein Emerson defines greatness as "the fulfillment of a natural tendency in each man" (8: 167). Moreover, he writes, "Men are ennobled by morals and by intellect"—although morality and intellect may well come into conflict with each other (8: 176). Greatness, then, lies in reconciling the two, in the name of social improvement: "What are these but the promise and the preparation of a day when the air of the world shall be purified by nobler society; when the measure of greatness shall be usefulness in the highest sense,—greatness consisting in *truth, reverence and good will*?" (8: 176–77, emphasis added). See also Alcott, *Little Women*, n278.

13. "Go then, my little Book, and show to all / That entertain, and bid thee welcome shall, / What thou dost keep close shut up in thy breast; / And wish what thou dost show them may be blest / To them for good, may make them choose to be / Pilgrims better, by far, then thee or me. / Tell them of Mercy; she is one / Who early hath her pilgrimage begun. / Yea, let young damsels learn of her to prize / The world which is to come, and so be wise; / For

little tripping maids may follow God / Along the ways which saintly feet have trod" (8). This epigraph is one further indication that Alcott intends to inspire a female readership to better understand their own experience.

14. The first line of this quatrain in *The Pilgrim's Progress* reads, "Fulness to such a burden is" (223).

15. Despite the differences between Apollyon's and Satan's physical descriptions, Arlette Zinck traces the parallels between Milton's *Paradise Lost* and *The Pilgrim's Progress* as being linked through the notion of resisting the temptations of evil: "Both literary works ... share two principal objectives: to illuminate satanic wiles and stratagems, and to instruct readers in the use of spiritual defences or armours" (46).

16. See "Over-Soul": "The soul that ascends to worship the great God is plain and true; has no rose-color, no fine friends, no chivalry, no adventures; does not want admiration; dwells in the hour that now is, in the earnest experience of the common day" (2: 171–72). Robinson connects the theology in "The Over-Soul" to "Experience" as a movement from the optimism expressed in Emerson's earlier work "towards ethical purpose and pragmatic action as the most reliable reconstitution of spiritual experience" ("Emerson" 168).

17. Gustaaf van Cromphout links Emerson's thinking to Foucault's analysis of Romantic constructions of the subject, observing that "Emerson also recognizes both that language is the necessary means of the mind's dialogue with itself and that this dialogue is needed for the achievement of self-awareness and thus selfhood" (324). Van Cromphout also notes, "Self-actualization depends on self-expression" (326).

18. David van Leer considers this to be a "pseudosyllogism" because the first premise "is harmless but intellectually trivial, especially since 'sign' is so poorly defined" (41). He considers far more important Emerson's Kantian implication that "consciousness presupposed the possibility (at least) of the experience of external objects" (42). Alcott's focus, however, seems to be on the relationship between Nature and Spirit.

19. The reference to a "state of the mind" prefigures Emerson's later work on "moods" and their relationship to experience in "Experience."

20. The precise quotation is as follows: "To believe your own thought, to believe that what is true for you in your private heart is true for all men,—that is genius" (2: 27).

21. Renee A. Aukeman notes that there are two rolls, the first given to Christian in the City of Destruction and the second given to him at the foot at the Wicket Gate in the presence of the cross. She complicates the allegorical nature of this second roll: "The roll is all of these—salvation, faith, Scripture, assurance of faith—and none of these, simultaneously" (72).

22. For a range of views on the troubled relationship between transcendentalism and feminism, see the following: Robinson, "Margaret Fuller"; Deese, "Emerson"; Crouse; and M. Elbert.

Works Cited

Alcott, Louisa May. *The Journals of Louisa May Alcott*, edited by Joel Myerson, Daniel Shealy, and Madeleine B. Stern, Little, Brown, 1989; U of Georgia P, 1997.

Alcott, Louisa May. *Little Women, or, Meg, Jo, Beth and Amy*, edited by Anne K. Phillips and Gregory Eiselein, Norton Critical Edition, W. W. Norton, 2004.

Alcott, Louisa May. *Moods*, edited by Sarah Elbert, Rutgers UP, 1991. First published K. Loring 1864.

Alcott, Louisa May. *The Selected Letters of Louisa May Alcott*, edited by Joel Myerson, Daniel Shealy, and Madeleine B. Stern, Little, Brown, 1987; U of Georgia P, 1995.

Aukeman, Renee Alida. "The Multiple Roles of the Roll in *The Pilgrim's Progress*." *Dulia et Latria*, vol. 1, 2008, pp. 65–79.

Bunyan, John. *The Pilgrim's Progress*, edited by W. R. Owens, Oxford UP, 2003. First published 1678.

Clark, Beverly Lyon. *Louisa May Alcott: The Contemporary Reviews*. Cambridge UP, 2004.

Crouse, Jamie S. "'If They Have a Moral Power': Margaret Fuller, Transcendentalism, and the Question of Women's Moral Nature." *ATQ*, vol. 19, no. 4, 2005, pp. 259–79.

Deese, Helen R. "Emerson from a Feminist Perspective: The Caroline H. Dall Journals." *Postscript*, vol. 12, 1995, pp. 1–8.

Deese, Helen R. "Louisa May Alcott's *Moods*: A New Archival Discovery," *New England Quarterly*, vol. 76, no. 3, 2003, pp. 439–55.

Elbert, Monika. "Elizabeth Palmer Peabody's Problematic Feminism and the Feminization of Transcendentalism." *Reinventing the Peabody Sisters*, edited by Monika M. Elbert, Julie E. Hall, and Katharine Rodier, U of Iowa P, 2006, pp. 199–215.

Elbert, Sarah. "Introduction." *Moods*, by Louisa May Alcott, edited by Sarah Elbert, Rutgers UP, 1991, pp. xi–xlvii.

Emerson, Ralph Waldo. "The Divinity School Address." *The Collected Works of Ralph Waldo Emerson*, vol. 1, edited by Alfred R. Ferguson, Harvard UP, 1971, pp. 71–93.

Emerson, Ralph Waldo. "Each and All." *The Collected Works of Ralph Waldo Emerson*, vol. 9, edited by Albert J. von Frank and Thomas Wortham, Harvard UP, 2011, pp. 14–15.

Emerson, Ralph Waldo. "English Literature." *The Early Lectures of Ralph Waldo Emerson*, vol. 1, edited by Stephen E. Whicher and Robert E. Spiller, Harvard UP, 1959, pp. 205–385.

Emerson, Ralph Waldo. "Experience." *The Collected Works of Ralph Waldo Emerson*, vol. 3, edited by Joseph Slater, Alfred R. Ferguson, Jean Ferguson Carr, Harvard UP, 1984, pp. 25–50.

Emerson, Ralph Waldo. "Greatness." *The Collected Works of Ralph Waldo Emerson*, vol. 8, edited by Joel Myerson, Harvard UP, 2010, pp. 167–77.

Emerson, Ralph Waldo. *Nature*. *The Collected Works of Ralph Waldo Emerson*, vol. 1, edited by Alfred R. Ferguson, Harvard UP, 1971, pp. 8–48.

Emerson, Ralph Waldo. "The Over-Soul." *The Collected Works of Ralph Waldo Emerson*, vol. 2, edited by Joseph Slater, Harvard UP, 1979, pp. 157–76.

Emerson, Ralph Waldo. "Self-Reliance." *The Collected Works of Ralph Waldo Emerson*, vol. 2, edited by Joseph Slater, Harvard UP, 1979, pp. 25–51.

Gilbert, Sandra M., and Susan Gubar. *Madwoman in the Attic: The Woman Writer and the Nineteenth-Century Literary Imagination*. Yale UP, 1984.

Hinson, E. Glenn. "The Progression of Grace: A Re-Reading of *The Pilgrim's Progress*." *Spiritus*, vol. 3, no. 2, 2003, pp. 251–62.

Hunt, Caroline. "The Pilgrim's Progress." *The Louisa May Alcott Encyclopedia*, edited by Gregory Eiselein and Anne K. Phillips, Greenwood, 2001, pp. 258–59.

James, Henry. Review of *Moods*, by Louisa May Alcott. *Louisa May Alcott: The Contemporary Reviews*, edited by Beverly Lyon Clark, Cambridge UP, 2004, pp. 35–39.

Kerber, Linda K. "Can a Woman Be an Individual? The Limits of the Puritan Tradition in the Early Republic." *Texas Studies in Literature and Language*, vol. 25, no. 1, 1983, pp. 165–78.

Lundin, Roger. "Natural Experience: Emerson, Protestantism, and the Emergence of Pragmatism." *Religion and Literature*, vol. 32, no. 3, 2000, pp. 23–67.

MacDonald, Ruth K. "The Case for *The Pilgrim's Progress*." *Children's Literature Association Quarterly*, vol. 10, no. 1, 1985, pp. 29–30.
MacDonald, Ruth K. *Christian's Children: The Influence of John Bunyan's "The Pilgrim's Progress" on American Children's Literature*. Lang, 1989.
MacDonald, Ruth K. *Louisa May Alcott*. Twayne, 1983.
Matteson, John. *Eden's Outcasts: The Story of Louisa May Alcott and Her Father*. W. W. Norton, 2008.
Matthiessen, F. O. *American Renaissance: Art and Expression in the Age of Emerson and Whitman*. Oxford UP, 1941.
Mott, Luther. *Golden Multitudes: The Story of Best Sellers in the United States*. Macmillan, 1947.
Phillips, Anne K. "The Prophets and the Martyrs: Pilgrims and Missionaries in *Little Women* and *Jack and Jill*." *"Little Women" and the Feminist Imagination: Criticism, Controversy, Personal Essays*, edited by Janice M. Alberghene and Beverly Lyon Clark, Garland, 1999, pp. 213–36.
Reisen, Harriet. *Louisa May Alcott: The Woman behind "Little Women."* Holt, 2009.
Robinson, David M. "Emerson and Religion." *A Historical Guide to Ralph Waldo Emerson*, edited by Joel Myerson, Oxford UP, 2000, pp. 151–77.
Robinson, David M. "Experience, Instinct, and Emerson's Philosophical Reorientation." *Emerson: Bicentennial Essays*, edited by Ronald A. Bosco and Joel Myerson, Massachusetts Historical Society, 2006, pp. 391–404.
Robinson, David M. "Margaret Fuller and the Transcendental Ethos: *Woman in the Nineteenth Century*." *PMLA*, vol. 97, no. 1, 1982, pp. 83–98.
Ronda, Bruce. "The Concord School of Philosophy and the Legacy of Transcendentalism." *New England Quarterly*, vol. 82, no. 4, 2009, pp. 575–607.
Seelye, John. *Jane Eyre's American Daughters*. Rosemont, 2005.
Shealy, Daniel, editor. *Alcott in Her Own Time*. U of Iowa P, 2005.
Shealy, Daniel. "The Friendship of Ralph Waldo Emerson and Louisa May Alcott." *Emersonian Circles: Essays in Honor of Joel Myerson*, edited by Wesley T. Mott and Robert E. Burkholder, U of Rochester P, 1997, pp. 225–35.
Urbanski, Marie Olesen. "Thoreau, Henry David." *The Louisa May Alcott Encyclopedia*, edited by Eiselein and Phillips, Greenwood, 2001, pp. 324–25.
Van Cromphout, Gustaaf. "Emerson on Language as Action." *Emerson: Bicentennial Essays*, edited by Ronald A. Bosco and Joel Myerson, Massachusetts Historical Society, 2006, pp. 315–33.
Van Leer, David. *Emerson's Epistemology: The Argument of the Essays*. Cambridge UP, 1986.
Walters, Karla. "Seeking Home: Secularizing the Quest for the Celestial City in *Little Women* and *The Wonderful Wizard of Oz*." *Reform and Counterreform: Dialectics of the Word in Western Christianity since Luther*, edited by John C. Hawley, Mouton de Gruyter, 1994, pp. 153–71.
Zinck, Arlette. "'Doctrine by Ensample': Sanctification through Literature in Milton and Bunyan." *Bunyan Studies*, vol. 6, no. 6, 1995–96, pp. 44–55.

"FAITHFULNESS ITSELF"
The Imperative for Hannah Mullet in *Little Women*

SANDRA HARBERT PETRULIONIS

The March family's live-in domestic servant, Hannah Mullet, occupies a curious place in *Little Women*. Appearing in over ninety scenes and quipping what may be the novel's best-known line, "Housekeeping ain't no joke" (94), Hannah is ubiquitous, especially in book 1, where she first appears as "old Hannah [who] cleared the table" (18), while Marmee and the girls get under way in planning their *Pilgrim's Progress* update in chapter 1. We learn in the next chapter that Hannah has been with the family for sixteen years, since Meg's birth, and is "considered by them all more as a friend than a servant" (20). Nevertheless, the narrator and others remind us, at times demeaningly so, of Hannah's subordinate status, albeit her character is more or less idealized after the manner of the March family generally—she is good-natured, loyal, and always ready to serve.[1]

And yet, the narrator renders Hannah Mullet utterly unmemorable, to the extent that most readers, and likely a majority of Alcott scholars, would be hard pressed to recall her full name. At times she appears as a nonentity or narrative device; at others, she evokes an amalgam of class-based disenfranchisement and solicitous servitude. Rarely do we perceive Hannah as a subject in her own right. She conveys no troubles, no joys, on her own behalf, but rather, expresses happiness, pride, and sorrow throughout *Little Women* on account of the Marches. What is Hannah's past? Does she have a family of her own? We don't know. Indeed, we are more than halfway through book 1 before we learn her full name. Until then, she is simply Hannah—"faithful," "old Hannah"—a stock female domestic laborer whose constancy and devotion are her primary virtues.[2]

Further, what is the scope of Hannah's job responsibilities? She appears to embody what studies of nineteenth-century household labor point to as the most common of domestic servants, the "maid of all work," who all day every day handles the full complement of cooking, laundry, sewing, and housecleaning (Sutherland 94). Moreover, after putting a delectable Christmas breakfast on the table in chapter 2—and therefore rising early before the others on this holiday morning—Hannah accompanies the Marches as they sacrifice her lovely breakfast to the impoverished Hummels. While the others carry the food, Hannah totes wood and kindles a fire when they arrive, after which she cleans "broken panes with old hats, and her own shawl" (21). Later that day, Hannah informs their wealthy neighbor's servant of the family's charitable act, in turn prompting Mr. Laurence to send over a sumptuous feast as compensation. It is Hannah who thereby sets in motion the story's essential relationship with these next-door acquaintances. As Nina Auerbach confirms, this Christmas meal "is less important in itself than as a liaison established between the two houses" (57). Thus, in the first two chapters of the novel, Hannah has prepared and cleaned up after family meals, joined the work of their community charity efforts, and initiated the plot's most important friendship.

For an author whose own laboring life and writings often attend to the concerns of working women, Alcott's narrator presents a regrettably flat and even debasing portrait of the woman whose unflagging, dutiful toil enables this story's central coming-of-age themes. If Marmee functions as *Little Women*'s most vital character in cultivating her daughters' development, then an observant reader would anticipate that the household worker who frees Marmee to sit by the hearth and dispense maternal wisdom deserves more than passing attention. Although the narrator refers often to the dear mother's unstinting work, in fact over the course of the novel Marmee shares household duties with Hannah only once, in chapter 11, "Experiments." Otherwise, Mrs. March's visible domestic exertions are limited to sewing, usually quietly in her corner. Does *Little Women*'s narrator model nineteenth-century society's cultural erasure of the servant in the house? To understand the extent to which her subjectivity is elided and her character devalued, this article first examines Hannah Mullet within the historical context of mid-nineteenth-century domestic servitude; it then looks at Alcott's biography for evidence of her and her family's attitudes toward both servants and household work itself. Finally, it interrogates several scenes in *Little Women* to assess the indispensable labor and other support Hannah provides to the March family as well as the self-effacing manner in which she is presented. Despite the narrator's suppression of her independent voice, this investigation makes abundantly clear that rather than peripheral to this saga, Hannah Mullet must be seen as an essential complement to Marmee. Without her bifurcated role as both family intimate and maid of all work, *Little Women*'s beloved mother-of-all-wisdom could not exist.

Contemporary reviewers of *Little Women* took no notice of Hannah. Rather, they laud the "noble, heroic mother" who transmits to her daughters "an appreciation of the dignity of labor"; they sing the praises of the "sensible, self-denying woman and loving mother, who, by her good example and ready sympathy, points out and leads them the way" (Clark 65, 83). Critical attention to Hannah has likewise been scant, with some references to an anonymous family "servant" rather than to Hannah by name.[3] Sarah Elbert is the unusual example who credits Hannah for both her counsel and her labor (200, 201). Peter Stoneley has also remarked on the "broad conceptual gulf" (140) between Hannah and her employer, similar to Susan Laird's claim that despite the narrator's insistence on their intimacy, Hannah operates "more [as] a domestic tool than a human character in the March girls' lives" (300).

Disappointingly, in studies attending to social class and/or work in *Little Women*, Hannah Mullet merits only brief mentions or is omitted entirely. Lorinda B. Cohoon valorizes Beth's housework and efforts in "managing the home" and nods to Hannah's "helping" role; in reality, though, Beth assists Hannah, who teaches Beth housekeeping skills. Nor do we see Beth at any time "manage" the household (159, 164). Other critics similarly overlook Hannah in studies where her character is optimal for appraisal. Stephanie Foote's insightful look at gender and class in *Little Women* neglects Hannah, the only figure in the March household of a different social class from the family members. Foote explains that by the mid-nineteenth century, "middle-class women become the guardians of the difference between economic class and social status" (68); she sees the March family's ambiguous genteel "social position . . . [as] strikingly incommensurate with their economic position"

(69), as was the case for the Alcotts themselves. Like Foote, Alice Kessler-Harris reminds us that class distinctions in nineteenth-century America depended on the types of labor performed by poor women versus women of means (40). With this disparity in mind, Hannah's presence as a live-in domestic servant actually elevates the Marches' class standing. What Foote describes as the family's "warmth," "domestic identity," and "nurturing qualities" (70)—markers of economic means—are possible because of Hannah's work.[4] Janis Dawson characterizes Alcott's "curiously skewed picture of working women's experiences" in fictionalizing her own family's saga in *Little Women* (116) and accurately contends that Alcott takes greater pains to "represent the 'genteel' working girl" (126) than to show the barren reality of many employed women's lives in the nineteenth century. Yet surely any discussion of women's work in *Little Women* should at the very least note the narrator's tunnel vision—that all the while Marmee and the girls hold forth on their daily labors, no one notices the backdrop of Hannah bustling in and out of the room, putting bread on the table, making the fire, hanging out the clothes, sending up the Christmas turkey, and otherwise laboring until, on occasion, falling asleep exhausted in a chair.

Critical studies focused on Marmee and the "normative mother" figure she projects similarly ignore Hannah. Shirley Foster and Judy Simons, for instance, describe the family's domestic space as a "women's world which Marmee and her four daughters inhabit" (87), forgetting that Hannah makes six in this residential female cohort. Richard Brodhead likewise homes in on the "loving parental presence, in an enclosed family space warmed by maternal affection and so oriented toward the mother's beliefs," an arrangement for which he credits a "regular set of substitutes" who fill in for Marmee, the "motherlike friends and advisors" (71, 72). Yet it is exclusively Hannah Mullet who serves as Marmee's surrogate, particularly during her absence to care for Mr. March. Further, Brodhead shows how easily Hannah can be rendered invisible when he posits that Marmee leaves the girls "home alone" in the opening chapter, despite the fact that we see Hannah there working as usual in chapter 1, clearing the table after dinner (72, 92). Like Foote, Brodhead skips the opportunity to discuss the embodied class distinction who resides in the March home—"old," "faithful" Hannah, who serves, labors, and is ever mindful of her subordinate "place."

Not surprisingly, the several film, stage, and radio adaptations of *Little Women* also reduce Hannah's role. Usually, she is cast as a middle-aged and generally good-natured servant, although some treatments present her less generously, as for instance in the 1933 George Cukor and 1949 Mervyn Leroy productions, in which Hannah more harshly mimics Marmee about poor Mrs. Hummel bringing yet another child into her family's destitution. In the 1949 film, actor Elizabeth Patterson as Hannah deplores the birth of the seventh Hummel, with a line that appears nowhere in Alcott's novel: "I believe in charity but why bring another child into the world and we have nothing to spare" (LeRoy). This Hannah also gossips ungenerously about Laurie, but like most cinematic Hannahs, she receives little screen time overall. Her character is overwhelmingly cast as a white servant; in limited examples, Hannah speaks with an Irish lilt, as in Gillian Armstrong's *Little Women* (1994). A 2001 stage version specifies Hannah on the cast list as "an Irish immigrant" (Asher n. pag.), while Irish actor Eleanor Methven plays Hannah in the 2017 BBC miniseries. In only one film adaptation, a 1987–1988 Japanese production by Nippon Animation, does Hannah appear as an African American. Stereotyped as a "Mammy" figure, this caricatured Hannah speaks with an overstated and inconsistent black dialect, a creation that led many viewers to object (Delamar 186). Hannah does not appear in Mark Adamo's 2001 opera of *Little Women*, while in the most recent big-screen film, Greta Gerwig's 2019 production, American actor Jayne Houdyshell brings Hannah to life. As is typical in many film adaptations of lengthy novels, minor characters like Hannah recede into the background, thus suppressing her character's pivotal role in the March family's story.

As with other levels of the idealized autobiographical scaffolding in *Little Women*, Hannah Mullet has no counterpart in Alcott's youth.[5] Only in their very early married life did Bronson and Abba Alcott employ a few domestic servants and a gardener. Before her marriage, the rather pampered Abba May likely had little if any experience with housework (Bedell 55, 65); by the time she was mother to four and often the lone breadwinner for her family of six, however, she and her daughters handled the domestic labor. Indeed, one acquaintance described Mrs. Alcott as "by nature a noble and charming woman, by profession a household drudge" (Bradford 391). As adolescents, Louisa and her older sister, Anna, contributed to family finances by sewing; by age eighteen, they both worked full-time, with Louisa trying out vocations as governess, teacher, seamstress, laundress, nurse, and, very briefly, domestic servant (Bedell 159, 269, 296; *Journals* 69). At no time did the Alcott girls benefit from the loving labor of a live-in servant such as Hannah.

At age eighteen, Louisa Alcott learned from experience the exacting conditions, dearth of respect, and low pay of servitude such as Hannah's daily grind. Humorously recounted in "How I Went Out to Service" (1874), the narrator finds that although hired to be a companion and to do light housekeeping, she is instead expected to clear paths through the snow, carry water from the well, split kindling, and tend the fire, particularly after rejecting her employer's suggestive desire for her rapt attention. Drawing the line at "blacking his boots," she stays out her term of seven weeks, only to be further insulted at receiving a pittance of four dollars as her total wages (360, 362). Unfortunately, as with the loose or nonexistent employment arrangements of most nineteenth-century domestic servants, no advance contract had stipulated the narrator's pay (Sutherland 103). As the story opens, the narrator states her preference to "scrub floors and take in washing" rather than teach. When her mother reminds her of the fall in social class such a position represents, and when her "highly respectable relatives" react in horror, she retorts that "every sort of work that is paid for is service" (*Little Women* 352). Such respect for Hannah's situation, however, is scarce in *Little Women*.

The Alcotts' distressed financial circumstances were public knowledge, quite often offset only through the charity of friends and family (Bedell 160–65, 240, 296; Willis 22). Placing "the domestic" Hannah as a socioeconomic prop in the fictional March household lessens the severity of this painful reality and allows Alcott to depict her protagonists as respectably genteel, their situation a considerable contrast to the squalid Hummels. Most important, Abba Alcott's fictional representation as Marmee appears in *Little Women* solely as a maternal counselor-comforter, a one-dimensional identity that depends absolutely on Hannah's dual role as servant and family intimate. As April Schultz contends, "domestic service was essential 'to the practice of sentimental domesticity'" (183); in other words, for Marmee to exemplify the norms of nineteenth-century "true womanhood"—"where the mother's presence seemed the sunshine of the circle around her; imparting a cheering and vivifying power" (Beecher 149)—Hannah must free her from household labor.

Examining Hannah Mullet in the historical context of mid-nineteenth-century domestic servitude in New England confirms the extent to which the narrator rose-tints her subordinate status and simultaneously hinders her development. As a female, live-in "maid of all work," Hannah takes part in a dismal labor force in which a "gaping social chasm" existed between employer and servant. Nearly all households that could afford to do so employed at least one servant for the "exhausting, backbreaking, unceasing" chores in an age that predated modern conveniences. By 1870 in Boston, a quarter of all families hired servants whose inferior position in the family was made manifest in their daily routine (Sutherland xii, 10, 46)—from taking meals in the kitchen, to using rear stairwells and back doors, to the speech used to address their employers' family members. Unlike Hannah's occasional social equality with the Marches, as when she is included in plans to attend a theatrical production with Meg (62), American servants did not often cross such boundaries.[6] Mostly, Hannah heeds these distinctions too. We frequently observe her in the kitchen or otherwise involved with meal preparation and service, but she is never viewed sharing a family meal.

Women comprised 90 percent of all household servants in mid- to late nineteenth-century America, in addition to which over half of all working women served in this capacity. Unlike Hannah, whom the narrator routinely calls "old," most "domestics" were young women; (presumably) like her, they were largely single (Sutherland 45, 55). The work Hannah performs in *Little Women* generally compares to servants' actual duties—cooking, serving, cleaning, laundering, and sewing/mending—although the March girls tend their own individual gardens (85). As with Hannah, who works both of the Christmas days that occur in *Little Women*, domestic servants in nineteenth-century America rarely received holidays or vacations (Sutherland 98, 99). So unusual was it to obtain a reputable, long-serving "domestic" that in her *History of American Housework*, Susan Strasser compares the fictional Hannah Mullet to "a needle in a haystack" (163). We remain ignorant of the basic provisions of Hannah's employment situation. What wages does she earn? Where in the home does she reside? Presuming she has a private room, we never see her in it. What are her rights, if any, in disputes with the Marches? To our knowledge, Hannah's employment agreement stipulates none of these terms.[7]

The Alcott family understood firsthand the plight of New England's poor working class. In addition to Louisa's own stint as a domestic servant, through which she certainly became aware that the cherished intimacy between the Marches and Hannah deviated greatly from any service norm of this time, Abba Alcott not only conducted neighborhood charity efforts as Marmee does in *Little Women* but also ran one of the first Boston employment offices tasked with finding jobs for the poor. In addition, she later served in the capacity of what many regard as the city's first female social worker (Bedell 282–85, 272 ff.). Popular household manuals, including those authored by Alcott acquaintances such as Catherine Beecher, Lydia Maria Child, and Catharine Sedgwick, offer copious advice to women on how to manage, retain, discipline, and train their "domestics." While these authors do urge mistresses to respect their servants and to exhibit patience while training them, they take for granted the employer's need to maintain class distinctions (Beecher and Stowe 314–16).[8]

Such household guides, and historical studies, establish the extent to which Irish immigrants dominated domestic service at this time, particularly in urban centers. During the second half of the nineteenth century, nearly one million Irish women arrived in the United States, most of them single, and they filled nearly half of these jobs in major cities like Boston (Schultz 180). Their preponderance as household maids gave rise to a wave of nativist sentiments, particularly anti-Catholicism and other xenophobic attitudes that rampantly affected employment practices. From the habitual "No Irish Need Apply" advertisements to deplorable stereotypes of loud, frazzled, dishonest "Bridget" and "Biddy" in popular media and literature alike, the Irish maid figures as a disrespected, often dehumanized, source of incomprehensible frustration to her employer (Beecher and Stowe 312; Dudden 65). By contrast, while excluding the Irish, "Help Wanted Females" advertisements often encouraged "Swede, German or Norwegian" applicants, in some cases requesting "A German girl who can speak English" (*New York Herald*, 1864 and 1871; *Daily Inter Ocean*, 1892). Such attitudes are blatant in the household manuals mentioned above, including the popular *American Woman's Home* (1869) by sisters Catherine Beecher and Harriet Beecher Stowe. As they lament the soaring influx of Irish women in domestic service in New England, the authors praise the American housewife's efficiency and intelligence over the muscle of the "common Irish servant," who will take a full day to do the work an American woman will knock off in a few hours. They pronounce the "raw Irish maid-of-all-work, [as] a creature of immense bone and muscle, but of heavy, unawakened brain" and find it remarkable that "with all the unreasoning heats and prejudices of the Celtic blood, all the unnecessary ignorance and rawness," the American home should reflect any "measure of comfort" (311, 313).[9]

Given this statistical and cultural reality, various sources have presumed that Hannah is Irish.[10] *Little Women*, however, affords no definite evidence identifying her ethnicity, race, or immigrant status, other than may be evoked by the fact that the surname "Mullet" derives from English and French (Hanks 633). Hannah's speech in the novel may reveal more about Alcott's amateur ability as a budding author to pen nonstandard English than it does about Hannah's identity. At times, she sounds respectfully British, as when she addresses Marmee as "mum" (*Little Women* 129, 130, 175). On occasion, her phrasing resembles caricatured African American dialect as seen in popular works like *Uncle Tom's Cabin*, from which Jo March misquotes in the "Burdens" chapter. For example, in chapter 10, Hannah claims she would "know which each of them gardings belonged to, ef I see 'em in Chiny" (85). Her letter to Marmee in chapter 16 presents additional examples: "I jes drop-a line to say we git on fust rate"; she hopes that Mr. March has recovered from his "Pewmonia"; she assures Marmee that the girls "hev coffee only once a week, accordin to your wish, and [I] keep em on plain wholesome vittles" (140). Karen Sands-O'Connor points out, though, that Alcott approved Frank Merrill's illustrations that appeared in the 1880 edition of *Little Women*; in these drawings, Hannah is sketched after the manner of the white characters (38n6). While these and other examples of her vernacular speech evidence Hannah's lack of education, they do not convey her specific ethnicity or race but, rather, demonstrate that regardless of her specific origins, the narrator presents Hannah as a stereotype of the oppressed and caricatured "other" who frequents nineteenth-century American fiction, including in this classic girls' story.

In contrast to their reformist sensibility on antislavery and women's rights, Alcott and her mother both expressed antipathy toward Irish men and women. Madelon Bedell argues, in fact, that Abba Alcott's prejudice at times equaled the most virulent of American nativist politics. In 1850, she decried their transforming Boston "into a 'New Ireland'" and doubted their prospect to "be Americanized" (qtd. in Bedell 275, 384), although in her capacity as social worker and employment agent, Abba also grew more aware that the root causes of immigrant poverty were low wages and lack of access to education. For her part, in her private writings, Louisa Alcott disparages the unprincipled "Irish incapables" (*Journals* 196; *Selected Letters* 273); in her fiction, she routinely portrays them negatively. Only three instances of Irish characters, two of whom are identified as such, occur in *Little Women*, the first in chapter 7, where "the sworn foes" of Amy and her schoolmates are "the little Irish children" who "exult over" the "contraband" limes she shamefully casts out the window when disciplined by her teacher (59). The second is Kitty, "an Irish lady [who] presided over the kitchen department" and "who took life 'aisy'" (305) in Meg and John's newlywed home; and the third figures as the object of Mr. Laurence's charity, a poor woman to whom he gives a fish while shopping in the market. In a dialect marking her as Irish, this woman thanks Mr. Laurence with a wish that his "bed in heaven would be 'aisy'" (42).

In Alcott's adult novel *Work*, the Irish domestic workers appear wholly unfavorably. Protagonist Christie Devon's prospective employer, Mrs. Stuart, appreciates learning that unlike the Irish applicants for the job, Christie does not object to working alongside the black cook, Hepsey Johnson. Christie's broad-mindedness, however, does not extend to the Irish, as she tells a subsequent employer, Mrs. Sterling, that she will do any task so long as "I need not do it with a shiftless Irish girl to drive me distracted by pretending to help" (19, 172). Christie is class conscious in her prejudice; as Sarah Lahey notes, she "refuses to work with Irish servants because she is 'unable to bear the contact with coarser natures which makes labor seem degrading.' Thus she sees the potential for uplift in labor only when one is able to consort with appropriate peers" (147). Ultimately, Christie decides to leave domestic service altogether rather than continue to "live with Irish mates" (30).

Though not subjected to this level of demeaning portrayal, poor German characters are also rendered unsympathetic in *Little Women*, demonstrating that in contrast to Professor Friedrich Bhaer, whom Jo marries, education, at least for Germans, can overcome class difference. The impoverished Hummels receive the Marches' charity throughout the novel in a one-sided relationship and are always portrayed harshly, their misery evident in every contact with them and their filthy hovel. Further, as Kristen Proehl argues, in addition to being desperately poor, the Hummels are repeatedly demeaned (113). When Meg's "cooking mania" fails, she bids Lotty to take the "batch of failures" to "the convenient stomachs of the little Hummels." Lotty herself, a servant who calls John Brooke her "master," has calmly watched the disastrous jelly episode "with Teutonic phlegm." Similarly, Amy dispatches the leftovers from her unsuccessful fancy luncheon to the "Hummels—Germans like messes" (218, 220, 221, 210). As these examples demonstrate, *Little Women*'s narrator commonly marks ethnic characters, whether Irish or German. That Hannah is not so identified, that her speech reveals a derisive mixture of ethnic exhortations, and, importantly, that her character's unflagging trustworthiness contrasts sharply with the disparaging portraits of all ethnic characters except Professor Bhaer makes it most probable that Hannah Mullet is poor, uneducated, white Anglo-European, and native born. Unfortunately, the narrator prohibits these and other authentic personal dimensions from developing Hannah into a fully actualized character.

In nearly one hundred appearances in *Little Women*, the truncated presentation of Hannah Mullet interweaves her role as a domestic servant whose duties align with the norm for this profession with more wide-ranging family responsibilities, added to which is an emotional closeness with the Marches that is both at odds with her position and occasionally the source of her serving as a stock figure of "comic relief" in the family dynamic. As already noted, in stark contrast to Marmee, whom we never actually observe doing housework, Hannah prepares delectable meals as well as daily turnovers and special treats; she irons, washes clothes, and readies "snowy muslins" (72) for Meg's "Vanity Fair" episode. Indeed, Hannah displays more than the requisite skills to tackle all domestic tasks. In book 1, she also relays messages to neighbors and escorts Jo and Meg home from the holiday ball, at which she scolds parentally when Meg sprains her ankle but refuses aid. Further, in both her encouragement of the March girls as well as her anger when they're wronged, Hannah reacts as a family intimate. When Mr. Laurence bestows on Beth the grand gift of a piano, for example, Hannah, who "always took a share in the family joys and sorrows," urges her, "Try it, honey; let's hear the sound of the baby-pianny" (56). Witnessing Beth muster up the courage to thank Mr. Laurence in person, Hannah voices everyone's amazement: "Well, I wish I may die, if it ain't the queerest thing I ever see! The pianny has turned her head; she'd never have gone, in her right mind" (56). She consoles the mortified Amy after the pickled limes episode and "shook her fist at the 'villain'" schoolteacher (60). For their part, the family occasionally has fun at Hannah's expense, as in chapter 10, "The P. C. and the P. O.," when the Laurences' gardener, "smitten with Hannah's charms, actually sent a love-letter to Jo's care," prompting them all—presumably the Marches and Laurences—to "laugh when the secret came out" (91). Hannah's reaction to this flirtation, and the ridicule, go unsaid.

In chapter 4, "Burdens," and chapter 11, "Experiments," Hannah's behavior complicates and augments Marmee's lessons to her daughters. As "Burdens" opens, the holidays have ended, and the girls grumble about resuming their normal routines, while Marmee is "very busy trying to finish a letter" (35). Only Hannah works in this scene, soldiering on in the kitchen despite having a rare instance of "the grumps" due to the holiday schedule causing her to keep late hours the night before. As Meg and Jo prepare to depart for their working day, Meg as a governess and Jo as crotchety Aunt March's companion, they savor the "institution" of Hannah's warm "turn-overs," which she "never forgot to make" (36). Intriguingly, the revised edition of *Little Women* (1880) intensifies Hannah's irritability in this scene. While in the first edition Hannah "bounced" into and out of the room to dispense the hot-from-the-oven turnovers, in the later edition she "stalked" (388), perhaps more firmly emphasizing her "grumps" and thereby an unusual streak of independence, and/or possibly evidencing the narrator's greater disdain for her moodiness. Whether bouncing or stalking, however, Hannah's morning labor in this episode contrasts not only with the girls' grievances about their workday "burdens" but also with Marmee's scolding when they interrupt her placid letter writing: "You drive me distracted with your worry," she exclaims to the girls (36). The resulting "momentary lull" when Hannah enters with the turnovers seems to reset everyone's spirits.

Since in this chapter we find out the salient detail of the family having suffered a reversal of fortune some years earlier as a result of Mr. March's aid to "an unfortunate friend" (36), the girls' litany of complaints here must be understood through their memory of a more privileged era, a time in their lives that Hannah also no doubt recalls, despite her "maid of all work" status then as now being the same. In "Burdens," we also learn that it is Beth's primary responsibility, not Marmee's, to "help Hannah keep home neat and comfortable" (*Little Women* 38), a division of labor that spawns one of gentle Beth's infrequent outbursts. Housekeeping, she declares, is the "worst work in the world" (12).[11] Marmee, meanwhile, spends the day "at the rooms" with other volunteers, sewing clothes to send to soldiers at the war front (42). As the chapter ends, the girls gather around her as usual in the evening and continue to sew, with Marmee fashioning a moral that calls attention to what they've already realized on their own: that wealth does not necessarily lead to happiness. As is the norm in these uplifting scenes, no one pays any mind to the servant in the house, who surely might beg to differ as to the privileges afforded by wealth.

"Experiments" provides another of Marmee's teaching moments, this one enabled by Hannah's absence as well as by her abiding presence. Additionally, this chapter marks the only time in *Little Women* that Marmee does share a portion of the housework, albeit which specific chores the narrator doesn't say. The girls luxuriate as the chapter opens at the prospect of idle summer weeks stretching before them and ask Marmee, sewing as usual in her "corner" (92), to be exempted for a time from their daily labors. Marmee assents with a week's reprieve, an "experiment" she privately anticipates will test the adage about "all work and no play." How does their mother put this "experiment" into operation? Not surprisingly, "with Hannah's help" (93). Although her employer doesn't ask whether Hannah is willing to take on extra tasks for an entire week, her compensation comes on the final day, when, to strengthen the impact of the lesson, Marmee relishes a day of solitude in her room and grants "Hannah a holiday" (94). "There was no fire in the kitchen, no breakfast in the dining-room, and no mother anywhere to be seen," when the girls arise that morning, the sole example in *Little Women* of Hannah having time off. Even the phrasing "gave Hannah a holiday" divulges that her work schedule, as was the norm for domestic servants in nineteenth-century America, does not include days off (Sutherland 98). We've already seen that Hannah works on Christmas Day; therefore, this "holiday" is extraordinary indeed. Even so, it's not quite a full day off; before leaving that morning, Hannah "left a pan of bread to rise" (*Little Women* 96).

By the end of the full week, the lesson of Marmee's "experiment" has been driven home, and the four girls gratefully take up their usual household tasks. "While Hannah and I did your work," Marmee explains, the girls learned "what happens when every one thinks only of herself" (*Little Women* 99). As a result of her essential supporting role in "Experiments," this chapter gives rise to rare critical mentions of Hannah. Equating Hannah's labor with that of Marmee, Kathryn Dolan notes that in addition to its central lesson about the importance of work-play balance, the girls also learn through their final day's "mishaps" "not to take Marmee and Hannah for granted" (46), thereby equating the two as domestic workers. Likewise, Sarah Lahey credits Hannah with coteaching the import of "Experiments," albeit she refers to the "household servant" (148) rather than to Hannah by name.

In book 1's consequential chapters 15 through 20, during which Marmee is absent from home to care for her wounded husband, Hannah becomes central to *Little Women*'s narrative, although her subordinate status is ultimately reestablished. She takes on all of Marmee's maternal responsibilities and more, as she must soon also manage the ensuing difficulty of Beth's grave illness. From her fearful relaying of "one of them horrid telegraph things" (129) in chapter 15, which missive announces Mr. March's sickness and sends Marmee packing, Hannah, wiping tears on her apron, "was the first to recover, and with unconscious wisdom she set all the rest a good example" and proceeded to "git your things ready right away, mum" (130). Earlier than usual the next morning, "Hannah's familiar face looked unnatural as she flew about her kitchen with her night cap on" (135), preparing breakfast for the traveler. Marmee entrusts Hannah with her daughters' "care" and directs eldest daughter Meg to "be prudent, watch over your sisters, [and] consult Hannah" as need arises (135). To be sure, Mrs. March also trusts Mr. Laurence for "protection" in "any perplexity," but Hannah is responsible for household management and routine caretaking of the four girls. In the initial hours after their mother departs, Hannah "wisely" gives them time to vent their feelings, makes coffee as a treat, and then, quite Marmee-like, urges them to "fall to work, and be a credit to the family." As they vow to be strong, Jo agrees that they will rely on Hannah during these trying days, while Beth confirms that she and Amy will keep house, because "Hannah will tell us what to do" (136).

Family's and friends' letters to absent Marmee in chapter 16 praise Hannah's care and efficiency, yet they also reinforce the narrator's consistent attention to the servant's subordinate class, despite her capable handling of increased responsibilities during these weeks. Meg pronounces Hannah "a perfect saint; she does not scold at all, and always calls me 'Miss Margaret,' which is quite proper you know, and treats me with respect" (137). In her epistle, Amy requests permission to instruct "Hannah to put more starch in my aprons and have buck wheats every day" (139). Old Mr. Laurence reports that Hannah "is a model servant, [who] guards pretty Meg like a dragon" (140), notwithstanding that with this caution, Hannah acts more like a mother than a servant. Meg's notice of Hannah's respectful address supports Susan Laird's critique of the "miseducation" of the March girls, in which Laird finds Hannah an exemplar of Marmee's "hidden curriculum in classism" (297). She argues that by "socializing her daughters to depend upon Hannah's domestic service without the simplest thanks, Marmee never teaches them any affectionate appreciation for Hannah's character or any reciprocal concern for the quality of her life" (297). Added to which, we see that Marmee herself seldom addresses Hannah directly, whether to thank, inform, or otherwise discuss family matters. Rather, for example, she instructs Jo to tell Hannah to get down her black trunk, volunteers Hannah to Meg for extra duty and childcare, and reminds all of them to rely on Hannah.

Original drawing of Hannah Mullet (Frank Merrill, 1880). Courtesy Concord Free Public Library

Her own letter to Mrs. March at the end of chapter 16 provides the lone occurrence in *Little Women* of Hannah's sustained perspective on the individual girls, even as it largely furthers the narrator's presentation of the servant's meek acquiescence of her station. First Hannah assures Marmee that "we git on fust rate." Then, in order of age, she characterizes their behavior. Meg's housekeeping talents are "surprising quick"; Jo "doos beat all for goin ahead, but she don't stop to cal'k'late fust, and you never know where she's like to bring up"; "Beth is . . . the best of little creeters, and a sight of help to me"; "Amy does well about frettin, wearin her best clothes and eatin sweet stuff." Next she turns to their neighbors: "Mr. Laurie . . . turns the house upside down frequent; but he heartens up the girls, and so I let em hev full swing"; and, finally, while she finds old Mr. Laurence's constant treats "rather wearin . . . [he] means wal, and it aint my place to say nothin." She closes by sending "my duty to Mr. March" (140). Here we see that though entrusted with household and family affairs, Hannah respectfully addresses their young friend as "Mr. Laurie" and remembers her "place." At last, however, as she closes the missive, Hannah writes herself into a full identity—especially given her uneducated status—"Yours Respectful, 'Hannah Mullet'" (140).

When Beth falls dangerously ill with scarlet fever after caring for the Hummels' dying infant, Hannah not only displays another vital skill as a nurse but must also make difficult decisions as to keeping the others safe, deciding whether or not to inform Marmee of the situation, and holding fast to her own judgment when challenged by Laurie. The girls' reliance on Hannah when confronted with this emergency is evident. The instant Beth discloses her condition, Jo rushes to "call Hannah; she knows all about sickness," whereupon Hannah, "the good soul . . . took the lead at once" (*Little Women* 143). She examines Beth, summons the doctor, reassures them all that "rightly treated, nobody died" of scarlet fever, and prepares Amy, the lone sister never exposed to this illness, to stay with Aunt March until the danger has passed (143). Gently consoling her patient, Hannah prods Beth to choose only Meg or Jo as her secondary nurse, again mindful of contagion. Though the older girls are conflicted about the decision not to notify Marmee, they accept Hannah's authority and rely on her nursing expertise. Initially, Dr. Bangs agrees with Hannah's appraisal that Beth won't be ill long, but soon they both realize she is "much sicker than any one but" the two of them "suspected" (146).

The narrator's somewhat ambivalent portrayal of Hannah at the helm during this urgent situation does not initially indicate whether she has usurped her position. Because old "Mr. Laurence was not allowed to see" Beth— presumably because of the potential for infection at his elderly age—"Hannah had everything all her own way" (*Little Women* 146). With this judgment, does the narrator criticize Hannah's overreach or uphold her authority? Soon we have our answer, as Hannah's management is undermined at this critical juncture. Keeping secret from their mother the knowledge of Beth's illness wears on the girls. Jo "could not think it right to deceive her mother, but had been bidden to mind Hannah, and Hannah wouldn't hear of 'Mrs. March bein' told, and worried just for sech a trifle'" (146), a decision all the more reasonable when they learn of their father's relapse from Marmee's recent letter. As Beth's condition worsens, however, the girls plead to tell their mother, and an exhausted Hannah, after sitting up all night with the patient, agrees to consider it while reassuring them that "there was no danger *yet*" (146). Just as she and the doctor agree they must alert Mrs. March, Hannah is relegated to her subservient role when Laurie and his grandfather telegraph Marmee a day before the doctor advises that they do so because they object to Hannah "overdoing the authority business." Joking with Jo, who is grateful for their action since she wants her mother home, Laurie adds that "Hannah most took my head off when I proposed a telegram," at which scolding he convinced his grandfather to take immediate action. "I never *can* bear to be 'marmed over,'" he reminds Jo (149), in a suggestive characterization of Hannah as proxy for Marmee. Thus, both upper-class Laurences make clear that rather than truly mistrusting her decision-making rationale itself, what they most disapprove of is Hannah acting in a manner beyond her servant station. Although Elizabeth Keyser credits Laurie for "helping sustain the family" in this episode when the family's "center" has been "displaced" (62, 56), in this instance, he countermands both the doctor and Hannah and takes action primarily because he resists Hannah's mothering behavior as well as her assumption of the authority with which Marmee has actually invested her.

The narrator renders Hannah's very competence in this episode as an emotional struggle for her. Ultimately, Hannah recognizes that she is powerless to prevail over the Laurences' class privilege and accepts the conditions of her station. Calling Laurie the "interferingest chap" (*Little Women* 149), Hannah nonetheless expresses "relief" that Marmee has been sent for. She remains vigilant, though "quite worn out," and sleeps at the foot of Beth's bed, while waiting for Marmee to return (150). As the crisis passes, we see Hannah's competence in one last scene. As Beth stirs, leading Jo and Meg to the "dreadful fear" that she has died, Hannah "started out of her sleep, hurried to the bed, looked at Beth, felt her hands, listened at her lips, and then, throwing her apron over her head, sat down to rock to and fro, exclaiming, under her breath, 'The fever's turned; she's sleepin nat'ral; her skin's damp, and she breathes easy. Praise be given! Oh, my goodness me!'" (150, 151). These details emphasize the degree of Hannah's nursing expertise, such that it seems anticlimactic when the doctor shortly confirms her diagnosis. By then, Meg and Jo have returned "to be kissed and cuddled by faithful Hannah" at Beth's side (151). Regardless of her pivotal role during these dire weeks, as they await Marmee, Hannah "knocked up a couple of pies in case of company unexpected" (149); on Marmee's return, sleepless "nodding Hannah mounted guard at the door" to prevent intruders from disturbing the family's reunion. Her customary station in the household has been restored as she "'dished up' an astonishing breakfast . . . finding it impossible to vent her excitement in any other way" (158), since as the narrator indifferently advances, for Hannah, "work was the panacea for most afflictions" (130).

As book 2 opens, three years have passed, and Hannah Mullet is the only resident of the March household for whom the narrator gives no update—all has apparently remained housekeeping duties as usual for "faithful Hannah." Throughout book 2 the narrator continues to depict Hannah's zeal to serve the March family alongside her character's undeveloped stasis. Instead, "five energetic women seemed to rule the house" (*Little Women* 190), declares our narrator, who elides the sixth woman in this busy home who labors rather than rules. Now her work for the Marches extends to newlywed Meg, as Hannah "arranged every pot and pan a dozen times over, and laid the fire all ready for lighting" before Meg and John marry (193). Prior to the wedding, Amy asks Meg whether she and John will hire servants, leading Meg to respond that in discussing the subject with Marmee, she has "made up my mind to try her way first." She explains that she expects to handle her housework "with Lotty to run my errands and help me here and there" (194). By "try her way first," Meg indicates that she will follow Marmee's example. But if this is the case, she will need to hire a full-time live-in servant like Hannah; making do with part-time Lotty does not replicate her mother's situation, whether now or in the past. How should we account for this discrepancy? Surely, the narrator does not forget Hannah's around-the-clock schedule in the current March household. Perhaps Meg refers to an earlier time in the Marches' married years, since they had hired Hannah when Meg was born. Yet these had been the glory years of the family's financial prosperity, when they likely employed several servants. Moreover, Marmee's contribution to this conversation reinforces Hannah's value. As a new mother, she had "learned of Hannah how things should be done, that my servants need *not* laugh at me" (194). While this scene's purpose is ostensibly to elevate the stature of the wife's domestic work, the incongruity between Marmee's actual "way" versus Meg's characterization of it mocks the young woman's naïveté even as it continues to disregard Hannah's full-time labor.

Amy's artistic experimentation and, especially, her social aspirations in book 2 intriguingly work against the narrator's self-abnegating depiction of Hannah. At the budding artist's "poker-sketching," when "smoke issued from attic and shed" and "red-hot pokers lay about promiscuously," only Hannah has the foresight to place "a pail of water and the dinner-bell at her door, in case of fire" (*Little Women* 203), though the narrator seems to tease at this overprecaution. Jo and Hannah are both "out of humor" as Amy's fancy luncheon "deranged" the usual work schedule. Referring to Hannah's ill humor as a "hitch in the main-spring of the domestic machinery" (207), the narrator reinforces her centrality to the running of the home. Yet on the day of "the grand event," in the novel's only such occurrence, "Hannah's cooking didn't turn out well; the chicken was tough, the tongue too salt, and the chocolate wouldn't froth properly" (207). Hannah wreaks further havoc with the menu when the cats make a meal out of the chicken she leaves "on the kitchen table a minute" (208). If Hannah has intentionally sabotaged Amy's party—perhaps because she shares Marmee and the girls' feelings about Amy's desire to impress the wealthier girls she's invited—the narrator is oblivious to this possibility of Hannah's agency. How do we know Hannah is out of sorts? Because her cooking goes awry. With the preparations under way by the girls and Hannah, Marmee's negligible contribution to the affair is standing on the porch, ready to welcome the guests (209), although as is typical in *Little Women*, Amy later declares about the day that "if it hadn't been for mother I never should have got through" (207).

Although repeatedly downplayed, Hannah's demonstrable competence as the all-knowing albeit self-effacing domestic manager ironically establishes her—rather than Marmee—as the household manager in *Little Women*, particularly in Meg's story. In chapter 5 of book 2, "Domestic Experiences," Meg imagines the ease with which she can turn out batches of currant jelly because "hadn't she seen Hannah do it hundreds of times?" (219), further reinforcing Hannah as the domestic ideal in *Little Women* rather than Marmee, who in fact had confided to Jo years before that she "never enjoyed housekeeping" (95). Following the jelly fiasco and Meg's marital doldrums after the twins displace John in commanding his wife's attention, Marmee steps in, as usual, to advise. Her solution? "Let Hannah come and help you; she is a capital nurse, and you may trust the precious babies to her while you do more housework. . . . Hannah would enjoy the rest" (308). Or as Meg later relays this "experiment" to John, "Hannah is to help me with the children, and I'm to see to things about the house more" (312). Nowhere in these conversations does anyone suggest asking Hannah or imagine that she should get some say in this significant shift in her job description. Indeed, as Elizabeth Keyser sees it, on Meg's behalf Marmee treats Hannah as "the family retainer" (75). We can but speculate whether Hannah—some twenty-five years away from caring for the young Marches—will share Marmee's opinion that it will be any kind of "rest" to care for infant twins in Meg's home, especially in light of how upset Hannah became when Amy's luncheon derailed her work routine. When relaying the new arrangement to John, Meg's diminishment of household labor in general, as with her explanation of her housekeeping plans to her sisters before marrying, is also noteworthy. While Marmee explains that Hannah will free her to do more "housework," Meg lightens this realignment to allowing me to "see about things about the house," tasks that, as with her mother, we never actually see Meg doing, other than the jelly calamity itself.

As in book 1, Hannah's emotional reactions in book 2 continue in relation only to the March family. At the birth of Daisy and Demi, Hannah joins others in "a peal of laughter," surprising Laurie as two, rather than one, infants are put into his arms; she pronounces Amy and Jo as "pretty as picters" as they prepare to make neighborhood calls; she is "afflicted" awaiting her hug from Laurie as he departs for Europe; she sorrowfully watches and waits as Beth deteriorates and "never wearied of concocting dainty dishes to tempt a capricious appetite, dropping tears as she worked"; and after Beth dies she understands approvingly that Jo hums Beth's old songs because "you're determined we shan't miss that dear lamb ef you can help it" (227, 230, 290, 324, 338). When newlyweds Amy and Laurie arrive home from Europe, Hannah marvels over the youngest daughter's stylish maturation—"Blest if she ain't in silk from head to foot; ain't it a relishin' sight to see her settin' there as fine as a fiddle, and hear folks calling little Amy 'Mis. Laurence!,'" a pronouncement followed by Hannah referring to "Miss Amy" (349, 350). Her devotion carries forward to Meg and John's children, whose care she now superintends: three-year-old Daisy's budding domestic talents "brought tears of pride to Hannah's eyes" (358).

A coming-of-age novel that made Louisa May Alcott's reputation as a beloved author, *Little Women* presents a heartwarming family story, at the center of whose loving home is a long-neglected maid of all work, Hannah Mullet. Thanks to Hannah's labor and devotion, Marmee can devote herself to the nurturing of her four girls as they mature into little women. The importance of working women looms large in Alcott's canon. From *Hospital Sketches* (1863), to "How I Went Out to Service" (1874), to *Work* (1873), Alcott dramatizes her own experiences as a nurse in a chaotic Civil War hospital, as a governess and teacher, and as a domestic servant. The end of *Work* culminates with an empowering and mutually supportive community of working women; but in *Little Women* and other children's works, servants like Hannah Mullet are left out of this fond circle. Although by the time she penned *Little Women*, Alcott well understood the vagaries and inequities of poor laboring women's lives, for the youthful readers of *Little Women*, she presents domestic tranquility and moral platitudes as the province of mothers; to a subordinate class belongs the household drudgery. As the final chapter unfolds, *Little Women* concludes where it began, the daughters gathered by Marmee's side, reminiscing about their childhood castles in the air. Hannah Mullet—whose devoted toil over the entirety of their lives has made possible this domestic comfort—is nowhere to be seen.

Notes

1. Thank you to Daniel Shealy, Greg Eiselein, and Anne Phillips for their initial encouragement of this topic, and to Noelle A. Baker for her thoughtful suggestions on a draft of this article. The final product benefitted tremendously from this generosity.

2. Presumably the same character, Hannah appears briefly in the other two books in the *Little Women* series. She and Marmee bake treats in *Little Men* (184), and her odd phrasing for little Dan's school of "hard knocks" maturation process is quoted in *Jo's Boys* (330).

3. I am grateful to Noelle A. Baker for pointing out that these readers are mimicking an attitude that the narrator invites by having stripped Hannah of any authentic identity or agency.

4. Further, Foote is mistaken in assessing that Mr. and Mrs. March reverse traditional domestic roles when he returns in book 2, such that Mr. March replaces his wife as the family counselor, and she often goes "out into the world" (83n2). Albeit such was certainly the case in the Alcott family, this does not accurately characterize the scenario in book 2 of *Little Women*. Mr. March occasionally advises his daughters, to be sure, but as in book 1, Mrs. March continues as the primary dispenser of wisdom, to which she now adds marital counsel to Meg. After Beth dies, Marmee supports the depressed Jo, who is further at loose ends after breaking Laurie's heart. We observe neither Mr. nor Mrs. March doing household labor, because as in book 1, Hannah remains the "maid of all work."

5. See Shealy, *Little Women*, for Lydia Hosmer Brown's recollection of the Alcotts in Concord as well as for other details regarding Hannah (56n7).

6. Daniel Sutherland suggests that on occasion female employers shared the housework with their servants, leading to closer relations (139), such as those the narrator maintains Hannah enjoys with the Marches, although as pointed out, Marmee is not seen handling her share of this labor in *Little Women*.

7. As in Alcott's time, so today do young immigrant women contribute substantially to America's domestic service; one recent estimate is that these women comprise over 7 percent of "the total labor force," many of them lacking the same rights and employment agreements as in the mid-nineteenth century, added to which are the perils associated with their often-undocumented status. See, for example, Huang; Sanchez.

8. Though Hannah's station in the March family is inconsistent, at times Alcott inverts the standard relations, as when Marmee confides that Hannah had taught her "how things should be done, that my servants need *not* laugh at me" (*Little Women* 194).

9. As in many New England communities at this time, in Concord, Massachusetts, where the Alcott family lived during many years of Louisa's childhood and where as a young adult she lived while writing *Little Women*, retaining a good servant, many of whom were Irish, could be a challenge. In early 1848, letters between Lidian Jackson (Mrs. Ralph Waldo) Emerson and her neighbor William Whiting flew fast and furious over Emerson's anger at the Whiting family having, in her view, enticed her servant Mary Collins to work for them instead: "What shall I say to one who has lightly taken it for granted that I could ask a poor uninstructed girl to commit a crime?" Whiting defends his and his wife's having hired Collins and accuses Emerson of both lying and of having intimidated her: "You accuse us of holding her in the bondage of fear. This Madam is a *grave charge*. . . . One circumstance I think I have omitted, which is *strong* proof to my mind, that she did not wish to leave my family is, that you were obliged to send to my house three several times . . . before you could obtain from her the *promise* which she says *you 'made her make'*" (L. J. Emerson 140; William Whiting to Lidian Jackson Emerson).

10. For examples that describe Hannah to be "of Irish descent" and "an Irish immigrant," see the current Wikipedia entry for *Little Women*; Asher; and my own inaccurate blog entry (Eiselein and Phillips).

11. Beth also aids Hannah in the important responsibility of handling household accounts, a task that reflects the trust Marmee places in their servant (140).

Works Cited

Alcott, Louisa May. *Hospital Sketches*. James Redpath, 1863.
Alcott, Louisa May. "How I Went Out to Service." *Alternative Alcott*, edited by Elaine Showalter, Rutgers UP, 1988, pp. 350–63.
Alcott, Louisa May. *Jo's Boys*. Roberts Brothers, 1886.
Alcott, Louisa May. *The Journals of Louisa May Alcott,* edited by Joel Myerson, Daniel Shealy, and Madeleine B. Stern, Little, Brown, 1989; U of Georgia P, 1997.
Alcott, Louisa May. *Little Men*. Roberts Brothers, 1871.
Alcott, Louisa May. *Little Women, or, Meg, Jo, Beth and Amy*, edited by Anne K. Phillips and Gregory Eiselein, Norton Critical Edition, W. W. Norton, 2004.
Alcott, Louisa May. *The Selected Letters of Louisa May Alcott*, edited by Joel Myerson, Daniel Shealy, and Madeleine B. Stern, Little, Brown, 1987; U of Georgia P, 1995.
Alcott, Louisa May. *Work*, edited by Joy S. Kasson, Penguin, 1994.
Asher, Sandra. *Little Women, or Meg, Jo, Beth, and Amy*. Dramatic Publishing, 2001.
Auerbach, Nina. *Communities of Women: An Idea in Fiction*. Harvard UP, 1978.
Bedell, Madelon. *The Alcotts: Biography of a Family*. Clarkson N. Potter, 1980.

Beecher, Catherine E. *A Treatise on Domestic Economy, for the Use of Young Ladies at Home and at School*, rev. ed., Harper & Brothers, 1846.

Beecher, Catherine E., and Harriet Beecher Stowe. *The American Woman's Home; or, Principles of Domestic Service. . . .* J. B. Ford, 1869.

Bradford, Gamaliel. "Portrait of Louisa May Alcott." *North American Review*, vol. 209, no. 760, 1919, pp. 391–403.

Brodhead, Richard H. *Cultures of Letters: Scenes of Reading and Writing in Nineteenth-Century America*. U of Chicago P, 1993.

Clark, Beverly Lyon, editor. *Louisa May Alcott: The Contemporary Reviews*. Cambridge UP, 2004.

Cohoon, Lorinda B. "'dishes and dusters': Valuing Beth's Labor in Louisa May Alcott's *Little Women*; or, Staying in for Service." *Critical Insights: "Little Women,"* edited by Gregory Eiselein and Anne K. Phillips, Salem Press/Grey House Publishing, 2015, pp. 159–73.

Dawson, Janis. "Little Women Out to Work: Women and the Marketplace in Louisa May Alcott's *Little Women* and *Work*." *Children's Literature in Education*, vol. 34, no. 2, 2003, pp. 111–30.

Delamar, Gloria T. *Louisa May Alcott and "Little Women": Biography, Critique, Publications, Poems, Songs and Contemporary Relevance*. McFarland, 1990.

Dolan, Kathryn Cornell. "Her Daily Bread: Food and Labor in Louisa May Alcott." *American Literary Realism*, vol. 48, no. 1, 2015, pp. 40–57.

Dudden, Faye E. *Serving Women: Household Service in Nineteenth-Century America*. Wesleyan UP, 1983.

Petrulionis, Sandra Harbert. "Chapter IV. Burdens." *Little Women 150. Louisa May Alcott's Little Women: A 150th Anniversary Celebration*, https://lw150.wordpress.com/2018/08/20/chapter-iv-burdens/.

Elbert, Sarah. *A Hunger for Home: Louisa May Alcott's Place in American Culture*. Rutgers UP, 1987.

Emerson, Lidian Jackson. *Selected Letters of Lidian Jackson Emerson*, edited by Delores Bird Carpenter, U of Missouri P, 1987.

Foote, Stephanie. "Resentful *Little Women*: Gender and Class Feeling in Louisa May Alcott." *College Literature*, vol. 32, no. 1, 2005, pp. 63–85.

Foster, Shirley, and Judy Simons. *What Katy Read: Feminist Re-Readings of 'Classic' Stories for Girls*. U of Iowa P, 1995.

Hanks, Patrick, editor. *Dictionary of American Family Names*. Oxford UP, 2006. Hathi Trust.

"Help Wanted—. Females." *Daily Inter Ocean*, 4 Dec. 1892.

"Help Wanted—. Females." *New York Herald*, 4 Mar. 1864.

"Help Wanted—. Females." *New York Herald*, 23 Apr. 1871.

Huang, Grace. "How to Make Sure Immigrant Women Aren't Left Out of Me Too." *HuffPost*, 30 June 2018, https://www.huffpost.com/entry/opinion-huang-immigrant-women-me-too_n_5b33f9dee4b0b5e692f3f7e6.

Kasson, Joy S. "Introduction." *Work*, by Louisa May Alcott, edited by Kasson, Penguin, 1994, pp. ix–xxxi.

Kessler-Harris, Alice. *Women Have Always Worked: A Concise History*. 2nd ed., U of Illinois P, 2018.

Keyser, Elizabeth Lennox. *Little Women: A Family Romance*. U of Georgia P, 2000.

Lahey, Sarah T. "Honeybees and Discontented Workers: A Critique of Labor in Louisa May Alcott." *American Literary Realism*, vol. 44, no. 2, 2012, pp. 133–56.

Laird, Susan. "Learning from Marmee's Teaching: Alcott's Response to Girls' Miseducation." *"Little Women" and the Feminist Imagination: Criticism, Controversy, Personal Essays*, edited by Janice M. Alberghene and Beverly Lyon Clark, Garland, 1999, pp. 285–322.

Little Women. Directed by Mervyn LeRoy, MGM, 1949.

"Little Women." *Wikipedia: The Free Encyclopedia*, 2021, Wikimedia Foundation, https://en.wikipedia.org/wiki/Little_Women.

Proehl, Kristen. "Sympathetic Jo: Tomboyism, Poverty, and Race in Louisa May Alcott's *Little Women*." *Sentimentalism in Nineteenth-Century America: Literary and Cultural Practices*, edited by Mary G. De Jong, Fairleigh Dickinson UP, 2013, pp. 105–20.

Sanchez, Rebecca Lee. "America's Domestic Workers, Mostly Female Immigrants, 'Undervalued and Underpaid.'" *GlobalPost*, 9 Dec. 2013, https://www.pri.org/stories/2013-12-09/americas-domestic-workers-mostly-female-immigrants-undervalued-and-underpaid.

Sands-O'Connor, Karen. "Anything to Suit Customers: Antislavery and *Little Women*." *Children's Literature Association Quarterly*, vol. 26, no. 1, 2001, pp. 33–37.

Schultz, April. "The Black Mammy and the Irish Bridget: Domestic Service and the Representation of Race, 1830–1930." *Éire-Ireland*, vol. 48, nos. 3 & 4, 2013, pp. 176–212.

Shealy, Daniel, editor. *"Little Women": An Annotated Edition*, by Louisa May Alcott, Harvard UP, 2013.

Stoneley, Peter. "Fashion and American Literature." *Nineteenth-Century Literature Criticism*, vol. 128, edited by Lynn M. Zott, Gale, 2004, pp. 138–46.

Strasser, Susan. *Never Done: A History of American Housework*. Pantheon, 1982.

Sutherland, Daniel E. *Americans and Their Servants: Domestic Service in the United States from 1800 to 1920*. Louisiana State UP, 1981.

Whiting, William. Letter to Lidian Jackson Emerson. Emerson Family Correspondence. ALS, MS Am 1280.226, Houghton Library, Harvard University, 3 Mar. 1848. Courtesy of the Ralph Waldo Emerson Memorial Association.

Willis, Frederick L. H. *Alcott Memoirs: Posthumously Compiled from Papers Journals and Memoranda. . . .* Richard G. Badger, 1915.

Mobilizing the Little Women
Images of Transport and the Domestic

Beverly Lyon Clark

Louisa May Alcott was an unusually mobile nineteenth-century woman. Not only did she travel to Europe twice and to Washington, DC, as a nurse, but she frequently changed domiciles in the Northeast. Her family lived in more than two dozen different dwellings between the time she was born and when, at age twenty-five, she and her parents moved into Orchard House in Concord, the home now usually associated with the family.[1] Yet even then she tried to reside there as little as possible: finding family responsibilities not entirely conducive to writing, she frequently rented rooms in Boston, moving back and forth and elsewhere several dozen times. In Alcott's *Little Women*, however, there's much less mobility. True, the two sisters who are the most independent do eventually travel, Amy to Europe, Jo to New York. Physical mobility is at least a partial metaphor for social and/or economic independence, even if both sisters are ultimately reined in, by men—and return home. What I'm going to focus on here is the gendering of mobility in the novel—specifically the gendering of transportation, mechanical and otherwise, as interpreted by illustrators. And I will play these depictions against illustrators' portrayals of what is usually perceived as an image of stasis and rootedness: the house.

Little Women, of course, is not an action-packed adventure story but rather centers on the dailiness of the ordinary lives of the four March sisters, and most of the more than 140 illustrators of English-language editions, whether they are men or women, have emphasized domestic stasis—often more than the novel itself does.[2] The most common scene chosen by illustrators—from May Alcott (1868), through Jessie Willcox Smith (1915, 1923), to Sophie Allsopp (2015)—clusters the four sisters, with or without their mother, in a circular composition that underscores the harmony of the family. Most of the other frequently illustrated scenes are likewise static, including Jo at a writing desk or under an umbrella with Professor Bhaer, Beth on her sickbed, Amy and Laurie amid the roses at Valrosa, and the four sisters sitting outdoors dreaming of their "castles in the air." Many illustrators seem particularly taken by the opportunity to depict fashion and romance and the generally decorative. Yet some have paid significant attention to modes of transportation—what mobility scholars would call mediated mobilities—including boats, trains, carriages, wagons, horses, and bicycles.

I don't see much change over time in depictions of transportation, but I have found that men have shown more interest in them than women artists. Of the eighty-four illustrated English-language editions that I have examined and that have an illustrator with an identifiable gender,[3] almost 60 percent of the men have included at least one illustration depicting a mode of transportation, compared to 40 percent of the women. In addition, the artist who created the most images depicting transportation is a man, Frank Merrill (1880), with twenty-three such images, by far the largest number; Louis Jambor (1947) comes second with seven.[4] And the artist with the largest percentage of images depicting transport is also male, Mark English (1967), with a remarkable 63 percent.

What is the function of these transporting images? Some modes of transportation were associated, in the mid-nineteenth century, with upper- and upper-middle-class privilege, especially horses and carriages. And while boats could be associated with the working classes, for the middle and upper classes they often denoted leisure. In the world of *Little Women*, horses are for the wealthy, including Laurie; boats are for leisure; and for the genteel poor such as the Marches, carriages are associated with emergencies and largesse, sometimes both (think of Laurie offering Meg a ride in his carriage after she sprains her ankle at the Gardiners' party).

In most of the references to boating in Alcott's novel, the boats are rarely used as vehicles to go to a particular place (unless for a leisure activity such as a picnic—or unless the boat is an ocean steamer). Boating is associated with leisure or exercise, or, when Jo rejects Laurie's proposal, provides a way to work through negative emotions. In artists' renditions, boats sometimes contribute to the picturesque—as in images of the Camp Laurence expedition or of Laurie proposing to Amy on the lake near Vevey in Switzerland. The latter, in particular, also offers an opportunity to query gender roles. In the novel Laurie proposes not "in the chateau garden by moonlight . . . but . . . exactly the reverse, . . . on the lake, at noonday, in a few blunt words," asking Amy if they "might always pull in the same boat" (*Little Women* 336). In this intentionally antiromantic passage, the two agree to a relatively gender-neutral, mutually powered mobility: both will be pulling the oars. Most artists, however, reromanticize the scene, whether they frame the couple with foliage and mountains, shade it with pastels, or adorn it with distant sails or a winging bird or a weathered pier. Often—contravening the text—they give Laurie control of the oars and thus traditional male dominance. A couple, including Derek James (1988), even forego the text's proposal scene in favor of that romantic chateau garden, replete with roses, arbor, and distant peaks.

The most intriguing boating image is by Elinore Blaisdell (1946), who provides not the usual distant view but a medium shot of Laurie and Amy in the boat, in a moment of stillness. She occludes the picturesque—no distant peaks—but also any sense of movement, instead using the outline of the boat as a frame. Our vantage is elevated, so we look down on the figures, hinting at the condescending mode of viewing the picturesque described by Nicholas Johnson and others.[5] But our perspective also enables the gunwale of the boat partly to frame the two, placing them almost in a bower—a framing that required some finessing of the angle between the presumably upright figures and the horizontal boat. Laurie is partly out of the frame, so is he trying to enter it? Or does the fuller framing of Amy, with the lines of Laurie's head and arm completing it, confine her? He looks at her, as if he's directing attention to her, while she pensively looks down and away. Amy is to be gazed at, as she often is in Alcott's text. Still, the two figures are about the same height and mass, egalitarian in that respect, even if his knee impinges on her space. And Amy has her own oar. More than other illustrators, Blaisdell captures egalitarian aspects of the proposal and de-emphasizes the romantically picturesque, even if her Amy remains demurely feminine.

More often, the depiction of transportation in the text and in the images indicates or implies movement through space. In a double-page illustration

Amy and Laurie (Elinore Blaisdell, *Little Women*, 1946)

of the wedding of Meg and John Brooke, Hodges Soileau (1985) shows not the usual static image of the solemnization but a scene in which the sisters appear about to frolic, perhaps to dance. A substantial portion of the upper recto is devoted to a horse and carriage in the background, facing to the right, the direction of a hopeful future for books in languages that read left to right. Thus does Soileau hint at the beginnings of a hopeful journey through life—although if one reads the image in tandem with the text, it's not clear whose hopeful journey it might be, since the textual Meg and John don't ride but walk to their new home.

Both boats and carriages offer fairly equal opportunities for mobility to men and women—even if the men are more likely to take the oars. Riding horseback, however, is for men, in the world of the Alcott text and its illustrations, and specifically for an upper-class man like Laurie.[6] Or at least riding a real horse is—an occasional illustration shows Amy or Jo riding the backyard tree branch that the sisters pretend is their horse. The character most often on horseback, however, is Laurie. The visual effect is to imply the greater scope that he has for movement compared with the March sisters.

Frank Merrill offers a visually complex set of equestrian images. An early chapter opens with Laurie "clatter[ing] by on horseback"—this is the moment when Amy commits her malapropism of calling him "a perfect Cyclops" when she means centaur (57). Merrill's image underscores the boy's mobility, and no girl is visible. Years later in Europe, Amy sketches the lounging Laurie and compares the image to an older one she'd done of him taming a horse. Most illustrators show the picturesqueness of the lounging, and Merrill does too. But he's one of only a couple who reproduce May's horse sketch—in an image that Alcott declared "Capital" ("Frank Thayer Merrill"). It depicts not the current action of the text but the action that the textual Laurie now lacks—in an illustration that is a partial mirror image of the earlier horseback one. It underscores the reversal of Laurie's earlier activity as it also converts Amy from an onlooker to a creator.[7]

Shortly before his lounging Laurie and his rendition of Amy's sketch, though, Merrill opens the chapter with an image that encapsulates the contrast between activity and inaction. Amy and Laurie go for drives near Nice and pass

> a bare-legged shepherd, in wooden shoes, pointed hat, and rough jacket over one shoulder, [who] sat piping on a stone, while his goats skipped among the rocks or lay at his feet. Meek, mouse-colored donkeys, laden with panniers

of freshly cut grass, passed by, with a pretty girl in a *capaline* sitting between the green piles, or an old woman spinning with a distaff as she went. (314–15)

Merrill reproduces the details as described (except for the attire of the shepherd—artists often take sartorial liberties with Alcott's text). Yet the image also has an emblematic function, anticipating the succeeding images of Laurie lounging and Laurie astride and also the contents of this chapter in which Amy chides the young man for his lazy inactivity. The man pictured here is lounging[8] and it's the women who are mobile, one even astride; the man's pipe is down but the women's stick and spindle are fully erect. Amy, too, is the character in this chapter who is active, verbally and artistically, as she urges Laurie to man up. For all that Laurie is the only major character shown on horseback, Merrill's depiction of modes of transportation in this chapter does not so much enact the character's mobility as underscore his passivity. Not the usual effect of horseback images in editions of *Little Women*.

Overall, if horses tend to favor males and endorse masculinity, despite Merrill's complex use of the creatures, some other modes of transportation facilitate movement by one of the novel's women, whether Marmee is boarding a carriage as she leaves home to tend her ailing husband in Washington, or Amy is aboard a ship heading to Europe or is in a carriage in Europe, or occasionally Jo is depicted on or boarding a train to or from New York. Although I won't dwell on most of these possibilities for mobilizing women, I will go on to address omnibuses, trains, and anachronistic bicycles. But first—

Consider a unique image of Meg's children created by Reisie Lonette (1950). Lonette's illustrations generally tend toward the decorative, yet she also provides some provocative subtexts. I don't much care for her image of Jo writing in a garret, which proffers a self-contained mobcapped prettiness that reminds me too much of John Everett Millais's *Cherry Ripe* (1897), whose overt little-girl innocence but underlying eroticism critics have happily expatiated on (see, e.g., Higonnet 132). As for Lonette's one image of mediated locomotion, Meg's small daughter Daisy is pulling her brother Demi in a wagon. The textual Daisy is subordinate to her twin: "Demi tyrannized over Daisy, and gallantly defended her from every other aggressor; while Daisy made a galley-slave of herself, and adored her brother, as the one perfect being in the world" (*Little Women* 358). Lonette does not depict, say, Demi hoisting Daisy in a basket hung over a chair and repeatedly bumping her head, as in the text, but invents the wagon scene. One could interpret this

XXXIX.

LAZY LAURENCE.

LAURIE went to Nice intending to stay a week, and remained a month. He was tired of wandering about alone, and Amy's familiar presence seemed to give a home-like charm to the foreign scenes in which she bore a part. He rather missed the " petting " he used to receive, and enjoyed a taste of it again; for no attentions, however flattering, from strangers, were half so pleasant as the sisterly adoration of the girls at home. Amy never would pet him like the others, but she was very glad to see him now, and quite clung to him, feeling that he was the representative of the dear family for whom she longed

Laboring or lazy? (Frank Merrill, *Little Women*, 1880)

image as showing Daisy once again serving Demi, his galley slave, but it also shows her taking an active role while he is passive. A role reversal that may, in part, be humorous but that also hints at the ways in which Alcott plays with gender, with her masculinized Jo, her feminized Laurie. Transportation here enables some feminine mobility and activity.

So far I've been examining individualized modes of mobility, but as Colin Pooley and his coauthors have suggested, women have generally used "slower and more public forms of transport" (257). Omnibuses, for instance, provide a mode of local transportation for the March women, enabling them to travel to the nearby city, whether to submit a manuscript or to buy a last-minute lobster for guests. Yet the interiors of public modes of transportation allow for potentially dangerous class mixing and class exposure.[9] When Amy is returning home with the lobster, she carefully conceals it in a basket, but it tips over, "and oh, horror! the lobster, in all its vulgar size and brilliancy, was revealed to the high-born eyes" of a young gentleman acquaintance (*Little Women* 209). Amy attempts to cover the embarrassment with some charming banter, and the charm and the banter are what Merrill foregrounds in his illustration of the scene (1880). Adolf Thiede ([1903?]) and Barbara Cooney (1955), however, both depict the moment of embarrassment, with the young gentleman poking at the lobster with a stick, perhaps his walking stick. Amy's class fragility—as someone who does not send a servant but herself fetches food from the market—has been exposed. The critic Lorna Shelley has argued that an omnibus journey can be "emblematic of women's modernity and increasing authority in city spaces," but in late Victorian writings it also fueled urban anxieties about "womanhood out of control in terms of sexuality, mobility, and class" (143, 141). An omnibus could be a dangerous space, exposing more than a woman wants to expose.

As for trains, I've found images of them in editions illustrated by six different artists. The historian Amy Richter notes that, in the nineteenth century, "the ideals of the railroad stood in opposition to those of 'respectable' womanhood. The first represented Victorian hopes of commercial, technological, and national progress; the second embodied a realm of moral and emotional rejuvenation beyond the reach of such social change" (1).[10] Or as the Victorianist Peter Bailey argues, the train itself was "the great engine of modernity in all its contradictions of constraint and liberation" (4). Clashing ideals were reinforced and partly reconciled by the creation of domesticated interior spaces on trains, which afforded both a public domesticity and technological mobility to women. As with omnibuses, the interior of a midcentury US train, with its large open cars rather than the smaller closed compartments of English trains, created considerable possibilities for class and racial mixing: a contemporary commentator deemed such a car "a wandering caravanseraï, in which eighty or a hundred persons of all classes and colors and ages are assembled together" ("American" 200).[11] Their size and openness could be "a teacher of democracy," although the opportunities for class and racial mixing meant that they also at times "exacerbated the differences that divided Americans" (Richter 12, 21). The train that Jo takes to New

York in *Little Women* allows for such an opportunity: it is a domesticated democratic space, where Jo interacts with fellow passengers, dropping gingerbread nuts over the back of a seat to pacify some Irish children.[12]

Although this railway trip occupies only two sentences in the novel, as recounted in Jo's letter home from New York, the passage merits close attention. It reads:

> When I lost sight of father's dear old face, I felt a trifle blue, and might have shed a briny drop or two, if an Irish lady with four small children, all crying more or less, hadn't diverted my mind; for I amused myself by dropping gingerbread nuts over the seat every time they opened their mouths to roar.
>
> Soon the sun came out; and taking it as a good omen, I cleared up likewise, and enjoyed my journey with all my heart. (262)

Given the extent to which Irish children are outsiders in the novel—think of the fate of Amy's contraband pickled limes, tossed out the schoolroom window to the Irish urchins outside—this railway car would seem to mediate between outdoors and indoors, as a place where one might venture beyond the home to try to tame or negotiate with or perhaps be amused by the denizens outside, however briefly.

Both Jo and Amy, in their respective scenes, deploy food items, which they toss through or over a barrier. Neither limes nor ginger is indigenous to North America, and neither is easily grown in temperate climates. Ginger was part of the early Spice Trade, and by the mid-nineteenth century was fully implicated in imperialist trade, as were limes (see, e.g., Woodward 188). Not homegrown like apples, both the limes in pickled limes and the ginger in gingerbread nuts mark their respective treats as for the privileged, signaling the relative privilege of Amy and Jo. Each sister thus uses edible products of imperialist trade in a transaction with immigrants (or their descendants) who have themselves been moved by the violence of imperialism—by, presumably, the potato famine of 1845–52. Scientists have recently traced the likely origins of the potato blight to South America, from which it was transmitted via North America, and noted that the ensuing famine was caused in part by "pre-existing poverty exacerbated by British policy" (Pappas). The presence of the Irish in both scenes, whether visible or not, whether emitting a roar or shout, underscores that mobility was not a universal good, not universally associated with freedom.[13] Whatever the immediate reason for the presence of these children on the train, their presence in the United States was the result of a globally interconnected food disaster exacerbated by the workings of British imperialism.

What then are we to make of Jo's account of the encounter in her letter? She is sad at leaving home and is tempted "to shed a briny drop or two"—the sentimentality of the potential act underscored by the flowery, indirect phrasing, the "briny drop." Ever eager to deflate the sentimental, Alcott then turns to a group she considered decidedly nonsentimental,[14] even as she deflects Jo's potential tears to these Irish children—not that they're necessarily shedding tears, given that crying can refer generally to loud vocalizing, not just that which produces "briny drops."

Jo is, in any case, "diverted" by the encounter and "amuse[s] herself" by dropping the gingerbread nuts. Both verbs can suggest a positive interaction (diverting, amusing), but they can also be neutral or worse (diverting one's attention). Indeed, any positive valence is neutralized by the way the sentence proceeds: Jo "amuses" herself not by direct interaction with the children but by a hands-off handing off. The ending of the sentence further clarifies that she drops the gingerbread nuts only in response to the children's noise, not as a simple act of kindness. She barters food for silence. Furthermore, although the children are initially described as crying, their cries become a roar. The distancing effects here are probably meant to be amusing, but the handing off of food across a barrier, indeed, dropping the food into open mouths, and then the choice of *roar*—all contribute to dehumanizing, bestializing, the children. And in case we still have any doubts whether the interaction might have been diverting and amusing in a positive way and thus perhaps chased away Jo's blues at parting from her family, the next sentence reveals that it was only when "the sun came out" that she "cleared up likewise."

Michel de Certeau points to the paradoxes of train travel, how it functions as a "travelling incarceration" (111). The passenger is separated from the world outside by the rail that allows one to move through that world and by the windowpane that allows one to see it. Jo's two sentences almost seem to move between these two modes, yet in her case the physical barrier, the seat mentioned in the first sentence, separates her not from the physical world outside the train but from the Irish fellow passengers, who are outside her world in a different sense. The sunlight, of course, comes through the window, a more welcome breaching of boundaries for Jo. Given the placement of "enjoyed my journey with all my heart"—its separation from the Irish children reinforced by both sentence and paragraph boundaries and its conjunction with the sun and the clearing up—what she enjoys is presumably the panorama outside her window. Illuminating an "exterior silence" that fosters interiority (de Certeau 112), the clearing of the sky enables Jo to clear up too, something that wasn't possible with the roaring children. Jo's epistolary account of her encounter with the Irish children ultimately underscores and exacerbates her differences from them.

As for the two illustrations of this scene that I have located, they suggest a more genial interaction than the text implies: in Merrill's 1880 image, which positions the viewer somewhat behind Jo, she is not disdainful but leaning forward while the Irishwoman (or "Irish lady," as Jo has the grace or irony to call her) who accompanies the children gazes benignly; in Tasha Tudor's 1969 image we are positioned across the aisle from Jo and can see enough of her face to know that she is smiling.[15] The two images differ, though, in their portrayal of implied movement. In Merrill's image the foreshortening, the orthogonal lines, and also Jo's leaning forward hint at the train's movement, toward the upper left, in keeping with his inclination in other illustrations to show activity and motion. Tudor borrows from Merrill but eliminates the diagonal, so that the image appears stationary, a moment caught in time; we focus on the three figures, the two children separated from Jo by the back of the seat and partly contained by its arm. Tudor's Jo is not leaning forward as much as Merrill's, does not overlap the children, and appears more genial than eager; she seems self-contained, even while the arm of her seat is oddly absent, an absence that allows for more display of her fashion sense but also places her under less physical constraint. Still, in both images Jo, like Alcott in later life, might seem to be the "children's friend."[16] Merrill and Tudor minimize Alcott's ambivalence about the democracy of the railway car, perhaps to promote a positive vision of Alcott's relationship to America's young.

Exterior views of trains appear in three editions of *Little Women*. Louis Jambor (1947), like Merrill, tended to favor movement and energy (see, e.g., Gannon 125) and provided a bustling image of a European train station, signaling Amy's movement about Europe. A 1997 edition published by Viking, containing both illustrations by Jame's Prunier and found images, includes four found images of trains—as if to show us what nineteenth-century trains looked like. One found image annotates the passage in which Laurie tells Jo that her mother will return from Washington on a late train that day. The image, however, is rather bizarre: its allegorical train is constructed of casks

Taming or befriending the Irish? (Frank Merrill, *Little Women*, 1880)

and other containers of alcohol. The caption indicates that it is "call[ing] attention to the increased consumption of alcohol.... But even people like the Marches would sometimes drink for medicinal reasons" (Adrien Lherm, trans. Barbara Brister, Prunier 229). So I suppose the image is to convey that Marmee is speeding home to nurse an ailing Beth—and maybe that when she'd left home she'd brought some wine with which to doctor her ailing husband? The intermixing of visual annotations and conventional illustrations in this edition is both illuminating and a bit disorienting, since I connect each with the text rather differently; this visual annotation is particularly disorienting because of its content and the difficulty of connecting the content to the text.

More apt is a train image by Mark English (1967), some of whose other evocative images I've discussed elsewhere (*Afterlife* 192–98). In this one, selected for the Society of Illustrators Annual Exhibition, a locomotive overwhelms Jo's leave-taking of Professor Bhaer in New York. Jo's dress is beribboned and befurbelowed in a way that Alcott's Jo would never allow, and, indeed, the fullness of her skirts would complicate her ability to sit on the

Taming or befriending the Irish? (Tasha Tudor, *Little Women*, 1969). Permission by Seth Tudor and Winslow Tudor

train—she's not exactly wearing traveling dress (the decorative impulse can be hard for Alcott illustrators to restrain). The professor's kissing of her hand is more intimate than formal, as befits his unexpressed feelings for her even if not his sense of decorum in the novel. But it's the train that dominates the image, dwarfing the couple, constraining them, yet also perhaps, in the way it surrounds them, embracing them. The image features an engine and not a passenger car—focusing our attention not on potential confinement but on the power of the locomotive. Nor are any nonelite potential passengers depicted, so we're not distracted by the dangers of class mixing. The engine looms with suppressed energy, its bell clanging, smudges of fire glinting through apertures, oranges and yellows swirling above it—thus perhaps hinting at Bhaer's suppressed fire and passion.[17] Maybe some of this suppressed energy belongs to Jo too, although she seems basically passive, looking up at Bhaer from beneath her lashes, even if she does allow her face to be intimately close to his. Still, it is she and not he who is about to embark, making her a mobile and modern nineteenth-century woman, compatible with the advanced technology of the time, even if the visual depiction here shows Jo as rather traditional. Like Soileau with his carriage, English hints at future movement, although one needs to read the text to realize which of the characters will embark. In one edition with English's illustrations, the image has the caption, "Early as it was, he was at the station next morning to see Jo off; and she began her journey with the pleasant memory of a familiar face smiling farewell...." (center gathering)—so it can be read as reinforcing the mobility of women. Nathalie op de Beeck argues that the 1926 picture book *Little Machinery* "reveals much about an era in which the myth of the innocent child in the bountiful garden collides with the perception of the child as a sophisticated cultural consumer, and a middle-class subject, in the teeming metropolis" (64). English's image, four decades later, shows a fiery steam engine as having intruded into and overwhelmed a potentially feminine, floral, and domestic space (like English's other *Little Women* illustrations, this one includes flowers, and a partial view of a house appears in the background): he offers another collision between the machine and the garden, between what has been called the "industrial revolution incarnate" (qtd. in Marx 191) and verdant femininity. If we view the image in isolation, the machine dominates. Yet in the corresponding text Jo is about to board and thus partly harness this mechanical behemoth. Text and image are in dialogue.

Now for the bicycles I've alluded to: I've found only two illustrations with them—not surprisingly, since bicycles aren't mentioned in the text.[18] One of the images is in a 2007 Italian edition, a redaction in the very popular Geronimo Stilton series (150 million copies worldwide)—and here I'm venturing beyond my attention to English-language editions of the novel. This version is "liberamente adattato" (freely adapted) by the murine Geronimo Stilton ([iv]): human characters have been transmuted into mice. In the bicycle scene we see the delivery "per posta" of a love letter purportedly from John Brooke to Meg (192). The first pedal bicycles were mass produced in France in 1868, and there was a velocipede craze in the United States in

1868–69, the years when parts 1 and 2 of *Little Women* were published (see Herlihy 102–26). Yet most of the 1860s cyclists engaged in their sport not on roads but in a rink, and indeed the craze soon dissipated, to be given new life a decade later by the penny-farthing, or high-wheel bicycle.[19] In any case, not only is the cheerful mail carrier imaged here riding a bicycle of a more recent vintage than the 1860s velocipede, but he seems undismayed by the ample covering of snow. Indeed, he leaves no track in it. Then, too, in Alcott's novel the ersatz letter was delivered not by the US post office but through the private post used by the Marches and Laurences, a repurposed bird house. The domestic and neighborly arrangements of the two families have here been superseded by an institutionalized and mechanized modern means of communication, the bicycle alighting like a displaced bird. The bicycle enables communication but not movement by the principals; its function seems rather to fix the March women in place, with things moving to them more than they themselves moving.

The bicycle serves a different function in its other appearance in *Little Women* illustrations, in one by, again, Mark English. In his depiction of the return from Camp Laurence, a picnic-and-croquet expedition, we see bicycles, straw boaters, and muttonchop sleeves, all associated with the 1890s rather than the 1860s. If the Geronimo Stilton illustration evokes a nostalgic sense of pastness that inscribes a traditional gendering of movement, something different happens in English's image. English does portray some anachronistic romanticizing of the past, but one can also borrow a phrase from the critic David Skilton, who has described an anachronistic illustration in a Dickens novel as creating a "chronological mermaid . . . , half in one time and half in another" (309). English himself has been paraphrased as saying that "his illustrations of fictional characters should prod a reader's imagination—not be exact description" (Bossert 19). His counterpoint of image and text here evokes an imprecise earlier era, the image rather romantic, visually beautiful. The center and left side of the image show women in flowing dresses, embowered in flowers. But in the upper right quadrant are three women with bicycles, which look like the Rover Safety Bicycles popular in the 1890s, specifically with the "drop frame," or lowered middle bar, that accommodated women with their cumbersome clothing. A man is behind them, but the three women are the ones in possession of the vehicles. In the 1890s, the bicycle became an emblem of independence for the New Woman: it fostered health and dress reform and also enabled independent mobility (see, e.g., Herlihy 266; Rubinstein, esp. 61–68; Wånggren 123–35). The suffragist Susan B. Anthony, interviewed by the intrepid Nellie Bly in 1896, claimed that bicycling "has done more to emancipate women than anything else in the world" (qtd. in Bly 136). I have no reason to believe that English saw the bicycles he depicts as having such a political function—he might simply have thought them picturesque—but he nevertheless chose to give women access to such mobility. The somber poise of the cyclists offers a visual counterpoint to the bright stasis of the women and flowers to the left and below, even as these generally more ethereal women do offer some hints of being more than merely decorative. The middle woman, for instance, wears a boater and tie that echo the attire of the cyclists, and her upright posture and forthright gaze suggest seriousness. Even the woman with flowing hair who is coyly drooping in the foreground is carrying a book. It's not clear who all these assembled women are—if I squint hard enough I can make out ten all together, but there were only seven in the pleasure expedition in the text. Nor is it clear who the three women with the bicycles are. Probably not March sisters, who lived right next door, and probably not the proper young British lady whose family is visiting Laurie. A hermeneutic mermaid, if you will, in addition to a chronological one. Yet the image in many ways empowers women, I'd argue, even if a bit ambiguously—not unlike Alcott's text as a whole.

Thus English and other artists often depict mobilities that empower female characters in *Little Women*; these images are frequently in counterpoint with images of immobility. The recurring image of a clustering of the four sisters, with or without their mother, endorsing the closeness of the family, is one example, as are many views of characters in interior, domestic settings. Of course, interior views, metaphors for the characters' interiority, also allow for complexity. Artists depict not just nostalgic images of domestic harmony but also indoor moments of anger, sorrow, disruption. As the architectural theorist Bart Verschaffel notes, "Modernity introduces exchange, movement and transport, change and openness . . . that . . . deconstructs the home," yet he also "points to a complexity that is included *in* the representation—in the construction of the meaning—of 'house' and 'home' itself, rather than being an effect of its de-construction" (153–54).[20] The interior of the home is always already contested space.

Yet houses are often seen as opposed to the kinds of mobility I have been discussing. As Rita Felski has noted, "The vocabulary of modernity is a vocabulary of anti-home. It celebrates mobility, movement, exile, boundary crossing" (23). Or as Marilyn Chandler has suggested of US literature, "Enclosure in a house ... runs counter to the inherent romanticism of some of our most deeply held collective values: autonomy, self-determination, mobility" (4; see also Roberson 3-4). Such an opposition is often implied in illustrators' depictions of houses, especially the frequent external views of houses imaged in their entirety and filling much of the space of the illustration—the house not, in short, contextualized in the world beyond it. The feminist geographer Doreen Massey critiques the "many readings of ... home, where there is imagined to be the security of a (false ...) stability and an apparently reassuring boundedness" (169). Moreover, in a penetrating study of the complexities of "domestication," one that calls for "blurring and overlap" in our thinking about the term, Rachel Bowlby argues that "the division of the domestic from its outside was previously sustained only through a literalization of the figure of the house within and separate from a surrounding world" (86). It's to such literal figures, often hypostatizing domesticity and against which the visual mobility I've so far been discussing frequently defines itself, overtly or implicitly, that I now turn.

Again, male artists are more likely than females to depict large-scale external views of houses—about 40 percent of the men, compared to 15 percent of the women. Perhaps they too, like Laurie early on, felt as if they were on the outside looking in, when the March family "forget[s] to put down the curtain at the window where the flowers are" (46). Some artists depict houses with windows that glow with inviting light; others don't so much invite us inside the house to join the family as dramatize its containment and constraint within the house. Often house images appear on covers, endpapers, frontispieces, or title pages, also in chapter heads. In short, they mark moments of stasis before an action starts. In the initial paratextual images, the view of the house may function as an establishing shot for the book as a whole, perhaps especially if the image includes more than one house. Images of single houses can do that too, even if they less clearly contextualize the house and may hint more at a symbolic function (and especially if they appear in the frontispiece or a chapter head): the domicile is often a metaphor for domesticity in the novel. Some late nineteenth-century editions of *Little Women* feature Orchard House in the frontispiece, reifying the connection between the semiautobiographical March family and the Alcotts (see Clark, "Writer" 32–34); the houses of later illustrators often depict or allude to Orchard House as well. Sometimes a house appears as backdrop for an action, such as Beth tossing mittens from the second floor to children below or Jo in the foreground sweeping or shoveling snow. Indeed, house scenes are often snowy, as if to enhance the picturesque and its distancing effects while physically insulating the house from the world outside with the layering of snow. And sometimes the house or houses are depicted with a sleigh or carriage passing by, perhaps to create visual tension but also heightening the contrast between mobility and immobility. Although almost all of the illustrators who ignore modes of transportation also ignore exterior views of houses, almost half of those who depict transportation also depict one or more full-scale house. Thus, not just in individual images, but in the books as a whole, there are tensions, with varying emphases, between stasis and mobility, between, if you will, private and public, or domesticity and independence. To exemplify contrasting approaches to housing the Marches, I turn to illustrations for two abridged editions of part 1 of the novel, both published in the 1980s.

For the 1987 Ladybird Children's Classics abridgment, Terry Gabbey provides endpapers showing a bird's-eye view of a snowy March family home (not resembling Orchard House) next to a more elaborate house, presumably the Laurences'. A small horse-drawn sleigh is entering diagonally from the middle right. An echo of this image, without the sleigh, heads the first chapter; the March family residence, especially, is here glowing with light that reaches the lawn and sidewalk. The tailpiece for the last chapter shows a pedestrian's view of the lower half of the March house, the upper half engulfed by blowing snow and the final words of the text. Again there's light emanating from within; this time we can see a wreath on the door and glimpse at least six figures through the front windows, the reunited family. Gabbey's endpapers establish the distanced picturesqueness of the scene (the snow, the elevated vantage point) and place the stationary houses in tension with the possibility for movement (he reprises a version of the sleigh near a brief mention of sleighing later on); then, inside the book, he frames the story with the houses, warmly inviting us in and then retreating as "the curtain falls on Meg, Jo, Beth, and Amy" (Gabbey 51). In between, he may do relatively little with modes of transportation, but his houses intimate, as they often do for male artists, a kind of anxiety of domesticity, as if he wanted to secure the house and its confines and distance himself from it to some degree. In keeping with Bowlby's arguments, I might argue that he literalizes the house in an attempt to enforce the domesticity of *Little Women*, keeping the family domestic, separate from the public sphere; the sleigh that he allows seems not to hint at the possibility of ingress or egress but simply helps to define the picturesque domestic containment.

Feminist scholars of house and home caution against romanticizing the opposition between private and public, between domesticity and adventure (see, e.g., Mezei and Briganti 843). If Gabbey's use of house images to frame and enclose the text seems an attempt to encapsulate both text and characters, to demarcate and reinforce boundaries between private and public, at least one artist finds visual ways to deconstruct the opposition. Gordon King does so in his 1984 illustrations. King includes a couple of background houses but no hypostatizing image of an isolated house; indeed, his endpapers show not a high-angle picturesque view of houses but a low-angle view of ice skaters (before Amy's accident), with a boathouse in the background to the left and Jo and Laurie skating toward the right.[21] The figures are not visually confined. Furthermore, King provides numerous images that show a breaching of the boundaries between inside and outside, especially doorways. Windows, of course, can allow a kind of access to the outside, and artists frequently portray windows in Alcott illustrations—when an ailing Beth is looking out at a snow maiden created by Jo and Laurie, for instance, or when Jo is outside and greets an ailing Laurie, who is at an upper-floor window in his house. Closed windows here generally enforce a separation between the person inside and the activities outside, a separation only reinforced when the person is disabled in some way and thus, in keeping with stereotypical views of disability, confined. Doorways, though, are a different matter. Few Alcott illustrators depict thresholds being crossed, but King provides not just one or two but six open doorways connecting indoors and outdoors. When the March family leaves home to present the impoverished Hummels with a Christmas breakfast, King depicts not the usual line of family members trooping across the page but Amy in a doorway, looking back at the servant Hannah, who is about to follow her, with another family member visible across the threshold. An image for a New Year's Eve party depicts what appears to be a verdant porch, with Jo in the doorway glancing back at the interior (oddly, no snow or shivering). Jo's first visit to the Laurence house shows her about to enter the front door. King's Marmee receives the telegram telling of Father's illness while standing in the front doorway, and when she returns home from tending him we see not the usual interior image of her reunion with the bedridden Beth but her arrival at the house, the wheels of a carriage visible through the doorway. Father's return is also framed by an open doorway. There's even an image of an anachronistic mail slot with a jutting newspaper, partly inside, partly outside, abrogating the boundary—and marking the return to the March household of a story that Jo had earlier sneaked out of the house to submit, another breaching of boundaries. The home here becomes intimately interlinked with mobilities; its meaning "derives, in large part, precisely from the specificity of its interactions with 'the outside,'" as Massey might note (169). Doorways and mail slots become transitional spaces reflecting the overlap and movement between domestic and public spheres. Unlike Gabbey, and indeed unlike most illustrators, King opens up houses to the world outside, not confining the March sisters but portraying a domesticity with permeable boundaries. The Adventure Classics edition that he illustrates is adventurous in a new key.

Overall, though, I don't see a trend over time in illustrations of *Little Women*—no increasing mobility for women figures, for instance, nor increasing deconstruction of mobility and stasis. The nineteenth-century Frank Merrill was already mobilizing women and girls, and the deconstructive work of a single illustrator, Gordon King, does not in itself constitute a trend. Indeed, scores of illustrators, including many recent ones, have too often opted for the decorative and the dainty, for a quaint but immobilizing nostalgia. One pattern I have noted is that male artists are the ones most likely to depict houses and also modes of transportation. But to what ends? Are they enforcing or ameliorating or defying the confinement associated with domesticity? Are they chafing against the text, specifically a quotidian stasis that they may see as dominating the novel? Or are they highlighting a level of activity that is already there, some possibilities for spatial and technological independence, maybe underscoring the potential that some women have for mobility? Mark English may simply be chafing, or more precisely, given his interest in formal visual elements, he may be primarily interested in the contrasts and tensions between the pastoral and the mechanical, the floral and the vehicular, and not so much in the politics of what the figures represent. Merrill strikes me as more attuned to the specifics of the text and the way that Alcott generally enables mobility and agency, including that of women. Certainly Alcott herself expressed enthusiasm for his work. King, in contrast, enables agency not just through the visual mobility of various figures but through his reframing of the domestic and its relationship with the rest of the world. Even artists who depict vehicles may also constrain their figures within the frame of boat or train. But illustrators sometimes hint at more complex meanings, as Reisie Lonette does when she reverses the roles of Demi and Daisy or as Elinore Blaisdell does in the proposal scene. Their Daisy and Amy gain some agency, I would argue, as does Merrill's Amy and English's Jo. Depicting certain mediated mobilities, and also blurring the boundaries between the domestic and the mobile, can enable the characters and us to be transported.

Notes

1. For discussion of several Alcott homes, including Orchard House, which was not actually Alcott's childhood home, see, e.g., Shealy 42n23. See also the chronology in Alcott, *Journals*, xvii–xxvii.

2. Indeed, like British novels that have often been classified as domestic fiction but are really antidomestic, as Deborah Epstein Nord argues, *Little Women* attends to leaving the home, to being "outward bound."

3. I'm excluding editions for which I've been unable to determine an illustrator's gender because he or she uses initials that I've been unable to parse, or there are multiple illustrators of mixed genders, or the illustrator hasn't been named (including books whose images are film stills). None of the illustrators I've identified seems to prefer nongendered pronouns, although some of those who use initials may, of course, be consciously avoiding gender identifiers. I also exclude multiple editions that reprint work by a single illustrator, such as Frank Merrill: each illustrator counts only once. Almost half of the gender-identifiable illustrators are women.

4. Although the 1997 Viking edition (first published in French, in France, in 1996) that is, in part, illustrated by Jame's Prunier contains at least fifteen images that foreground modes of transportation, most are found images; only three of Prunier's own illustrations clearly include vehicles.

5. Johnson argues that if Amy finds Europe picturesque in ways that by then were rather hackneyed, the narrator transgresses picturesque conventions in this scene: instead of sentimentally condescending to laboring-class figures in the landscape, she portrays middle-class US surrogates for the reader—"a portrait of bourgeois sentimentality" (47). I'd add that situating Amy and Laurie in this scene is also a way of condescending to them, making them part of a picturesque landscape. Alcott may revalue the picturesque, yet the picturesque also revalues Amy and Laurie.

6. For discussion of the aristocratic associations of horseback riding in, for instance, eighteenth- and nineteenth-century Britain, especially the associations with leisure, wealth, and power, see Linley, esp. 84.

7. A barely discernible unerased line in the first image, to the left of Laurie's right arm, provides a palimpsestic trace that not only reminds us that Merrill's drawing is a drawing but could imply an earlier position for and hence movement of Laurie's arm, thus hinting at even more action in the image.

8. And making music—an activity that Laurie has been prone to indulge in even though his grandfather doesn't consider it one of the "more important things" that Laurie should commit to (50).

9. For more on buses and "the gendering of transport exclusion," see Adey 141–46; Adey's book provides a useful overview of mobility studies. Relatively little has been written on mobility and *Little Women*, but see Gaul, who argues that Alcott contains the anxieties raised by women's travel in the nineteenth century through letter writing that connects women to the home (esp. 103, 107).

10. Trains could also be sites of physical and moral danger for women (see, e.g., Beaumont 125–53), but neither Alcott nor her illustrators foreground such danger.

11. Such mixing was especially unavoidable before the introduction of Pullman cars after the Civil War. For an illuminating discussion of the differences between European and US passenger carriages in the nineteenth century, see Schivelbusch 93–114. For further discussion of US passenger cars, see Richter, esp. 65–74.

12. Jo doesn't specifically label them Irish, and it's possible that the Irishwoman accompanying them is a nursery governess for non-Irish children, but it seems likely that on an extended train trip at this time "an Irish lady with four small children" (262) comprise a family group.

13. See, e.g., Pritchard's discussion of how the rhetoric of mobility provides "a wholly inadequate index of freedom and development," occluding differences in the meanings of mobility for differently situated persons (57). See also Parkins on the dangers of some versions of mobility for nineteenth-century women, specifically "fallenness" and purposeless wandering (esp. 13, 62); and Ahmed for the debunking of mobility as always transgressive and of the fixity of the boundaries of home (esp. 338–39).

14. Alcott was not overly fond of the Irish and never sentimentalizes about them: she mentions in her journal having to "trot after" servants that she describes as "Irish incapables" and writes in a letter that, as nursery maids, "the Pats [Irish] are strong but have no principle" (June, July, Aug. 1875, *Journals* 196; 9 Oct. [1883?] letter to Elizabeth Wells, *Selected Letters* 273).

15. In a third illustration of the interior of a railroad car, in contrast, Judith Cheng (1982) provides a waist-high shot of Jo alone, showing little more of the car than the back of her seat, as she gazes, half-smiling, at the bunch of violets that Professor Bhaer gave her when she left New York to journey home. No Irish children here, or indeed anyone else, to interrupt her dreaming—instead, a fully romanticized domesticated interior.

16. The phrase was associated with her as early as 1875 (see, e.g., Clark, *Afterlife* 27–28).

17. See Bailey on the frequent gendering and sexualizing of trains in nineteenth-century literature (7).

18. Only later, in *Jo's Boys* (1886), do bicycles figure in the world of the March family, as vehicles for various boys in Jo and Bhaer's school. For discussion of the many mobilities in this later novel, including bicycles, and their associations with geographical detachments and freedoms, see Eiselein, esp. 87, 95–105.

19. It's also unlikely that a US mail carrier would have been delivering mail to a nonurban home like that of the March family during the Civil War, given that "free" delivery of mail didn't happen in (some) cities till 1863—and in rural areas till 1896 and usually later (see "Free City Delivery" and "Rural Free Delivery (RFD)"). See also Henkin, esp. 90.

20. For the classic statement on the ambiguous gendered valences of houses and homes, see Young. For a poetic evocation of the spaces of Alcott's novel, see Standing; for an account of its internal architectures, see Watters; for discussion of its questioning of the material norms of domesticity, see Hellman; for an account of the multivalent meanings of the Orchard House museum, see West.

21. The cover, however, is a different matter: it shows Jo looking at Meg dancing at a dance, with an inset depicting the four sisters and their mother reading a letter from Father. Heteronormative and domestic.

Works Cited

Adey, Peter. *Mobility*. 2nd ed., Routledge, 2017.
Ahmed, Sara. "Home and Away: Narratives of Migration and Estrangement." *International Journal of Cultural Studies*, vol. 2, no. 3, 1999, pp. 329–47.
Alberghene, Janice M., and Beverly Lyon Clark, editors. *"Little Women" and the Feminist Imagination: Criticism, Controversy, Personal Essays*. Garland, 1999.
Alcott, Louisa M. *Little Women, or, Meg, Jo, Beth and Amy*, edited by Anne K. Phillips and Gregory Eiselein, Norton Critical Edition, W. W. Norton, 2004.
Alcott, Louisa May. *The Journals of Louisa May Alcott*, edited by Joel Myerson, Daniel Shealy, and Madeleine B. Stern, Little, Brown, 1989; U of Georgia P, 1997.
Alcott, Louisa May. *The Selected Letters of Louisa May Alcott*, edited by Joel Myerson, Daniel Shealy, and Madeleine B. Stern, Little, Brown, 1987; U of Georgia P, 1995.
"American Railway Travelling." *Putnam's Magazine*, Feb. 1870, pp. 195–205. *Internet Archive*, https://archive.org/details/putnamsmagazine00projgoog/page/n207.
Bailey, Peter. "Adventures in Space: Victorian Railway Erotics, or Taking Alienation for a Ride." *Journal of Victorian Culture*, vol. 9, no. 1, 2004, pp. 1–21.
Beaumont, Matthew. "Railway Mania: The Train Compartment as the Scene of a Crime." *The Railway and Modernity: Time, Space, and the Machine Ensemble*, edited by Matthew Beaumont and Michael Freeman, Peter Lang, 2007, pp. 125–53.
Blaisdell, Elinore. Illustrations. *Little Women*, by Louisa M. Alcott, vol. 1 of *Chronicle of the March Family*, Little, Brown, 1946.
Bly, Nellie. "Champion of Her Sex: Miss Susan B. Anthony." *New York World* (2 Feb. 1896). Rpt. in *Around the World in Seventy-Two Days and Other Writings*, by Nellie Bly, edited by Jean Marie Lutes, Penguin, 2014, pp. 130–37.
Bossert, Jill. *Mark English*. Madison Square, 2002.
Bowlby, Rachel. "Domestication." *Feminism beside Itself*, edited by Diane Elam and Robyn Wiegman, Routledge, 1995, pp. 71–91.
Certeau, Michel de. "Railway Navigation and Incarceration." *The Practice of Everyday Life*, by Certeau, translated by Steven F. Rendall, U of California P, 1984, pp. 111–14.
Chandler, Marilyn R. *Dwelling in the Text: Houses in American Fiction*. U of California P, 1991, *UC Press E-Books Collection*, 1982–2004, http://ark.cdlib.org/ark:/13030/ft167nb0r5/.
Clark, Beverly Lyon. *The Afterlife of "Little Women."* Johns Hopkins UP, 2014.
Clark, Beverly Lyon. "The Writer, the Family, or the House? Visualizing Jo March's Genius in the Nineteenth Century." *Story Time: Essays on American Children's Literature from the Betsy Beinecke Shirley Collection*, edited by Timothy Young, Beinecke Rare Book & Manuscript Library/Yale UP, 2016, pp. 23–39.
Eiselein, Gregory. "Modernity and Louisa May Alcott's *Jo's Boys*." *Children's Literature*, vol. 34, 2006, pp. 83–108. *Project MUSE*.
English, Mark. Illustrations. *Little Women*, by Louisa May Alcott, condensed (1967). Rpt. in *Reader's Digest Best Loved Books for Young Readers*, Choice, 1989.
Felski, Rita. "The Invention of Everyday Life." *New Formations*, no. 39, 1999–2000, pp. 15–31.

"Frank Thayer Merrill Drawings to Illustrate Roberts Brothers 1880 Edition of Louisa May Alcott's *Little Women*, [1880]." Finding Aid. *Concord Public Library Special Collections*, https://concordlibrary.org/special-collections/fin_aids/Merrill_Alcott.

"Free City Delivery" and "Rural Free Delivery (RFD)." *Reaching Out to Everyone. The History of the United States Postal Service*, Publication 100, *The United States Postal Service—An American History 1775–2006*, Nov. 2012, http://www.warlca.com/documents/postal%20history_pub100.pdf.

Gabbey, Terry. Illustrations. *Little Women*, by Louisa M. Alcott, retold by Joan Collins, Ladybird Children's Classics, Ladybird Books, 1987.

Gannon, Susan R. "Getting Cozy with a Classic: Visualizing *Little Women* (1868–1995)." Alberghene and Clark, pp. 103–38.

Gaul, Theresa Strouth. "'The Precious Home Letters': Letter-Writing in *Little Women*." *Critical Insights: "Little Women,"* edited by Gregory Eiselein and Anne K. Phillips, Salem Press/Grey House Publishing, 2015, pp. 97–112.

Gavin, Adrienne E., and Andrew F. Humphries, editors. *Transport in British Fiction: Technologies of Movement, 1840–1940*. Palgrave Macmillan, 2015.

Hellman, Caroline Chamberlin. *Domesticity and Design in American Women's Lives and Literature: Stowe, Alcott, Cather, and Wharton Writing Home*. Routledge, 2011.

Henkin, David M. *The Postal Age: The Emergence of Modern Communications in Nineteenth-Century America*. U of Chicago P, 2006.

Herlihy, David V. *Bicycle: The History*. Yale UP, 2004.

Higonnet, Anne. *Pictures of Innocence: The History and Crisis of Ideal Childhood*. Thames, 1998.

Johnson, Nicholas. "*Kennst du das Land?* Learning the Language of Landscape in *Little Women*." *Children's Literature*, vol. 34, 2006, pp. 37–58.

King, Gordon. Illustrations. *Little Women*, by Louisa May Alcott, retold by Jane Carruth, Adventure Classics, Exeter Books, 1984.

Linley, Margaret. "The Living Transport Machine: George Eliot's *Middlemarch*." Gavin and Humphries, pp. 84–100.

Lonette, Reisie. Illustrations. *Little Women, or, Meg, Jo, Beth and Amy*, by Louisa May Alcott, Literary Guild of America, 1950.

Marx, Leo. *The Machine in the Garden: Technology and the Pastoral Ideal in America*. Oxford UP, (1964) 1972.

Massey, Doreen. *Space, Place, and Gender*. U of Minnesota P, 1994. *ProQuest Ebook Central*.

Merrill, Frank. Illustrations. *Little Women; or Meg, Jo, Beth, and Amy*, by Louisa M. Alcott, Little, Brown, 1880, 1896. *Internet Archive*, https://archive.org/details/littlewomenormeg00alco2/page/n1.

Mezei, Kathy, and Chiara Briganti. "Reading the House: A Literary Perspective." *Signs*, vol. 27, no. 3, 2002, pp. 837–46. *JSTOR*.

Nord, Deborah Epstein. "Outward Bound." *Nineteenth-Century Gender Studies*, vol. 3, no. 2, 2007, n. pag., http://www.ncgsjournal.com/issue32/nord.htm.

Op de Beeck, Nathalie. "'The First Picture Book for Modern Children': Mary Liddell's *Little Machinery* and the Fairy Tale of Modernity." *Little Machinery: A Critical Facsimile Edition*, by Mary Liddell, Wayne State UP, 2009, pp. 63–99.

Pappas, Stephanie. "Irish Potato Blight Originated in South America." *Live Science*, 3 Jan. 2017, https://www.livescience.com/57363-irish-potato-blight-originated-in-south-america.html.

Parkins, Wendy. *Mobility and Modernity in Women's Novels, 1850s–1930s: Women Moving Dangerously.* Palgrave Macmillan, 2009.

Pooley, Colin, Jean Turnbull, and Mags Adams. "The Impact of New Transport Technologies on Intraurban Mobility: A View from the Past." *Environment and Planning A*, vol. 38, 2006, pp. 253–67.

Pritchard, Elizabeth A. "The Way Out West: Development and the Rhetoric of Mobility in Postmodern Feminist Theory." *Hypatia*, vol. 15, no. 3, 2000, pp. 45–72. *JSTOR*.

Prunier, Jame's. Illustrations. *Little Women*, by Louisa May Alcott, Viking, 1997.

Richter, Amy G. *Home on the Rails: Women, the Railroad, and the Rise of Public Domesticity.* U of North Carolina P, 2005.

Roberson, Susan L. *Antebellum American Women Writers and the Road: American Mobilities.* Routledge, 2011. *ProQuest Ebook Central*.

Rubinstein, David. "Cycling in the 1890s." *Victorian Studies*, vol. 21, no. 1, 1977, pp. 47–71. *JSTOR*.

Schivelbusch, Wolfgang. *The Railway Journey: The Industrialization of Time and Space in the Nineteenth Century.* Hanser, 1977; U of California P, 2014. *ProQuest Ebook Central*.

Shealy, Daniel, editor. *"Little Women": An Annotated Edition*, by Louisa May Alcott, Harvard UP, 2013.

Shelley, Lorna. "'Buses should . . . inspire writers': Omnibuses in *fin-de-siècle* Short Stories and Journalism." Gavin and Humphries, pp. 136–50.

Skilton, David. "The Relation between Illustration and Text in the Victorian Novel: A New Perspective." *Word and Visual Imagination: Studies in the Interaction of English Literature and the Visual Arts*, edited by Karl Josef Höltgen et al., Universitätsbund Erlangen-Nürnberg, 1988, pp. 303–25.

Standing, Sue. "In Jo's Garret: *Little Women* and the Space of Imagination." Alberghene and Clark, pp. 173–83.

Stilton, Geronimo [Annalisa Strada et al.], adapter. *Piccole donne*. Italian translation of *Little Women*, by Louisa May Alcott, illustrated by Maria Rita Gentili et al., Edizioni Piemme, 2007.

Verschaffel, Bart. "The Meanings of Domesticity" (2002). Rpt. in *The Domestic Space Reader*, edited by Chiara Briganti and Kathy Mezei, U of Toronto P, 2012, pp. 153–56.

Wånggren, Lena. "The 'Freedom Machine': The New Woman and the Bicycle." Gavin and Humphries, pp. 123–35.

Watters, David H. "'A Power in the House': *Little Women* and the Architecture of Individual Expression." Alberghene and Clark, pp. 185–212.

West, Patricia. *Domesticating History: The Political Origins of America's House Museums.* Smithsonian Institution Press, 1999.

Woodward, Penny. "Herbs and Spices." *Encyclopedia of Food and Culture*, edited by Solomon H. Katz, vol. 2, Scribner, 2003, pp. 187–95.

Young, Iris Marion. "House and Home: Feminist Variations on a Theme" (1997). Rpt. in *On Female Body Experience: "Throwing Like a Girl" and Other Essays*, Oxford UP, 2005, pp. 123–54. *ProQuest Ebook Central*.

"This Was Something Altogether New"
On Jo March's Adulthood and *Little Women*'s Final Chapters

ANNE K. PHILLIPS

As Carolyn Heilbrun famously argued and an ongoing scholarly chorus agrees, "Alcott betrayed Jo" (144). According to their readings of *Little Women*, Jo March is a lively, original heroine who refreshingly eschews conventional feminine performance and aspires to attain literary fame and adult independence—but then sacrifices all of her hopes and interests in order to care for her family, marry an eccentric German professor, and have babies. Whether as Angela M. Estes and Kathleen Margaret Lant have argued, Alcott has been "forced to wage war upon her protagonist" (567), subsequently compelling "Jo to assume a kind of death in life, to impersonate the dead Beth" (578), or has coerced her heroine "to subordinate [her] needs for artistic expression to the needs of [her] famil[y]" (602), as Elizabeth Keyser among others has asserted, or capitulated to publisher and reader pressures, as she herself suggests in her letters and journals, Jo meets a fate in the final chapters of the novel that seems for many readers utterly incongruous with her younger self. Much of the critical and most of the fan conversation about *Little Women* consists of fierce arguments regarding Jo's romantic entanglements, particularly her refusal of Theodore "Laurie" Laurence's proposal (not to mention his subsequent, and for many readers infuriating, marriage to Jo's youngest sister,

Amy), and Jo's eventual marriage to Friedrich Bhaer. One hundred and fifty years after the novel's initial appearance in print, conversations about these topics continue to be lively.[1]

For many readers, marriage as it is commonly understood—what Kate Chopin refers to in "The Story of an Hour" as a "powerful will bending [one's own] in that blind persistence with which men and women believe they have a right to impose a private will upon a fellow-creature" (426)—is simply unacceptable for such an independent spirit as Jo March. As Elizabeth Langland explains:

> Marrying entails a sacrifice of those things she values: personal ambition, autonomy, and identity; her community of women at home; and her role as provider within that home. Mature sexual love, including marriage and motherhood, means a loss of Jo's identity and role as family mainstay, a loss of female community in which that identity and role are played out, and a sacrifice of parity with men. (125)

Alcott's letters fan these flames, particularly because she comments to Elizabeth Powell, a friend and Vassar College instructor, that "'Jo' should have remained a literary spinster but so many enthusiastic young ladies wrote to me clamorously demanding that she should marry Laurie, *or* somebody, that I didn't dare to refuse & out of perversity went & made a funny match for her" (*Selected Letters* 125). Daniel Shealy has insightfully addressed Alcott's possible motivations for making these comments to Powell, "a strong, independent activist and champion of woman's rights and racial justice": "Did Alcott think Powell would approve her insistence that Jo March not marry and that the author only acquiesced to her editor's desires?" (367). Also, Alcott suggested in a January 1869 letter to her uncle, Samuel May, that "publishers are very *perwerse* & wont let authors have thier way so my little women must grow up & be married off in a very stupid style" (*Selected Letters* 121–22)—but as Shealy also has emphasized, no specific dictates from Roberts Brothers' editor Thomas Niles to Louisa regarding the characters' fates have ever been found. "The marriage decision was all Alcott's," he concludes (367).

What exactly is funny about the match? What message is Alcott sending about reader expectations in her resolution to the novel? Further, how is Alcott herself regarding and complicating her depiction of Jo's marriage and motherhood? Scholar Donna M. Campbell has noted that "Alcott's method in *Little Women* is both to evoke and to transcend the broad outlines of what Susan K. Harris calls 'the dominant novelistic subgenre of the 1850s and 1860s'"—sentimental, domestic fiction (118). The specific means by which Alcott does so has remained elusive. Focusing on the text, particularly its final chapters, we see that Alcott employs purposeful word selection, contradiction, triangulation, and omission to provoke amusement while also subverting conventional expectations. At the same time, she offers meaningful observations about the relationship of an individual to herself, her family, and her community.

This multiplicity of purposes leads to unusual juxtapositions in the novel's final chapters. Jo is made to play a romantic heroine, yet she also retains significant independence. Her union with Friedrich may be "funny" in some aspects; yet we are expected to take it seriously. Jo and Friedrich are committed partners, but Jo also retains an intense, intimate bond with Laurie. Indeed, Jo's interactions with Laurie and Friedrich reveal that she needs and thrives in proximity to both men. And, while Jo leans into marriage and motherhood, much associated with those developments remains entirely offstage, forcing readers to think carefully about what Alcott omits and includes—and why. Creating an innovative, original representation of female individualism, marriage, and community, Alcott remains in control of her material all the way to the final paragraph of her enduring novel. Readers, including representative illustrators, often have overlooked or overruled essential elements of that material. Only to varying degrees have they been able to take in and keep up with Alcott's innovation and insight.

In staging the scenes and crafting the prose of her novel, Alcott subverts conventional expectations while adding complexity to her representation of marriage. As Alison M. Parker has observed, Alcott "consented to marrying off each sister—but with as little fanfare as possible" (694)—and, I would add, with the characterization of the bride driving the depiction. Even the most prominent wedding in the novel has been manipulated to emphasize the needs and preferences of the bride. Claiming "I don't want a fashionable wedding, but only those about me whom I love, and to them I wish to look and be my familiar self" (*Little Women* 198), Meg foregoes the orange blossoms that would be a sign of a fashionable wedding in her era and gives her first kiss as a married woman not to her husband but to her mother. Elegant Amy's wedding, though entirely offstage and alluded to only after the fact, takes place in Paris, with an ensuing honeymoon at Valrosa that is appropriate for Amy and

Laurie, given their tastes and history together. Jo's wedding and the birth of her children also occur offstage, which is appropriate given her disinterest in performing conventional femininity. As Michelle Massé has noted, "Neither proposal, nor wedding, nor children prompt closure. Indeed, the last two are noteworthy in not being represented but simply reported after the fact" (339).

On one hand, these choices demonstrate Alcott's ambivalence regarding the expectation that her characters should grow up, get married, and have children. On the other hand, they suggest the ways in which she was rethinking what it means to become a wife and mother and offering a new way of talking about those roles, even while writing at a fierce pace that she estimated might be a chapter a day (*Journals* 167). One of her strategies involves the omission of language traditionally used in sentimental, romantic literature. Tracing the use of the word "wife," for instance, readers will discover that there are only four instances of it in the first twenty-three chapters. The term "housewifely" appears in reference to Beth and her domestic impulses in "Burdens": "She was a housewifely little creature, and helped Hannah keep home neat and comfortable for the workers, never thinking of any reward but to be loved" (*Little Women* 38). Elsewhere in the first part, "wife" appears within the girls' family newspaper and elsewhere alludes to the spouse of the barber, who convinces him to cut and buy Jo's hair (133). The final instance references Marmee as she and Mr. March silently commune about Meg's emerging affection for John Brooke. "Wife" in these instances conveys domesticity, attention to family concerns, and some authority, particularly in the latter examples.

In the second part of the novel, Alcott's avoidance of conventional romantic terminology continues. While there are numerous usages of "wife," all of those references allude to Meg in her marital relationship with John or, in the final chapters, to Amy after she has married Laurie. Significantly, not one reference to Jo as a wife appears in *Little Women*. Further, there are only two references to Friedrich as a "husband." In "Under the Umbrella," Jo says, "I couldn't bear a rich husband!" (*Little Women* 372), and at the very end of the novel, she says "'I'm far happier than I deserve,' . . . glancing from her good husband to her chubby children, tumbling on the grass beside her" (380). Of the handful of references to "wedding" in the novel, all but two apply to Meg and Amy. Laurie comments that he could happily dance at Jo's wedding to Friedrich (356), and the narrator makes the comment that the apple harvest of the final chapter occurs "five years after Jo's wedding" (377).

Thus Alcott is crafting new ways to talk about an adult woman who has committed to a marital union. There are no wedding preparations, no ceremonies, and no social upheavals associated with this occurrence. Alcott was capable of writing enthusiastically about weddings, marriages, and anniversaries, as evidenced by Meg's wedding in *Little Women* and by scenes in other works, such as the golden wedding celebration in her earlier novel *Moods*. For Jo, though, Alcott provides an appropriately simple and matter-of-fact approach, maintaining the character's independence and selfhood even after she is well into her marriage. Alcott's refusal to allude to Jo as a bride or wife and her minimal reference to Jo's wedding contribute to the purposeful lack of emphasis on conventional romantic tropes throughout the novel. Further, for Jo it is far more important to emphasize the marriage, a productive partnership of two people committed to their important work, than the ceremony of the wedding. Alcott also wrote to Powell that "publishers wont let authors finish up as they like but insist on having people married off in a wholesale manner which much afflicts me" (*Selected Letters* 125). Throughout the second part, she effectively thwarts those expectations, but she nonetheless has invested care and thought in the way that she develops her characters' adult trajectories.[2]

Alcott finds the writing of the second part of the Marches' saga to be an opportunity to flesh out her principles about adult identity, familial/societal bonds, and vocation. Having recently published "Happy Women," a sketch of four independent, productive (single) adult women, where she detailed her thoughts regarding adulthood, vocation, and relationships, she must have regarded the second volume of *Little Women* as an opportunity to further showcase those perspectives. Writing about specific women's lives, choices, and purposes, Alcott provides additional comment on what marriage should and shouldn't be. "M." for example has had the opportunity to marry, but the young man was "her inferior in all respects," and she states, "I want to look up, not down . . . I must let it go, for I dare not sell my liberty" ("Happy Women" 204). Concluding the sketch, Alcott advises, "If love comes . . . , accept it in God's name and be worth[y] of His best blessing. If it never comes, then in God's name reject the shadow of it, for that can never satisfy a hungry heart" (206). Here, then, Alcott provides a framework for reflecting on her depiction of marriage and motherhood, including those described in *Little Women*: marriage should seem a divine blessing, give both partners confidence and uplift, foster interdependence, and result in mutual satisfaction.

Any assessment of what occurs in the final chapters of *Little Women* also must be grounded in Alcott's convictions about the nature of the family. The conception of the family that Alcott developed and exalted in her works is an idealized version of her personal experiences that is also influenced by reform impulses of the period in which she came of age. Charles Strickland has demonstrated that "profound changes were occurring during Alcott's lifetime (1832–1888) in relations between husbands and wives, in relations between parents and children, and in relations between the home and the marketplace" (2). "Family" at the end of *Little Women* thus includes blood relatives, romantic partners, in-laws, and an extended network of children and adults, with each individual engaging and committed to the welfare and values of the larger community. While Alcott's own family adhered in principle to this ideal, individual family members fell short in practice. There was patriarchal abdication of financial responsibility by Louisa's father Bronson, but he maintained a deep, ongoing investment in the rearing of his children that was unusual in the era in which he lived. Louisa's mother "Abba" assumed oversight of the family's finances, also perhaps unusual in her era, while providing emotional and psychological support and practical advice for her daughters as well as neighbors, acquaintances, and total strangers. The Alcott siblings labored to support and provide each other with what was needed throughout their lives—and Louisa in particular needed to be needed. Often, she recorded her efforts on behalf of her sisters: "Sewed a good deal getting May's summer things in order," she wrote in 1861 (*Journals* 105). Following Anna's marriage, the Alcott family expanded to include her husband John Bridge Pratt and subsequently her sons John and Freddie. Louisa was intimately involved with the raising of these nephews throughout their childhoods, noting in a journal entry for February 1864, for instance, "I shall love to have baby here" (128), and in 1873, "Had Johnny for a week, to keep all quiet at home. Enjoyed the sweet little soul very much" (187). While often renting rooms in Boston in order to write and escape household drudgery, Louisa remained deeply committed to her family, and familial dedication and identification are infused throughout her depictions of the March family.

Additional demonstration of Alcott's ideal of the family community is alluded to in an 1873 letter to Lucy Stone of the *Woman's Journal*. Addressing her support for women's suffrage, Alcott described her household's responses in support of the cause, quoting enthusiastic comments by her parents Bronson and Abba but also emphasizing that both of her nephews are "mustered in" on behalf of female suffrage. "Such being the temper of the small convention of which I am now President," she reported, "I can not hesitate to say that though I may not be with you in body, I shall be in spirit" (*Selected Letters* 179). For Alcott, the individual maintains an intimate, complex, and essential relationship to others in the family, and each of the individuals within the community should have the liberty to participate, if willing, in the family's activities and decisions. Moreover, even those who are not blood relatives can commit themselves to and be included in these "small conventions." Scholar Anne Dalke, acknowledging the importance of this interdependence in *Little Women*, notes that Alcott's novel offers perspective on two journeys: "the first individual and the second communal" (557). That understanding of social configurations translates directly to her depiction of Jo March's marriage and motherhood.

In the final chapter of the novel, this companionate extended family is clearly in evidence. We are privy to the conversation as the "Marches, Laurences, Brookeses, and Bhaers" (*Little Women* 377) mull Jo's announcement that she intends to open a home for boys at Plumfield, which she has inherited from Aunt March. The cues that denote the intimate, devoted relationship among those gathered here are both verbal and nonverbal. Mr. Laurence, who "had been longing to lend the lovers a hand" (374), calls out, "tell us all about it" (374). Amy's eyes and demeanor indicate her approval, while Marmee reaches for Jo's hand, confirming her support with that gesture (374). Sketching her plan for Plumfield, Jo anticipates and exults in Friedrich's and Mr. March's projected pedagogical contributions, then pays tribute to her other partner, Laurie, whom she knows she will be able to rely on: "You love good and beautiful things, enjoy them yourself, and let others go halves, as you always did in the old times" (375). Laurie immediately credits his grandfather and wife for his positive attributes, placing "one hand gently on his grandfather's white head, the other on Amy's golden one, for the three were never far apart" (375). Even Aunt March's spoiled fat poodle, which Jo "had adopted, out of respect to his former mistress" (373), is included within the "small convention" of this family.

As Alcott is constructing a new family of the "Marches and Laurences and Brookses and Bhaers," so she is constructing new relationships and alliances between Jo and her love interests. While much of the energy of the critical conversation has settled on Jo's refusal of Laurie and her acceptance of Friedrich, not enough scholarship has acknowledged their interdependence.

As Alcott finds her way to the conclusion of her novel, she triangulates Jo's relationship with both in ways that are particularly innovative. Both are friends; both love her; both are loved by her. Building her adult life within an expanded community modeled on her family, Jo March establishes what she needs to be happy as she builds distinctive, intimate relationships with both of them.

Throughout much of the second part of the novel, Alcott triangulates the relationship between Jo, Laurie, and Friedrich. Even in her first letters to her family from New York, when Jo is absorbed in describing Friedrich's appearance, behaviors, and encounters, she comments regularly about Laurie, writing comments such as "Is Teddy studying so hard that he can't find time to write to his friends?" (*Little Women* 268) or "A happy New-Year to you all, my dearest family, which of course includes Mr. L. and a young man by the name of Teddy" (270). Describing the professor and Tina as Bottom and Titania, Jo notes that they are "'quite a landscape,' to use a Teddy-ism" (272). Returned to the family fold after completing her governess stint in New York, she describes Friedrich to Laurie as "the best friend I've got—next to you" (285). And Friedrich admits, following Jo's commitment to marrying him, that he would have asked her earlier except that he believed that she was betrothed to Laurie. They are linked from Friedrich's first references in "Jo's Journal" through the final page of "Harvest Time"—and throughout the second part of the novel, Jo seems to need something from both of them that takes her relationships with them beyond the expected boundaries of a standard marriage plot.

Alcott leaves open why Jo begins to reconsider and seek new connections with these men. Perhaps she does so because of the loneliness and despair she experiences after Beth's death, "when she thought of spending all her life in that quiet house, devoted to humdrum cares, a few poor little pleasures, and the duty that never seemed to grow any easier" (*Little Women* 337). Alternately, Meg's domestic contentment may prompt Jo to consider the possibility of marrying: "Marriage is an excellent thing after all. I wonder if I should blossom out, half as well as you have, if I tried it, always '*perwisin*' I could" (338). Alcott confirms how much Jo loves her niece and nephew, Daisy and Demi, who are "Meg's most effective arguments" in support of a domestic arrangement and a more conventional womanhood (339). As Jo ponders these possibilities, she participates in poignant, intimate scenes with Laurie and then Friedrich, further developing her triangulated coming-of-age process across the final chapters of the novel. While those significant scenes have often been alluded to by scholars, they operate and correspond to one another in ways that have not been previously understood.

Although Jo could not accept Laurie's proposal of marriage and does not see herself as his romantic partner, there remains between them an intense, loving intimacy.[3] Using strategies that have heightened readers' affinities for Jo's relationship with Laurie, Alcott casts him in some scenes as a more romantic partner than Friedrich. Indeed, given how much of Jo's courtship with Friedrich remains offstage, the scene in which Laurie returns from Europe and reconnects with Jo takes on additional significance. Jo and Friedrich do not exchange vows before readers—but Jo and Laurie do.

In "Surprises," Jo awakens to find Laurie standing over her, returned from Europe and intent on telling her that he has married Amy. This scene provides the necessary resolution that enables Jo and Laurie to move forward in their relationship. In it, they work to find their way back from the precipice that Laurie's marriage proposal to Jo and her refusal cast them upon in "Heartache." Laurie's marriage to Amy alters their relationship and makes it possible for Jo to reestablish her relationship with him. Now, neither looks for a marital relationship, but they can move forward within what may be one of the most intimate and satisfying, but not sexual, male-female relationships in literature. Alcott's treatment of Jo's relationship with Laurie anticipates her observation about the protagonist of her 1873 novel *Work*, Christie Devon, who "was a woman who could change a lover to a friend, and keep him all her life" (440).

A number of elements of the scene in "Surprises" convey profound intimacy. No longer barricading Laurie from her couch, or pummeling him with her horsehair pillow, as she attempted during their "Tender Troubles," Jo addresses him as "Teddy," and he acknowledges, "No one ever calls me that but you" (*Little Women* 344). They attest that their love for each other will endure: "I never shall stop loving you" (346). Their comments are evocative of how a bride and groom might speak during a wedding, including a question and a response: "'I could honestly share my heart between sister Jo and wife Amy, and love them both dearly. Will you believe it . . . ?' 'I'll believe it, with all my heart'" (346). During these "vows," they both put aside childish things, as it were, and acknowledge their relationship as adults: "We are man and woman now, with sober work to do. . . . I shall miss my boy, but I shall love the man as much, and admire him more" (346). Wedding ceremonies often end with a kiss. Here, an equally intimate physical gesture binds Jo and Laurie together at the conclusion of their conversation: "He did not say a word, but took the hand she offered him, and laid his face down on it for a minute, feeling that out of the grave of a boyish passion, there had risen a beautiful, strong friendship to bless them both" (346). In this fashion, Alcott gives readers a "wedding" of souls—not exactly a romantic commitment, but a union nonetheless. Sarah Wadsworth perceptively notes in her discussion of heterosexual friendship in Alcott's works that Alcott is "presenting Jo and Laurie as kindred spirits, or 'second selves,' and complementary halves of an ideal duo" (389)—and although Wadsworth suggests that the friendship strains after Jo and Laurie come of age (390), they clearly find their way back to being "complementary halves" before the final chapters of the novel.

While giving the friends a symbolic wedding, Alcott takes a quite different approach in depicting the lovers. Gregory Eiselein has noted that Alcott frequently employs contradiction "to engender new meaning" (6). Alcott particularly engages in contradictions in her descriptions of Friedrich Bhaer. While "in no respect what is called fascinating, imposing, or brilliant," he was "as attractive as a genial fire" (*Little Women* 276); "always poor, yet always appeared to be giving something away"; "a stranger, yet every one was his friend; no longer young—but as happy-hearted as a boy; plain and odd,—yet his face looked beautiful to many" (276). These contradictions continue throughout their courtship. In the penultimate chapter, Alcott stacks up contradictory details as the lovers enjoy "the magical moment that bestows youth on the old, beauty on the plain, wealth on the poor, and gives human hearts a foretaste of heaven" (368). Readers might ask, what "new meaning" is engendered through these descriptions? Alcott, attentive to the way that readers will respond to Professor Bhaer, gives him attributes that they might dislike or eschew, but in every case, she follows those details (about his appearance, poverty, lack of status, etc.) with attributes that are of greater significance. She knows that she is not giving readers what they want, thus teasing them, but she is also affirming values dear to her heart and principles while rebutting their objections.[4] Further, the contradictory constructions—not that, but this—give additional emphasis to the values and qualities that she wants to extol in portraying Friedrich Bhaer.

Writing Jo and Friedrich's commitment scene, Alcott withholds almost all of the elements that one might associate with a proposal, and the ones that she includes are manipulated for comedic effect. Jo, who otherwise has become more than competent in relation to many of the domestic arts, and is alluded to earlier in the second part of the novel as "mantua-maker general to the family" (*Little Women* 228), suddenly becomes hapless while shopping for sewing supplies with Friedrich. Normally, "Jo rather prided herself upon her shopping capabilities, and particularly wished to impress her escort with the neatness and dispatch with which she would accomplish the business" (366). However, as Professor Bhaer observes, "She upset the tray of needles, forgot the silesia was to be 'twilled' till it was cut off, [and] gave the wrong change," generally humiliating herself (366).

Friedrich's eventual announcement of his love for Jo is stripped of all of the elements readers might expect for an equally comic effect. He can't kneel (they are standing in a muddy street). They have no privacy and are in a precarious position (indeed, the omnibus almost hits them). Friedrich, rather than Jo, is holding the bouquet (posies intended for Daisy that Jo has accidently flung in hailing the bus) as they give voice to their feelings. His hands are full of bundles and thus he cannot reach for her (contrasting with the physical proximity Laurie and Jo share in their "wedding" scene). He doesn't even utter what most readers might regard as a conventional proposal. Instead of some variation of "Will you marry me?" he asks, "I haf nothing but much love to gif you; I came to see if you could care for it.... Can you make a little place in your heart for old Fritz?" (*Little Women* 368). Granting that "it was certainly proposing under difficulties" (368), the narrator makes the only explicit identification of what is taking place in the scene. Given the rain and mud that surround Friedrich and Jo as they wander through the business district (rather than a more romantic country lane), Alcott makes the scene as comical as possible: "There actually seemed to be little rainbows in the drops that sparkled on his beard. . . . she looked far from lovely, with her skirts in a deplorable state, her rubber boots splashed to the ankle, and her bonnet a ruin" (368). Altogether, they are indeed "a pair of harmless lunatics" (368). Nonetheless, Jo "trudged beside him, feeling as if her place had always been there, and wondering how she ever could have chosen any other lot" (368). Alcott achieves quite different tones and effects in these scenes—but despite the comedy, Jo determinedly gives her hands and kiss to Friedrich. Nonetheless, both Laurie and Friedrich are essential to the conception of family that Jo needs and seeks in the final chapters.

Those who complain that Jo has become someone other than she was in the earlier portions of the novel need to appreciate the revitalization she undergoes following the return of Laurie and Friedrich to her life. While she has been constrained by grief and loss and despair following the death of her sister, Jo rebounds in the final chapters. Whether she is making a fool of herself while shopping with Professor Bhaer (a characterization in keeping with her burning of Meg's hair and her rambunctious behavior at the Gardiner party) or demonstrating a certain energetic, harum-scarum quality during the harvest festival at Plumfield, the Jo of the final chapters must be acknowledged to be active, secure in her identity, and happy—not, as Estes and Lant have argued, "a false Jo, a broken doll, a compliant Beth" (582). Describing her plan for Plumfield, Jo demonstrates a returning joyfulness and zeal "in the old enthusiastic way, which they had not seen for a long while" (*Little Women* 374). At the harvest festival, "Jo was in her element . . . and rushed about with her gown pinned up, her hat anywhere but on her head, and her baby tucked under her arm, ready for any lively adventure which might turn up" (378). Sharing reminiscences with her mother and sisters, Jo concludes that she "never was so jolly in my life" (380)—a return to the slang she has exulted in using throughout the earlier chapters of the novel.

Further, there is a purposeful, productive emphasis on liveliness, liberty, and play throughout the final chapter. While it may seem less pronounced because a portion of it is rendered through the narrator's commentary rather than from immediate delivery by the central characters, it is nonetheless prominent throughout the chapter. Further, it contrasts purposefully with the characterization of Jo at the beginning of the novel. While scholars have often traced the connections between the thirteenth chapter, "Castles in the Air," and "Harvest Time," as the sisters reflect on the goals they once discussed, the first chapter, "Playing Pilgrims," offers equally essential insight in evaluating the final chapter. In the beginning, Jo is contained indoors. She is frustrated with the social boundaries that seem to be closing in upon her: "I hate to think I've got to grow up and be Miss March, and wear long gowns, and look as prim as a China-aster" (*Little Women* 12). She chafes because instead of making a more active contribution to the war effort, she "can only stay at home and knit like a poky old woman" (13). Attempting to help prepare for the family supper, Jo "set chairs, dropping, overturning, and clattering everything she touched" (16). The overall impression, initially, is of an awkward, gangly, adolescent girl who is anxious about having to give up her freedom, conform to societal expectations, and perform conventional femininity.

However, building from Jo's insistence in the penultimate chapter, "I'm to carry my share, Friedrich, and help to earn the home. Make up your mind to that or I'll never go" (*Little Women* 372), Alcott emphasizes in "Harvest Time" Jo's independence, her interdependence with family and community, and her characteristic enthusiasm. "Think what luxury; Plumfield my own, and a wilderness of boys to enjoy it with me!" (374), she exults. The meal that everyone shares in this final chapter, capably staged by a no-longer-awkward Jo, occurs outside rather than inside (in what is clearly an ongoing custom at Plumfield), and there is an undeniably carnivalesque quality to the celebration: "The lads were not required to sit at table, but allowed to partake of refreshment as they liked,—freedom being the sauce loved best by the boyish soul" (378). Finally, there is artistic, performative activity, in keeping with the numerous examples of play modeled by the Marches in the early chapters. Following the meal, the Plumfield children serenade Marmee from the trees, and the narrator explains that they are singing "something altogether new": "the little song Jo had written, Laurie set to music, and the professor trained his lads to give with the best effect" (379). Here, Jo is still writing, still creative—and her partners both contribute to the success of her surprise for Marmee. While other scholars have seen in the relationship of *Work*'s Christie Devon and David Sterling Alcott's "most thoughtful and mature statement about marriage and the family" (Strickland 113), her innovative representation of Jo's status and experiences as wife, mother, and schoolmistress at the end of *Little Women* deserves additional consideration.

Alcott is thus satisfying and thwarting reader expectations while also upholding ideals of individualism, liberty, interdependence, and community. Jo has attained the life that she desired and needed. She retains her strong bond to her family. She is fulfilled by diverse kinds of friendship and love. She remains independent within her personal and professional community. She remains creative, as evidenced by the song that she has written in collaboration with her best friend and her husband. She manifests exuberance and remains unconventional, demonstrating a consistency in the character throughout both parts of the novel that has not often been acknowledged by readers and critics.

"Harvest Time" offers perspective on the larger Plumfield community, including fathers and husbands and students, but its lens then narrows, offering a final vignette that bookends the first chapter's familiar, oft-depicted tableau of Marmee with her daughters. With the grandchildren near at hand, Marmee, Meg, Jo, and Amy commune, reviewing their history, evaluating their current status, and counting their blessings. These are the final images that readers take from the novel and retain as they reflect upon it. How, then, have representative illustrators represented that concluding imagery? Have they acknowledged the larger community while still conveying the centrality of the mother and her daughters? What aspects of the characters' commentaries are most often perpetuated in the illustrations? The following analysis is not intended to be a comprehensive survey of illustrators' approaches. Rather, it demonstrates that some illustrators, attentive to the text, can accommodate its innovations and eccentricities. Others, however, seek through their images to make the text conform to more conventional romantic or domestic expectations.

The initial illustrator of the second part of the novel, Hammatt Billings, provided only four illustrations. His frontispiece depicts Amy and Laurie in Valrosa, reflecting events of the sixteenth chapter. Other illustrations include Jo in the vortex, a delightfully energetic depiction (212)[5]; Friedrich and Tina; and Jo and Beth at the seashore. Billings does not offer any perspective on the events of the final chapters, although attentive readers might notice the alignments between Friedrich in his study (264) and Jo at the seashore (292). In particular, both characters are associated with books, and both demonstrate devotion to younger, more dependent characters. In both images, Friedrich and Jo attract attention, affection, and trust: the cat leans into Friedrich, while Beth has snuggled up to Jo. Chronologically, the final image is of Laurie and Amy, but the most intimate relationship captured by Billings is Jo nestling with Beth. Alcott's editor Thomas Niles might have expressed disappointment with this image,[6] but it demonstrates Billings's awareness that Jo's connection with Beth is essential to her characterization.

In 1880, Frank T. Merrill provided more than two hundred illustrations for an edition that incorporated both parts of Alcott's novel.[7] In his edition, Merrill has prepared multiple images per chapter, including often-comical small headpieces and tailpieces at the beginning and ending of each chapter. Susan Gannon has aptly noted that "Merrill defuses the potential sentimentality of the novel very much as Alcott does, by stressing moments of absurdity and unexpected humor" (116–17). The headpiece for the penultimate chapter demonstrates Merrill's close attention to and emphasis on the text. Indeed, readers can always identify the exact passage that has inspired Merrill's drawing while appreciating how he highlights and emphasizes aspects of Alcott's text. In the chapter 46 headpiece, Jo and Friedrich are depicted "enjoying promenades" (Merrill 558) down a country road, which

Beth and Jo at the shore (Frank Merrill, *Little Women*, 1880)

is appropriate because no matter which path Jo took, "she was sure to meet [Friedrich], either going or returning" (558).

Within that chapter, Merrill also depicts the moment when Jo looks up and sees Friedrich holding the umbrella over her. Happily, and in contrast to numerous other depictions of the lovers under the umbrella, Merrill enables us to see their faces. Here, the professor is holding the umbrella over Jo, not seeming to care that he is getting wet. Merrill chooses the moment when the lovers first encounter each other to build some suspense, in keeping with Alcott's use of such delaying tactics as her cataloging of Professor Bhaer's thoughts about the many different tones used by Jo during their conversation, or her detailing of the many errands they conduct before admitting their love for each other. However, Merrill is also purposefully linking this image to an earlier illustration to heighten Jo's strong connection to Friedrich. Previously, in "Beth's Secret," Merrill has included an umbrella in a full-page illustration of Jo and Beth at the seashore (Merrill, tipped-in opposite page, 449), where Jo protectively holds the umbrella over Beth. The text doesn't specify this detail; it is something that Merrill has added. Having seen Jo and Beth posed intimately under the umbrella, at a time when Jo asserts, "I don't care what becomes of anybody but you, Beth" (*Little Women* 294), readers are perhaps

Jo modeling shawl (Frank Merrill, *Little Women*, 1880)

more likely to appreciate the way in which Friedrich will provide sustaining love for Jo when they see him holding the umbrella over his beloved.

Merrill then depicts Jo modeling the shawl that Friedrich will purchase for Tina's mother (when she enjoys letting the clerk assume that they are a married couple; Merrill 565). It is only after Jo and Friedrich have reached an understanding that Merrill depicts them together under the umbrella, facing away from the reader (573). Curiously, Jo appears to be wearing the same shawl (with its distinctive diagonal stripe and fringe) that she has modeled in the earlier scene set at the store. It wouldn't make sense that Jo would wear that shawl home, but what Merrill may be conveying is the now-impending change in her marital status and the fact that although she was playing at being Friedrich's partner in the store, she is actually committed to him by the end of the chapter. The layout of this sketch also gives the lovers privacy. Finally, the tailpiece to the chapter shows Professor Bhaer's umbrella folded up and leaning against the door, as if to convey that he is indeed "home."

Under the umbrella (Frank Merrill, *Little Women*, 1880)

In the final chapter, Merrill initially emphasizes the communal aspect of life at Plumfield. Offering a vignette of the community in his headpiece, he depicts more than a dozen children and several adults engaged in the harvesting of the apples in Plumfield's orchard (575). The children are of varying ages, and they include girls as well as boys. In the far right portion of the scene, there are very young children and a mix of women and men, denoting the location where Marmee and her daughters will converse in the final pages of the chapter. This is an active scene, with boys climbing ladders, hauling baskets, gathering apples that have been dislodged from the trees, and more. There also are plenty of apples in those trees, conveying the fertility and bountifulness of the orchard at Plumfield.

Two other illustrations round out Merrill's work in the final chapter of the novel, and they add to Merrill's acknowledgment of the breadth of the

Harvest time (Frank Merrill, *Little Women*, 1880)

community while also highlighting the intimacy between Marmee and her daughters. The first of these images shows a younger child being carried piggyback-style on an older child's back (582). Below, four boys are playing leapfrog in the orchard. The former highlights the students' tendency to carry off Jo's youngest son, Teddy: "Nothing ever happened to him, and Jo never felt any anxiety when he was whisked up into a tree by one lad, galloped off on the back of another, or supplied with sour russets by his indulgent papa" (*Little Women* 378). This is an image that runs vertically down the left side of the left page. Theorist Molly Bang has asserted that vertical shapes "are more exciting and more active" (54), and these vignettes of boys playing certainly emphasize their energy. Further, they offer a delightful conclusion to the motif Merrill has established at the beginning of his edition. In the first chapter, as the March sisters are recalling their childhood game of pretending to be pilgrims en route to the Celestial City, Merrill illuminates the right side of the right page with a vertical illustration of four little girls wending their way up rounded flights of stairs, burden-bags on their backs and staffs and scrolls in their hands (11). (This is an image that Roberts Brothers used widely in advertising and also added to the cover of some later editions of Alcott's novel.) The image in the final chapter complements this earlier image and offers confirmation that the next generation is beginning its journey.

It also affirms the importance of play and activity in a healthy child's life across generations.

Merrill's final image focuses on Marmee, Meg, Jo, and Amy, along with five children (opposite 583). They are nestled together on a blanket, with baskets and other picnic paraphernalia nearby. Some of the characters are in shadow and some are in the light. It would seem that Jo is positioned at the left in this scene, with Teddy sitting next to her, rapturously churning his fist in the milk jug, and Rob is stretching out on the grass across from Teddy. (The placement of the children in the scene helps readers determine the identities of the women.) There are small deviations in the image from Alcott's text—for instance, Merrill depicts Amy's young daughter sitting up, seemingly awake and alert, while Alcott describes Amy's daughter sleeping "in her arms" (*Little Women* 380). Generally, though, Merrill attends to as much of Alcott's description as possible, showing that Daisy is in proximity to Amy's daughter, that Teddy and Rob are "tumbling on the grass beside [Jo]" (380), and that Marmee is closest to the center and positioned just a little higher than any of the other characters, as befits her status within the family and the scene—consistent with what picture theorist William Moebius has explained: "Figures may be strengthened or weakened depending on whether the character is centred or in the margin, large ... or small" (149). Merrill strikes a nice balance between the harvest activities of the larger community of the "Marches and Laurences and Brookses and Bhaers" at the beginning of the chapter and the intimate gathering of Marmee and her daughters at its end. In choosing to highlight these moments in his final images, he acknowledges Alcott's emphases on activity, community, and familial love. Satisfyingly, as Gannon has also noted (118), Merrill completes his pilgrim motif with the tailpiece for the final chapter, an image of a hat, staff, scroll, and burden-bag, denoting the conclusion of the quest. His images respect Alcott's text. They highlight the characters' individuality as well as their interdependence. They celebrate the liveliness of the characters without forcing them into artificial proximities or behaviors.

In contrast, other illustrators, seemingly less attentive to or equipped to appreciate Alcott's innovations, impose more conventional arrangements on the characters in the final chapters. As scholar Beverly Lyon Clark has acknowledged, "Illustrators of *Little Women* have often emphasized the decorative and romantic and domestic" (197). Frances Brundage's 1929 edition of *Little Women* exemplifies this tendency. Providing fewer illustrations than in Merrill's edition but more than in Billings's, Brundage was

Marmee with daughters and grandchildren (Frank Merrill, *Little Women*, 1880)

particularly known for depictions of endearing, sentimentalized children ("Frances"), and she brings a conventional sensibility to her illustration of Alcott's novel. In the final chapters of her edition, there are only two illustrations. In the penultimate chapter, Brundage devotes a full-page illustration to Friedrich and Jo under the umbrella with all of their bundles and baskets (608). Depicted at the upper left of the scene, they are moving toward the left, which, as Moebius would suggest, conveys that they are heading toward a more secure footing (149). Friedrich faces the reader as he turns toward Jo. Jo looks straight ahead.[8] The focus is to some extent withdrawn from them, though, because Brundage has added two other groups who are also under umbrellas: a dog, girl and boy, with their own basket, pointing and looking toward Jo and Friedrich, and another group of three umbrella-bearing youngsters, who seem to be enjoying the inclement weather. The caption for the image alludes to Friedrich and Jo's bliss: "Little they cared what anybody thought, for they were enjoying the happy hour which gives human hearts a foretaste of heaven" (609). However, in adding the other clusters of children and umbrellas, Brundage also emphasizes the lovers' inattention to what is happening around them (while finding a way to incorporate more of the rounded, playful children from which she had built a highly successful career). Brundage thus plays up the comic aspect of the moment, extending the comic representation of the lovers fostered by Alcott in her text.

Brundage's final scene for the volume appears four pages from the conclusion (627), and it offers a striking contrast to the corresponding image in Merrill's edition. Brundage depicts the March grandchildren bringing Marmee gifts and celebrating her birthday—emphasizing a quite different moment from the ones depicted by Merrill. The larger community is hinted at through the addition of one additional male child to this scene, in addition to figures that are assumed to be Daisy, Demi, Rob, and Teddy. The wheelbarrow of gifts sits at the left, and Marmee sits at the right, facing the children at the center. Most interestingly (and understandably, given Brundage's affinity for depicting children), Jo and Friedrich are positioned together behind Marmee at the right, gazing adoringly at the children. For Brundage, then, it is important to allude to Marmee's birthday and her successful fostering of generations of offspring (evoked in the parallel positioning of Marmee and Jo). She also seems to find it necessary to assure readers of Jo's happy marriage and motherhood—hence, emphasizing Friedrich's proximity to Jo. This is a notable deviation from the text, since Friedrich and Jo are independently attending to different tasks throughout most of the final chapter of Alcott's novel. Brundage's composition reflects her recognition of the gaps in Alcott's text regarding Jo's nearness (or lack thereof) to Friedrich. Responding to those omissions or absences by imposing a more conventional representation of Alcott's heroine in proximity to her husband and children, Brundage is representative of the way that numerous illustrators have chosen to subvert Alcott's emphasis on Jo's liberty and independence in her conclusion while heightening and emphasizing Jo's marriage and motherhood.[9]

Closely reading the final chapters of Alcott's novel, studying their composition, and attending to the way that they have been received by scholars, fans, and representative illustrators, readers can appreciate how innovative Alcott's depiction of Jo March's adulthood, marriage, motherhood, and vocation really is. While recognizing fans' desires and perhaps encountering some editorial direction, Alcott negotiates her own path while establishing the consistency of Jo's character, her realization of a mature femininity that remains distinctly her own, her attainment of work that she finds satisfying, and her realization of the kinds of relationships and social configurations that satisfy her. In writing the first part of her novel, Alcott moved through

Jo and Friedrich (Frances Brundage, *Little Women*, 1929)

Marmee's celebration (Frances Brundage, *Little Women*, 1929)

noticeable stages, including resistance—"Never liked girls or knew many, except my sisters" (*Journals* 165–66); resignation—"Lively, simple books are very much needed for girls, and perhaps I can supply the need" (166); cautious enthusiasm—"It reads better than I expected" (166); and confidence—"Pleasant notices and letters arrive, and much interest in my little women" (167). Depicting Jo's path to womanhood in the second part, Alcott also famously resists: "I *won't* marry Jo to Laurie to please any one" (167). As well, in a letter to her editor regarding the title, she writes, "A jocose friend suggests 'Wedding *Marches*' as there is so much pairing off, but I dont approve" (119). Soon, though, she is enjoying the prospect of finding out more about her characters: "As I can launch into the future, my fancy has more play" (167). Only a few weeks later, she reports being "so full of my work, I can't stop to eat or sleep" (167). Launching Jo into her adult life, Alcott acknowledges her heroine's hardships and sorrows but also provides her with meaningful personal and professional goals and paths to their attainment. Representing her protagonist's distinctive configuration of heterosexual relationships and marriage, Alcott offers purposeful, meaningful, original commentary on friendship, romance, partnership, and parenthood. Readers may not always have gotten exactly what they wanted from the conclusion of *Little Women*. Alcott, negotiating a path through and around reader responses and editorial guidance, may not always have gotten exactly what she wanted. But careful consideration of the final chapters of the novel demonstrates that Jo March, rather than being betrayed by her author, gets what she needs.

Notes

1. See, for example, Barker; Rizzuto; Zehr.

2. Other nineteenth-century women writers were also envisioning and writing about marriage without forcing their heroines to conform to stereotypical romantic tropes. See, for example, Fulton's analysis of depictions of marriage in the works of Jewett and Phelps.

3. For a sampling of scholarly assessments of Jo and Laurie's relationship, see Brodhead; Dalke; Fetterley; MacLeod; Susina; and Tuck.

4. For a range of perspectives on Friedrich's relationship with Jo, see Campbell; Doyle; Massé; Minadeo; Reardon; Showalter; and Strickland.

5. Page numbers for the illustrations refer to editions catalogued by illustrator in the Works Cited; quotations from Alcott's text are taken from the Norton edition of the novel catalogued under her name.

6. On 4 Apr. 1869, Niles wrote to Alcott, "I like all the pictures but one, Beth & Joe [sic] on the Sea Shore, which is rather a failure" (qtd. in Alcott, *Little Women* 422).

7. For further analysis of Merrill's illustrations, see Clark; Gannon.

8. Indeed, Brundage's composition of Friedrich and Jo and her choice of caption appear quite closely modeled on Jessie Willcox Smith's depiction of Friedrich and Jo under the umbrella (1915).

9. See, for example, Reisie Lonette's edition of *Little Women* (1950), in which the final image is a close-up of (a conventionally lovely) Jo cuddling her (cherubic) youngest son (375). Here, the final image of Alcott's lively heroine entirely reduces her to sentimental motherhood.

Works Cited

Alcott, Louisa May. "Happy Women." *Alternative Alcott*, edited by Elaine Showalter, Rutgers UP, 1988, pp. 203–6.

Alcott, Louisa May. *The Journals of Louisa May Alcott*, edited by Joel Myerson, Daniel Shealy, and Madeleine B. Stern, Little, Brown, 1989; U of Georgia P, 1997.

Alcott, Louisa May. *Little Women, or, Meg, Jo, Beth and Amy*, edited by Anne K. Phillips and Gregory Eiselein, Norton Critical Edition, W. W. Norton, 2004.

Alcott, Louisa May. *Moods*, edited by Sarah Elbert, Rutgers UP, 1991.

Alcott, Louisa May. *The Selected Letters of Louisa May Alcott*, edited by Joel Myerson, Daniel Shealy, and Madeleine B. Stern, Little, Brown, 1987; U of Georgia P, 1995.

Alcott, Louisa May. *Work: A Story of Experience*. Roberts Brothers, 1873.

Bang, Molly. *Picture This: How Pictures Work*. Rev. and expanded 25th anniversary ed., Chronicle Books, 2016.

Barker, Elise. "Alcott's 'Funny Match' for Jo." *Critical Insights: "Little Women,"* edited by Gregory Eiselein and Anne K. Phillips, Salem Press/Grey House Publishing, 2015, pp. 189–203.

Billings, Hammatt, illustrator. *Little Women*, by Louisa May Alcott, W. W. Norton, 2004.

Brodhead, Richard H. "Starting Out in the 1860s: Alcott, Authorship, and the Postbellum Literary Field." *Cultures of Letters: Scenes of Reading and Writing in Nineteenth Century America*. U of Chicago P, 1993, pp. 69–106.

Brundage, Frances, illustrator. *Little Women*, by Louisa May Alcott, Saalfield, 1929.

Campbell, Donna M. "Sentimental Conventions and Self-Protection: *Little Women* and *The Wide, Wide World*." *Legacy*, vol. 11, no. 2, 1994, pp. 118–29.

Chopin, Kate. "The Story of an Hour." *The Norton Anthology of American Literature*. Shorter 8th ed., vol. 2, W. W. Norton, 2013, pp. 425–27.

Clark, Beverly Lyon. *The Afterlife of "Little Women."* Johns Hopkins UP, 2014.

Dalke, Anne. "'The House-Band': The Education of Men in *Little Women*." *College English*, vol. 47, no. 6, 1985, pp. 571–78.

Doyle, Christine. "Singing Mignon's Song: German Literature and Culture in the March Trilogy." *Children's Literature*, vol. 31, 2003, pp. 50–70.

Eiselein, Gregory. "Contradiction in Louisa May Alcott's *Little Men*." *New England Quarterly*, vol. 78, no. 1, 2005, pp. 3–25.

Estes, Angela M., and Kathleen Margaret Lant. "The Horror of *Little Women*." *Little Women, or, Meg, Jo, Beth and Amy*, edited by Anne K. Phillips and Gregory Eiselein, Norton Critical Edition, W. W. Norton, 2004, pp. 564–83.

Fetterley, Judith. "*Little Women*: Alcott's Civil War." *Feminist Studies*, vol. 5, no. 2, 1979, pp. 369–83.

"Frances Brundage." *Wikipedia: The Free Encyclopedia*, 28 May 2019, Wikimedia Foundation, https://en.wikipedia.org/wiki/Frances_Brundage.

Fulton, Valerie. "Rewriting the Necessary Woman: Marriage and Professionalism in James, Jewett, and Phelps." *The Henry James Review*, vol. 15, no. 3, 1994, pp. 242–56.

Gannon, Susan R. "Getting Cozy with a Classic: Visualizing *Little Women* (1868–1995)." *"Little Women" and the Feminist Imagination: Criticism, Controversy, Personal Essays*, edited by Janice M. Alberghene and Beverly Lyon Clark, Garland, 1999, pp. 103–38.

Heilbrun, Carolyn G. "Alcott's *Little Women*." *Hamlet's Mother and Other Women*. Columbia UP, 1990, pp. 140–47.

Keyser, Elizabeth. "'Portrait(s) of the Artist': *Little Women*." *Little Women, or, Meg, Jo, Beth and Amy*, edited by Anne K. Phillips and Gregory Eiselein, Norton Critical Edition, W. W. Norton, 2004, pp. 600–623.

Langland, Elizabeth. "Female Stories of Experience: Alcott's *Little Women* in Light of *Work*." *The Voyage In: Fictions of Female Development*, edited by Elizabeth Abel, Marianne Hirsch, and Elizabeth Langland, UP of New England, 1983, pp. 112–27.

Lonette, Reisie, illustrator. *Little Women*, by Louisa May Alcott. Children's Classics, 1950.

MacLeod, Anne Scott. *American Childhood: Essays on Children's Literature of the Nineteenth and Twentieth Centuries*. U of Georgia P, 1994.

Massé, Michelle A. "Songs to Aging Children: Louisa May Alcott's March Trilogy." *"Little Women" and the Feminist Imagination: Criticism, Controversy, Personal Essays*, edited by Janice M. Alberghene and Beverly Lyon Clark, Garland, 1999, pp. 323–46.

Merrill, Frank T., illustrator. *Little Women*, by Louisa May Alcott. Little, Brown, (1880) 1896.

Minadeo, Christy Rishoi. "*Little Women* in the 21st Century." *Images of the Child*, edited by Harry Eiss, Bowling Green UP, 1994, pp. 199–214.

Moebius, William. "Introduction to Picturebook Codes." *Word & Image*, vol. 2, no. 2, 1986, pp. 141–58.

Parker, Alison M. "The Alcotts and the Wilders: Revealing Family Histories." *Reviews in American History*, vol. 38, no. 4, 2010, pp. 689–95.

Reardon, Colleen. "Music as Leitmotif in Louisa May Alcott's *Little Women*." *Children's Literature*, vol. 24, 1996, pp. 74–85.

Rizzuto, Lauren. "'Jo March Is Pregnant and Laurie's The Father': Re-Visioning *Little Women* in Fan Fiction." *Critical Insights: "Little Women*," edited by Gregory Eiselein and Anne K. Phillips, Salem Press/Grey House Publishing, 2015, pp. 204–18.

Shealy, Daniel. "'Wedding Marches': Louisa May Alcott, Marriage, and the Newness of *Little Women*." *Women's Studies*, vol. 48, no. 4, 2019, pp. 366–78.

Showalter, Elaine. "*Little Women*: The American Female Myth." *Sister's Choice: Tradition and Change in American Women's Writing*. Clarendon, 1991, pp. 42–64.

Strickland, Charles. *Victorian Domesticity: Families in the Life and Art of Louisa May Alcott*. U of Alabama P, 1985.

Susina, Jan. "Men and *Little Women*: Notes of a Resisting (Male) Reader." *"Little Women" and the Feminist Imagination: Criticism, Controversy, Personal Essays*, edited by Janice M. Alberghene and Beverly Lyon Clark, Garland, 1999, pp. 161–72.

Tuck, Donna-Marie. "Blurring the Boundaries: The Sexuality of *Little Women*." *Working with English: Medieval and Modern Language, Literature and Drama*, vol. 2, no. 1, 2006, pp. 82–88.

Wadsworth, Sarah. "'New Friendship Flourished Like Grass in Spring': Cross-Gender Friendship in *Moods* and *Little Women*." *Women's Studies*, vol. 48, no. 4, 2019, pp. 379–92.

Zehr, Janet. "The Responses of Nineteenth-Century Audiences to Louisa May Alcott's Fiction." *American Transcendental Quarterly*, n.s. 1, 1987, pp. 323–42.

MARRIAGE IN THE NINETEENTH CENTURY
The Influence of Margaret Fuller's "The Great Lawsuit" on *Little Women*

CHRISTINE DOYLE

One of Louisa May Alcott's earliest childhood memories involved Margaret Fuller, a transcendentalist and friend of the Alcott family in Concord who worked for a time with Bronson Alcott at his Temple School. Late in her own life, Alcott recalled an occasion when Fuller visited her parents in Concord, and "the conversation having turned to the ever interesting subject of education, Miss Fuller said: 'Well, Mr. Alcott, you have been able to carry out your methods in your own family, and I should like to see your model children.'" Fuller's wish was granted momentarily, when "a wild uproar approached, and round the corner of the house came a wheelbarrow holding baby May arrayed as a queen; I [Louisa] was the horse, bitted and bridled and driven by my elder sister Anna, while Lizzie played dog and barked"—at which point, Mrs. Alcott commented, "Here are the model children, Miss Fuller" (Alcott, "Recollections" 35). By the time Fuller died in an 1850 shipwreck, she was a close enough friend to Abba Alcott for Abba to lament her early death in her journal, calling it "too tragic to think of" (qtd. in LaPlante 156). In the larger cultural context, Elizabeth Cady Stanton and her feminist cohorts chronicling the *History of Woman Suffrage* in 1881 commented that "Margaret Fuller possessed more influence upon the thought of America, than any woman previous to her time" (801). It might seem strange, then, that Louisa May Alcott, a committed nineteenth-century feminist who often mentions writers and role models in her journals and letters, hardly ever refers to this woman who would logically have been a role model to her, as they had much in common: Fuller was a champion of women's rights in the nineteenth century; like Fuller when Alcott knew her, she hadn't married; she had a career as a writer and even foreign correspondent to the New York Tribune; and she refused to be restrained from joining a war effort, participating in the Italian Revolution of 1848.

Their age difference may account for some of this absence, as Fuller was closer to Alcott's parents' age than she was to Louisa's (Fuller was born in 1810, Louisa May Alcott in 1832), had moved to New York and then to Europe so she wasn't in the immediate vicinity during Alcott's teen years, and when she died, Alcott was only seventeen. Her published letters and journals, though, make no mention of Fuller's horrific death, an event that consumed the popular press when it occurred (see Capper 2: 498–520) and clearly touched some of Alcott's most admired Concord neighbors—at Ralph Waldo Emerson's urging, and with his financing, Henry David Thoreau spent nearly a week on Fire Island searching for her body. Nevertheless, the lone references to Fuller in Louisa May Alcott's published journals, like the "model children" recollection above, come toward the end of her life. In 1880, having read the memoirs of the Frenchwoman Madame de Remusat (1780–1821), known for her intelligence and her beauty, she commented, "Not very interesting. Beauties seldom amount to much. Plain Margaret Fuller was worth a dozen of them" (*Journals* 224, Feb. 1880); in 1882, she commented that the female tourists showing up for the grand opening of her father's School of Philosophy comprised "M. Fullers in white muslin" (235, July 1882). Two brief mentions of Fuller in her published *Selected Letters* are even more tangential. Still, we might surmise that Alcott may have spoken aloud her praise for Fuller's life and work, since according to Katie Kornacki, "Fuller's formative influence on Alcott is a connection frequently noted by contemporary women writing about the famous author's early life." Kornacki quotes a writer who called Fuller Alcott's "earliest teacher," and another who listed Fuller among writers Alcott particularly enjoyed reading (144).

But we needn't rely only on the testimony of others. In her creative work, if not in her journals and letters, Alcott frequently alludes to Fuller's life and work. The "model children" scene above, for example, is incorporated into

Little Men (1871), in chapter 11, when Laurie pays a visit to Plumfield and is regaled by similar antics played out by Daisy, Bess, and Nan. Fuller's series of Conversations, study groups for women she organized and conducted between 1839 and 1844, which Stanton and company celebrated as "a vindication of woman's right to think" (801) are clearly the model for the work Christie Devon urges her friend Bella to devote herself to in 1873's *Work* (see Doyle 132; Kornacki). On a more somber note, Fuller's death in a shipwreck just off the coast of New York is reinvented as Adam Warwick's death in the 1864 version of *Moods*.

In what may have been her first textual reference to Fuller, however, Alcott draws from Fuller's most well-known work, her essay published in the *Dial* as "The Great Lawsuit" (1843) and then as a book, *Woman in the Nineteenth Century* (1845). In the back of her personal copy of Goethe's *Wilhelm Meister's Apprenticeship*, which Alcott records in her journal as Emerson giving her as a gift in 1850 (making her a Goethe fan for life!), Alcott seemingly sums up Goethe's groundbreaking novel with words from the end of Fuller's essay about the women Wilhelm encountered in the progress of his bildungsroman: "M. Fuller says . . . as Meister grows in life & advances in wisdom, he becomes acquainted with women of more & more character, rising from Mariana to Natalia who expresses the Minerva side of things, Mignon, the electrical, inspired lyrical nature."[1] It is fitting that Alcott's most direct acknowledgment of Margaret Fuller is not from her life but from Fuller's most famous work. In fact, there may be no greater tribute to the legacy of Margaret Fuller, and especially to her important essay "The Great Lawsuit," than Alcott's *Little Women*, which concerns itself with the development of American girls into women in practical ways as Fuller's essay does in theoretical ones. This is especially true of part 2 of the novel, when Alcott grapples with the possibilities open to US women in the nineteenth century as they prepare for and ultimately enter into marriage. *Little Women*, part 2, repeatedly and specifically draws upon Fuller's essay in turning the "little women" of part 1 into "good wives." Even more, Alcott demonstrates how the individual development of *both* women and men greatly enhances their potential for good *marriages*.

In many ways, Margaret Fuller's most famous essay can itself be seen as a response to Emerson's essay "Self-Reliance," which had been published as one of the twelve essays collected in his first volume of *Essays* in 1841. In it, Emerson argues for each human being to develop himself to his fullest potential by finding his own individual path forward, eschewing societal expectations like conformity and consistency as well as societal institutions like religion, property, and travel—anything that would link a person to someone else's already-formed ideas rather than one's own. This was, to Emerson, the path to "genius" (210).

None of these ideas could have been new to Fuller when they first appeared in print. Emerson's essays were drawn from ideas in his journals that he had tried out in public lectures before publishing them. Further, Fuller had had close connections with Emerson since she sought him out after his famous essay *Nature* appeared in 1836 and, drawn to transcendentalist ideas, had worked with him to edit the *Dial* from its founding in 1840 until 1842. Indeed, the very terms "self-reliance" and "self-dependence" appear multiple times in Fuller's own essay. But Fuller's "The Great Lawsuit" is a response to, rather than a repetition of, Emerson. Emerson writes from a philosophical point of view, proposing ideas to human beings generally in what probably seemed to him to be a nongendered way. But as Fuller was well aware, US culture in her day had very different expectations for men than it had for women. It might be all well and good for Henry David Thoreau to go out to Walden Pond and camp for two years, but it would simply not be acceptable for a woman to do so. Fuller's essay, then, might be conceived of as "'Self-Reliance' for Women." It addresses women's lives in practical as well as philosophical ways. To be sure, one of the most striking passages in "The Great Lawsuit" is the story of a woman Fuller calls "Miranda" (a thinly veiled version of Fuller herself), a woman who has been raised by a doting father to be independent and self-reliant.[2] But when Miranda is asked why every woman can't merely use her as a model and go forward independently, Miranda notes that "self-dependence, which was honored in me, is deprecated as a fault in most women. They are taught to learn their rule from without, not to unfold it from within" (735). Miranda proposes that this is mostly due to the fact that men themselves are not fully developed ("Man is as generous towards [woman] as he knows how to be" [736]). And although, like a good transcendentalist, she looks at the world with optimism for a future that will see society advancing as men and women "prophesy to one another" as they "love in one another the future good which they aid one another to unfold" (737), she is fully cognizant of the fact that, so far, the United States has not fulfilled its promise and teems with all sorts of injustice (730), of which the oppression of women is just one aspect.

Miranda's independent status notwithstanding, Fuller writes much of this essay with the implicit assumption that most of her readers, if not yet married, will be one day. Like the essay itself, this is a nod to practicality; in the mid-nineteenth-century United States, 93 percent of women married, a figure that "dipped" to 91 percent after the Civil War (Smith 121) and then to an all-time "low" of 87 percent for women who came of age at the end of the century (Theriot 117).³ No matter how you look at it, the overwhelming majority of US women would one day marry (Capper asserts that it is "almost certain" [365] that Fuller married the father of her child before their ill-fated 1850 sea voyage, but she was unmarried when she published "The Great Lawsuit"); the essay speaks to that assumption with the facts of life in the United States in mind. For example, it lays out the dire legal situation for wives concerning inheritance, property rights, and children before the Married Women's Property Act and similar reforms were enacted; this list of legal impairments is embedded within an imagined "debate" between a married "trader" (whether of enslaved persons or of general merchandise is not explicitly stated, but the conversation appears among several references to similarities between slavery and the condition of women) and an advocate for women's right to vote and to hold office. Most of her multiple examples from life and literature involve married women. Close to the end of the essay, she recounts a conversation between a husband and wife from Robert Southey's *The Curse of Kehana*, in which the husband resists educating their daughter too fully because it will be too hard for her to find a husband and then comments on several of the female companions Wilhelm Meister encounters in his progress toward finding the perfect wife in Goethe's *Wilhelm Meister's Apprenticeship* (the very words that Alcott had inscribed into her own copy of *Meister*). At the very end, when some "profound thinker" concludes from the preceding discussion that "no married woman can represent the female world," that the representative woman must be a virgin, Fuller objects that "that is the very fault of marriage, and of the present relation between the sexes" (759). Nevertheless, she proposes, the revolutionary atmosphere present in Europe has propelled society into a "transition state about marriage" as to whether it will ultimately be "a union of souls, or merely a contract of convenience and utility" (744), the former of which would necessitate that men and women enter into marriage with an assumption of equality. Meanwhile, the essay presents examples of marriages in her own time that point toward that promising future and also proposes advice to effect women's self-development, development that will mean that when they do marry, it will be on egalitarian terms.

It is quite likely that, as influenced as she may have been by Fuller generally and from an early age, Alcott had much more reason to consider the details of "The Great Lawsuit" as she began to write *Little Women*, part 2 than when constructing her original novel. It is not that there is no interest in or discussion of marriage in the first volume. In chapter 9, for example, after Meg has returned from the "Vanity Fair" of a party at the home of the well-to-do Moffatts, where she has heard speculations of her mother's "plans" to marry her off to Laurie for his money, Marmee proposes that, while money is "needful and precious," it's more important to her to see them settled as "happy, beloved, [and] contented" wives who have "self-respect and peace." Spurred on by Jo, she even allows that it would be "better [to] be happy old maids than unhappy wives" (84). But the March girls are only sixteen, fifteen, thirteen, and possibly twelve[4] as the novel begins, and it ends one year later, with Meg's proposed three-year engagement, before any actual marriage takes place. It was a children's novel, much more so than its sequel, which ultimately takes the story at least fifteen years further into the future,[5] when marriage would have been assumed to be a virtual certainty for her characters.

So Alcott had good reason to be considering—however reluctantly—the parameters of marriage for women as she wrote the sequel. Her grousing about having to "marry off" her heroines is well known, both from her journals and from letters she wrote at the time. She complained mightily about fans who "write to ask who the little women marry, as if that was the only end and aim of a woman's life" (*Journals* 167, 1 Nov. 1868) and of "publishers [who] wont [sic] let authors finish up as they like but insist on having people married off in a wholesale manner which much afflicts me" (*Letters* 125). To complicate things as she was faced with the looming marriage plot, her own life would not be of help going forward in ways it had been previously, since only her eldest sister Anna had married at the time; she and her other surviving sister, May, remained single. But however much Alcott resisted, she ultimately made marriage, and her thoughts on marriage, a recurring interest in her sequel. As part 1 showed, young girls have many different ways of becoming women. Part 2 was to explore in detail several different patterns for marriage. To a large extent, the marriages in *Little Women* were to be applications of the specific types of marriages Margaret Fuller had described in "The Great Lawsuit."[6]

Fuller's first type of marriage equality is what she terms the "household partnership," in which each partner has a separate but equally important role in making the relationship function, and it runs with "mutual esteem, mutual dependence" (745). Marmee and Mr. March's marriage is a version of this pattern, and this is the pattern Marmee helps Meg eventually to achieve. The older Marches' marriage has long been a topic of scholarly conversation, with it often being suggested that Alcott virtually wrote Mr. March out of the story, resulting in the novel's power being almost entirely vested in women. He is away as a Civil War chaplain through most of the first volume, and even when he returns to make the Christmas joy complete at the end, he remains well in the background of the novel, then as well as when it continues in the sequel. Anne Phillips makes a compelling argument that Mr. March is still very important as the spiritual head of that family (see "Prophets and Martyrs"); however, what we see of their marriage seems to be built upon a division of labor, albeit an unusual one for the time period. It is Marmee who takes on the traditional role of the "man" of the family in many ways. She is the head of the household while Mr. March is away; she goes off to work every day; she boldly goes to the army hospital in Washington to bring her invalid husband home when he becomes ill (not wounded) during the war. Conversely, he supposedly teaches his wife how to manage their young children when they come along ("He never loses patience,—never doubts or complains,—but always hopes, and works and waits so cheerfully" [*Little Women* 69]). They do work as a unit at some points—John Brooke speaks to both of them about marrying Meg, for example—but to the extent that the reader sees their relationship, it does look like each has a separate role in the marriage.

Meg's marriage in the second volume is even more clearly a household partnership—eventually. Although sixteen-year-old Meg was given an additional three years to grow and prepare herself for marriage, two chapters in the novel demonstrate how very difficult that can be once the couple "discovered that they couldn't live on love alone" (*Little Women* 218). The first real quarrels in their married life result from disruptions in the idealized marriage partnership they seem to have imagined. First, Meg finds herself less capable of the practical side of homemaking than she had anticipated and exchanges sharp words with her husband when he brings a friend home for dinner unannounced while she is in the middle of trying unsuccessfully to make jelly. Once they bridge that impasse, Meg's earlier longing for luxuries leads her to purchase silk for a dress that she can't afford, impugning John's abilities as a wage earner in the aftermath. That is, it seems to each of them that the other does not "esteem" their labor. In this chapter, Meg remembers her mother's words to "be the first to ask pardon if you both err, and guard against the little piques, misunderstandings, and hasty words that often pave the way for bitter sorrow and regret" (222)—that is, that's the wife's job!—and takes it upon herself to begin conversations that lead to better understanding between them. The chapter ends with the birth of twins Daisy and Demi as if to confirm their reconciliation.

Alcott leaves Meg's story alone for the next ten chapters of the novel, chapters in which all her sisters have extremely dramatic experiences: Amy goes off to Europe, Jo moves to New York, from whence she returns to reject Laurie as a lover, and Beth articulates to her family her understanding that she is going to die. No wonder Alcott titles the chapter in which she returns to Meg's story "On the Shelf"! In this chapter, Alcott shows astute insight as she delineates the dramatic changes to the marital relationship that the arrival of children entails. The twins are now a year old, and while Meg is "more admired and beloved than ever," she is also "entirely absorbed in her children, to the utter exclusion of everything and everybody else" (*Little Women* 305). The housework is neglected, the cooking is turned over—horror of horrors!—to an Irish cook, and John finds he can neither effect amusement at home nor convince his wife to go out for pleasure (Meg cries, "Leave my children for pleasure, never!" [305]). Ultimately, John takes refuge where he had done before, with their childless neighbors, the Scotts. Meg's initial relief to have one less claim on her attention soon turns to a feeling of abandonment, unrealized by her husband. This time, remembering Marmee's words is not enough; Marmee herself gets involved, urging Meg, "Don't shut [John] out of the nursery, but teach him how to help in it" (307) and "Take an interest in whatever John likes.... understand what is going on, and educate yourself to take your part in the world's work" (308). The sermon is delivered to Meg, but as the rest of the chapter indicates, this time both of them work at equalizing the parenting (even though John's participation is more as the traditional disciplinarian) and both work at taking an interest in the other's activities: as John thinks to himself, "She is trying to like politics for my sake, so I'll try and like millinery for hers—that's only fair" (312). Not unlike Marmee's more "masculine" role in her own household, John's move toward coparenting in his and Meg's is even more progressive than what Fuller described as the "household partnership,"[7] but that is fundamentally what it is—a home where there is "division of labor" and "real home-love and mutual helpfulness" (313). As Fuller puts it, this "is good as far as it goes" (745).

Fuller pairs the next two types of marriage equality in a way that suggests "a closer tie" but at the same time a limitation: "intellectual companionship, or mutual idolatry" (745). Her further discussion of both of these "ties" suggests that the first is all cerebral without passion, the second all passion without much else. She dispenses quickly with the "mutual idolatry" model, suggesting that the couple only has eyes for one another: "To themselves they seem the only wise, to all others steeped in infatuation" (745). She considers the "intellectual companionship" model to be the opposite of idolatry—deep friendship without passion—but allows that it can be productive in that "They work together for a common purpose" (747). Much of her commentary on "mutual idolatry" could easily apply to Amy and Laurie's relationship and marriage, so far as we see it in *Little Women*. Laurie and Amy had already laid some groundwork for a connection in part 1, when Amy stayed with Aunt March in order to avoid any possibility of her contracting scarlet fever from Beth. It is Laurie's considerable charm that is called upon to make this happen with as little fuss as possible; Amy doesn't want to go but is persuaded when Laurie vows he will come every day to apprise her of Beth's condition, take her "out gallivanting" (144), and escort her to the theater. The reader should recall, here, that Amy being left out of exactly these activities was what had led to her burning Jo's manuscript earlier, so we might imagine them as being particularly attractive to young Amy. He is faithful to his promise, and we see Laurie's ability to charm her as well as Aunt March in this chapter; we also see Amy's interest in finery, as she dresses up in her aunt's castoff but elegant brocades and longs for her beautiful turquoise ring, which she receives at the end of the ordeal, when Laurie pronounces her "a capital little woman" (*Little Women* 158). All of this sets the stage for their later encounters while Amy is traveling as a guest of her Aunt Carrol in Europe.

While Alcott's depiction of Laurie and Amy's relationship does not descend to the potential for unmitigated passion that Fuller's description might imagine as an extreme, there is no doubt that it focuses on physical attraction and that they separate from those around them as they become more and more enamored with one another. The "New Impressions" chapter, for example, in which Laurie first reencounters Amy in Nice (post-Jo breakup), is replete with references to physical attraction and appearance. As Laurie walks the Promenade, seeking the little sister he left behind in

America, both men and women who see him are struck by his handsome appearance: "Sundry pairs of feminine eyes . . . look approvingly after him, and sundry dandies . . . envy him" (*Little Women* 296). But Laurie notices none of them, because he is looking for Amy—who storms on to the scene, scandalizing the locals by driving her own carriage. The chapter is filled with their reassessments of one another—Amy finding Laurie "handsomer than ever" (298); Laurie gazing at Amy with new eyes, eagerly taking in "the soft hue of her dress, the fresh color of her cheeks, the golden gloss of her hair" (299). The narrator spends several paragraphs describing Amy's "prink[ing]" (299) for the Christmas ball that night: "She had seen her old friend in a new light . . . as a handsome and agreeable man, and was conscious of a very natural desire to find favor in his sight" (299). They greet one another that night in godly terms—as "Diana" and "Apollo"—and although the premise, and their relationship, is still on familial terms, Amy is not above "pity[ing] the four plain Misses Davis from the bottom of her heart" (300–301) as she makes her entrance with her handsome companion. By the end of the evening, the narrator is commenting on the "new impressions" of one another the two "were unconsciously giving and receiving" (304), and Laurie stays a month in Nice instead of the week he had intended.

Laurie's ultimate departure from Nice also suggests his increasingly romantic relationship with Amy, prompted partly by Amy's admission that she intends to accept Fred Vaughan's marriage proposal, when it comes, even though she doesn't love him, partly by Laurie's admission that his noticeable listlessness is due to the fact that Jo has rejected him—and finally, by Amy's scolding Laurie about his despondency: "Wake up, and be a man" (*Little Women* 322). The questions of love and marriage embedded in their quarrel intimate a growing potential for a romantic bond between them, and Laurie's farewell note to Amy, announcing his intention to take her advice, calls upon another "epic" relationship, if still not the appropriate one, as he refers to himself as "Telemachus" and her as "Mentor" (323).

Their time apart reinforces and furthers the developing love between the two of them, marked by the final closing off of their other romances: Laurie finally accepts Jo's rejection, and Amy rejects marrying Fred for his money. This leads to an intensifying epistolary relationship between the two of them. The narrator teases the reader about their letters: "As few brothers are complimented by having their letters carried about in their sisters' pockets, read and reread diligently, cried over when short, kissed when long, and treasured carefully, we will not hint that Amy did any of these fond and foolish things" (*Little Women* 332). From the way this paragraph continues to note that Amy "did grow a little pale and pensive," spent more time alone, went sketching and either produced nothing or else pictures that are clearly memories of Laurie (332), the reader can infer that she was doing *exactly* those "fond and foolish things" mentioned first and that their friendship is rapidly changing, not only to a romance but to the deeply passionate and inner-focused romance that Fuller had talked about. When Laurie finally reconnects with Amy in Vevey, the view of Amy again focuses on her physical appearance, and especially a "little ebony cross at her throat" that Laurie had given to Amy and that she wears now as her *only* accessory, since she is in mourning over Beth's death (333–34). As before, their past connection in America is a bond that already separates them from those around them, but the brother/sister relationship has changed to romance. The fact that their engagement becomes a reality on a rowboat ride past the castle at Chillon seems to emphasize their isolation from the world even more, as does their decision to marry at once, in Europe, not even letting their families know until their return: "We were so absorbed in one another we were of no mortal use apart" (345), as Laurie puts it. The two of them refer to one another as "my lord" and "my lady," and although Laurie avers that Amy rules him at this point but "by and by we shall take turns," Jo dismisses that thought with "You'll go on as you begin, and Amy will rule you all the days of your life" (347).

Further, the circumstances of their union reinforce that inward focus of mutual admiration. Although their initial plan is for Laurie to go into his grandfather's business, and for Amy to become a society wife with general philanthropic aims, the two of them quickly shift to a very similar plan: Laurie wishes to help young men like the "talented fellows making all sorts of sacrifices, and enduring real hardships, that they might realize their dreams," and Amy responds that she wants to aid "ambitious girls . . . [who] often have to see youth, health, and precious opportunities go by just for want of a little help at the right minute" (*Little Women* 357). Though both have a general interest in sharing their wealth, and though it is abundantly clear that it is Laurie's money that will accomplish their aims, even their aims seem very much the same rather than individualized. Finally, their only child, Bess, is as fragile as her namesake, a situation that also "bound them closely together" (380). The marriage of Alcott's second little woman, then, has much in common with Fuller's second example of marital equality, one that has a basis in "mutual idolatry." Laurie and Amy are bonded together in intimate ways, as suggestively passionate as Alcott ever gets in her children's fiction. Although Alcott seems to make the relationship a far more positive one than Fuller's dismissive comments suggest, Amy and Laurie's nearly identical life goals, and their bond over their frail little girl, do make this relationship, at least by the close of *Little Women*, seem very inward looking in the ways Fuller herself had noted as characteristics of this particular type of marriage "equality."

Perhaps no subject has caused more consternation among readers of *Little Women* throughout the 150 years of its existence than that of Jo's marriage to Friedrich Bhaer. Alcott herself defiantly wrote in her journal that she would not "marry Jo to Laurie to please any one" (*Journals* 167, 1 Nov. 1868) and to Vassar professor Elizabeth Powell that since she didn't dare leave Jo a spinster, she "made a funny match for her" for which she expected "vials of wrath to be poured out upon [her] head" (*Letters* 125, 20 Mar. 1869). Few commentators over the last 150 years have been able to resist weighing in on this union, from early reviewers to contemporary critics. Despite the overwhelmingly laudatory contemporary assessments of *Little Women*, for example, writers allowed that "we do not feel quite satisfied with [Jo's] destiny" (rpt. in Clark 80), and one even related that her friend was more upset by Jo's refusal of Laurie than Laurie himself had been, "for he got over it, and our friend has not yet ceased grumbling!" (rpt. in Clark 77).[8] Contemporary feminists have more commonly objected that Jo, who repeatedly swore herself to literary spinsterhood, had married at all. Elizabeth Keyser, in reading the ending as Alcott's grim assessment of the lack of choice for women in her time, with neither spinsterhood nor marriage being fulfilling, refers to Jo's choice as "self-immolation" (80); Estes and Lant read it as a "horror."[9] However, some more recent critics, having come to terms with the fact that the March girls do marry, have seen marriage in *Little Women* more positively. In particular, both Daniel Shealy and Anne Boyd Rioux allude to the marriages in *Little Women* as egalitarian, with both writers generally asserting Fuller's influence. Rioux writes, "With Bhaer, Alcott made an argument for the kind of companionate marriage advocated by Margaret Fuller and that her [Alcott's] mother had hoped for with her father" (201). Indeed, "The Great Lawsuit" provides a rather specific primer not only for the marriage into which Jo eventually enters but for Jo's progress toward and preparation for it. Fuller's discussion of equality in marriage culminates in what she terms "the higher grade of marriage union, the religious, which may be expressed as pilgrimage towards a common shrine" (748). She continues, "This includes the others; home sympathies, and household wisdom, for these pilgrims must know how to assist one another to carry their burdens along the dusty way" and also includes a pitch for "intellectual communion" (748) between the partners.

But Fuller, though a transcendentalist and so by definition an optimist, was not so romantic as to suppose that this kind of union could just "happen." Instead, she proposes as a true ideal what Mary Rigsby calls an aesthetic of "being-in-dependence" (v), which recognizes "the essential need for both (1) independence, self-fulfillment through unfettered challenge and experience, and (2) *in*-dependence, self-fulfillment through mutually-supportive relations with others" (6). Fuller had previously suggested the desirability of the "being" part of Rigsby's premise with her "Miranda" story. Here, she follows her definition of the highest form of marriage with several ideas that specifically address additional avenues toward self-development—female authorship, spinsterhood, and a time of isolation from one's ordinary life—all of which Alcott specifically addresses in *Little Women*.[10]

Fuller, for example, sees "the triumphs of female authorship" as a way that women can develop independence in exploring "provinces for which men had pronounced them unfit" (749). Indeed, the fictional Jo March's adventures as a writer have long been one of the recognized attractions of the novel for many real women writers who came after her; they also, however, mark her development as a character. The reader had already seen how important writing was to Jo in part 1, where Amy burning her manuscript resulted in a vehement response that was nearly fatal to her younger sister. In part 2, the "Literary Lessons" chapter furthers Jo's development not only as a writer but also as a self-realized human being. Thrilled with some success at publishing stories that bring her money, but also urged by her father to "aim at the highest" (214), Jo sees her first novel into print, but "in the hope of pleasing every one, she took every one's advice" and ultimately published a work that left her bewildered as to whether she had "written a promising book, or broken all the ten commandments" (216, 217). This experience, which in many ways echoes the real Louisa May Alcott's experience with her novel *Moods*, shows that the fictional Jo isn't mature enough yet to assert her true self in her writing. Later, in New York, she writes sensation stories for the money. This once again highlights an uncertain sense of self, in that they are published without her name attached; while the money she receives for them brings her pleasure and comfort, even she realizes that "she was beginning to desecrate some of the womanliest attributes of a woman's character" and was "living in bad society" that even though imaginary, "its influence affected her" (275). These unconscious intuitions stay hidden until Professor Bhaer calls sensation fiction "trash" (280), resulting in a struggle with her conscience. Ultimately—perhaps in an echo of Amy's action in part 1—she herself burns her manuscripts. Her writing process after this leads her to dabble uncomfortably in several different genres of writing until she finally "cork[s] up her inkstand" until she has learned more about life and can write in a more "honest" way (281). The connection between her writing and her self-development culminates when, after she returns from New York and nurses Beth through her last illness, she returns to her writing, produces a novel with "heart" and "truth" in it—and discovers her "style at last" (340). Her creative journey had no doubt taken her to places even she deemed "unfit," but ultimately it leads her to a mature, independent version of herself, both as a writer and as a person.

Fuller's comments in "The Great Lawsuit" on behalf of "old maids" are also worth examining in that they, too, find expression in *Little Women*. While acknowledging that "marriage is the natural means of forming a sphere, of taking root on the earth" (750), Fuller takes it upon herself not only to speak up for the worth of those who do not marry—"the business of society has become so complex, that it could now scarcely be carried on without the presence of these despised auxiliaries"—but to suggest there may be a developmental advantage in the unattached life: "They thus gain a wider, if not so deep, experience. They are not so intimate with others, but thrown more upon themselves," which "may be of inestimable benefit. The person may gain, undistracted by other relationships, a closer communion with the One" (751). Fuller even goes so far as to suggest that, even for those who will eventually form unions, a time of withdrawal from relationships could be a useful step toward the development of self-reliance in the individual and make the resulting relationships richer in the long run. She writes, "If any individual live too much in relations, so that he becomes a stranger to the resources of his own nature, he falls after a while into a distraction ... from which he can only be cured by a time of isolation, which gives the renovating fountains time to rise up." She continues, "To be fit for relations in time, souls, whether of man or woman, must be able to do without them in the spirit." It is in this same passage that she avers, "Union is only possible to those who are units" (757).

While Fuller eventually did probably marry, Alcott remained single all her life, so it should not be a surprise that the topic of "old maids" interested her as well. Indeed, just a few months before writing the first part of *Little Women*, Alcott had published a sketch in *The Ledger* titled "Happy Women," a short piece that describes the lives of four "old maids" who live their lives independently, usefully, and—as the title indicates—happily. Shortly thereafter, she briefly took up the subject of "old maids" in *Little Women*, part 1, in the "Vanity Fair" chapter discussed earlier. Part 2 revisits "old maids" in chapter 43, on the eve of Jo's twenty-fifth birthday,[11] and even though it is mostly a two-page lecture to the young reader on being nice to such persons (the narrator ultimately apologizes for what she assumes was probably a sleep-inducing lecture!), it actually begins with an assertion that a spinster could "get on quite happily if one has something in one's self to fall back upon" (343)—that is, that time outside a spousal relationship might be time in which self-development could take place. Further, the connection between living outside one's usual relationships and developing the "resources of [one's] own nature" is taken up repeatedly as Alcott explores marriages in *Little Women*. The only March daughter to marry *without* doing so, in fact, is Meg, and to a large extent, her marital difficulties, described earlier, all seem to be related to her not having developed the practical or spiritual resources necessary before she married. She ultimately navigates her way to a solid relationship through some on-the-job training, but her journey toward marriage equality in the novel is described as much more of a struggle than those of either of her sisters.

On the other hand, Amy and Jo both remove themselves from their usual surroundings, not like Thoreau out at Walden Pond but in ways more plausible for nineteenth-century women, and develop independence because of it. Amy's trip to Europe is supervised by her Aunt Carrol, but we see her literally taking the reins (of a pony cart), somewhat scandalizing a proper "French mamma" and causing Laurie to observe that "her native frankness was unspoiled by foreign polish" (*Little Women* 297, 299). She tries to develop her art, comes to a realization that "talent isn't genius," and resolves to "polish up [her] other talents, and be an ornament to society," which the narrator allows captures the ambition of youth but is an ambition with "a good foundation" (317). The sense of self she is developing allows her to scold her lifelong friend into action toward his own self-development and, while she is most on her own, to refuse a marriage proposal from a man who is wealthy but whom she doesn't love. All of these developments help her to progress into marriage from a position of personal strength. For his part, Laurie, spurred on by Amy's scornful depiction of him as "Lazy Laurence," has also gone off on his own, worked through his grief over Jo, attempted to develop his own art, and become a more mature, developed young man in the process. And how ironic is it that Fuller herself described the retreat from society as a space in which "rowers are pausing on their oars, [and] they wait a change before they can pull together" (757)—which is a *literal* description of Amy and Laurie's proposal scene? Comparatively flawed though their marriage might be in terms of its inner-directedness, it does proceed from a place in which both partners are well-developed "units."

But it is Jo and Friedrich's marriage that most exemplifies Fuller's description of the highest level of equality, and both partners in this relationship also exhibit self-development before coming together as a unit. The reader doesn't learn many details of Friedrich's developmental backstory, although we are told that he was a respected professor in Berlin who had sacrificed his position there to come to America, where he could work only as "a poor language-master" (*Little Women* 276), because he promised his deceased sister to educate her two sons in America. At minimum, we are being informed that Friedrich too has launched into a completely new realm of experience where his core values will be developed and tested.

We are privy to more details of Jo's time away, however. She herself proposes her journey to New York, on the premise that she is "restless, and anxious to be seeing, doing, and learning" (*Little Women* 259). Admittedly, Jo will be working as a seamstress and governess under the roof of a family friend, and admittedly, her move is prompted in part by the realization that Laurie is becoming more fond of her than she likes, as well as by a sense of denial concerning the severity of Beth's illness. Nevertheless, with the new experiences, both in writing, as discussed previously, and in living among unfamiliar and sometimes hostile people (others in the boardinghouse disparage her position as a governess), she herself notices changes in her outlook; she writes home, "I'm cheerful all the time, now, work with a will, and take more interest in other people than I used to" (272). By the time she is ready to leave New York, the narrator says she was "laying a foundation for the sensation story of her own life" (282). This comment both marks Jo's hiatus in her writing and foreshadows her movement toward marriage but uses the same word, "foundation," that had referred to Amy's development in Europe. Jo does develop a relationship with Friedrich and deems him "a friend worth having" (283), but the New York experience benefits her individual growth as well. She demonstrates this when she returns to deal with rejecting Laurie's proposal and to see Beth through her final illness—both of which she was in denial about before her journey, both of which test the "foundation" of the woman she is becoming.

With this kind of preparation in terms of individual development, it should come as no surprise that Jo and Friedrich's marriage fulfills so much of Fuller's egalitarian ideal. As with Mr. and Mrs. March, and as with Meg and John, their unique working out of the "household partnership" calls to mind once again Fuller's contention that "there is no wholly masculine man, no purely feminine woman" (756). Although experience has certainly softened the tomboy Jo, it is she who is perpetually rambunctious and he who is described as gentle and even sentimental; it is her inheritance and her plan to set up Plumfield as a school, whereas he is the one who is adored by children—and he darns his own socks (if badly)! On the other hand, Jo describes her imagined school as "a good, happy, home-like school, with me to take care of them, and Fritz to teach them" (*Little Women* 374). That is, in work and in life, they don't need to be doing exactly the *same* thing (which is more the case with Laurie and Amy) but, in Fuller's words, are on a "pilgrimage towards a common shrine" (748).

The sense of "intellectual companionship" is also present in their relationship. Friedrich is certainly more educated than Jo, but they clearly share an intellectual life based on mutual respect for each other's talents. Jo is in awe of Friedrich when he defends religion at a symposium of intellectuals in New York; he gives her a copy of his collection of Shakespeare as a gift, and it is Jo's poem about Beth that ultimately brings him to her door. Fuller's quote from "an observer" of one of her ideal couples, the Count Zinzendorf and his wife, seems to apply to this marriage as well: "She was not made to be a copy; she was an original; and, while she loved and honored, him, she thought for herself on all subjects with so much intelligence, that he could and did look on her as a sister and friend also" (qtd. in Fuller 749). Their intellectual relationship does not seem so much like Emerson and Fuller sitting around sharing transcendentalist philosophy but perhaps more like the one Alcott herself had with the various thinkers she admired: she took the philosophy and made practical application of it in her fiction. Although Jo has taken a break from her writing at the end of *Little Women*, she doesn't herself consider it to be permanent ("I may write a good book yet" [379]), and we do find, in *Jo's Boys*, that she becomes a successful writer. I imagine Mrs. Jo, similarly to Alcott herself, not necessarily writing theoretical treatises but writing books that put her version of the theory into practice.

Finally, it is common for readers objecting to Jo's marriage to comment on the "companionate"—that is, not passionate—nature of their relationship, since Friedrich is older than she. Admittedly, Alcott's writing outside the sensation genre mostly skirts questions of passion. Nevertheless, even if one could discount the fact that they quickly produce two children once they marry, the scene in which they first confess their love is full of romance, despite the fact that it takes place in a pouring rainstorm. Friedrich is so happy that Jo returns his feeling for her that "the only way in which he could express his rapture was to look at her, with an expression which glorified his face to such a degree that there actually seemed to be little rainbows in the drops that sparkled on his beard," and even in her bedraggled state, he considers her to be "the most beautiful woman living" (*Little Women* 368). They walk along, oblivious to the rain like a pair of "harmless lunatics" (368). She refers to his offer of love as "the one precious thing I needed" (372), takes him (finally!) out of the rain with a "Welcome home," after which she "led her love in, and shut the door" (373). All of this is much more emotionally and romantically charged than the friendly regard that many critics consider to be the sum total of their relationship.

Perhaps the actual summation of their relationship can be read in Jo's ultimate response to Friedrich's proposal, in the way it so specifically echoes Fuller's description of the "higher grade" of marriage when she writes that "these pilgrims must know how to assist one another to carry their burdens along the dusty way" (*Little Women* 748). Not only does Fuller's language call to mind the centrality of *The Pilgrim's Progress* motif throughout *Little Women*, but Jo actually says to Friedrich, "No one can say I'm out of my sphere now,—for woman's special mission is supposed to be drying tears and bearing burdens. I'm to carry my share, Friedrich, and help to earn the home. Make up your mind to that, or I'll never go" (372). Their way may be more muddy than "dusty" at the moment, but they fully intend to share the burdens. Jo's reference to the concept of separate spheres adds yet another dimension to her speech, for according to Tiffany Wayne, "Fuller's primary feminist statement at the Conversations was a refusal to discuss 'woman's sphere' as a legitimate or useful rhetorical concept. Instead, she

... encouraged [women] to consider as part of their 'sphere' any activity that they deemed themselves capable of or which interested them" (26). Jo's immediate reference is to a "womanly" duty of drying tears, but it's clear that neither of them intends to be restricted, for each of them immediately asserts individuality: Friedrich, who has accepted a college teaching job in the West in order to secure his nephews' financial futures, cautions, "I must go away and do my work alone ... because even for you I may not break my word to Minna" (*Little Women* 372); Jo, who had made a deathbed promise to Beth to take care of their parents and see them through their grief, replies, "I have my duty also, and my work. I couldn't enjoy myself if I neglected them even for you" (373).

Jo and Friedrich's year apart, working at their separate tasks, writing copious letters, and preparing for marriage, is never proposed as easy; neither Fuller nor Alcott proposed that marriage would be. Nevertheless, in her most important work, each writer contemplated the institution that the large majority of their readers would enter at some point in their lives, and what Fuller proposed as theoretical bases for equality in marriage, Alcott used her beloved characters to work out as realistic situations, at times even going beyond the possibilities Fuller suggested. *Little Women*, part 2 was published as *Good Wives* in England, a title that wasn't initially used in the United States but that nevertheless foregrounds its interest in the types of marriages the March girls would form. As Alcott had shown her readers a variety of ways to come into womanhood in her original novel, in the sequel she showed them a variety of ways in which men as well as women might be parts of "good marriages"—joining together people who in Margaret Fuller's words "love in one another the future good which they aid one another to unfold" (737).

Notes

1. I can't be certain when Alcott wrote this note, whether it was upon her first reading when Emerson gave her the book, which would mean in 1850 (see *Journals* 60, 9 Oct. 1847), or upon rereading it at a later date. Nor can I be absolutely certain whether her text for Fuller was the original *Dial* essay from 1843 or the expanded book published in 1845. What she writes, however, is slightly misquoted but almost identical to Fuller's words in the *Dial* essay; Fuller used some of this language in the expanded version, but there it is *much* expanded, going on for two pages to say what is here in a few brief sentences. Therefore, I will assume Alcott was referencing the earlier version and use the *Dial* version as my reference for the remainder of this essay.

2. The name "Miranda" shows up fairly often as a name for an independent woman in nineteenth-century literature by women. It draws from Shakespeare's heroine in *The Tempest*, who was raised away from society due to her father Prospero's exile on an island.

3. These statistics should be understood as pertaining to *white* women specifically, since enslaved persons were not permitted to marry civilly, and groups such as Native Americans were not typically counted in census data.

4. The narrator merely tells us that Amy is the "youngest," while giving ages for the other three girls (*Little Women* 13–14).

5. Indeed, *Little Women*, part 2 may be the most "adult" of any portion of the March family trilogy. Although time continues to march forward, *Little Men* refocuses on childhood by taking up the stories of the children at Plumfield, and *Jo's Boys* repeats that focus, with the addition of girls as Plumfield expands to the co-ed Lawrence College.

6. Fuller's essay even provides us with a parallel to the future of Beth, who will die in part 2. In proposing that there is equality in heaven, where there is "no marrying nor giving in marriage, [but] each is a purified intelligence, an enfranchised soul" (742), Fuller draws upon the example of Mignon from *Wilhelm Meister's Apprenticeship*—a child who dies in the novel. Fuller calls her "a prophetic form, expressive of the longing for a state of perfect freedom, pure love. She could not remain here, but was transplanted to another air. And it may be that the air of this earth will never be so tempered, that such can bear it long. But, while they stay, they must bear testimony to the truth they are constituted to demand" (742). She sounds like a truly kindred spirit to Beth as Alcott portrays her in *Little Women*!

I would also like to point out here that Fuller's influence regarding the egalitarian marriages in *Little Women* has not gone totally unnoticed, especially recently. Both Daniel Shealy's and Anne Boyd Rioux's excellent scholarship on this subject is cited later in this essay. Rather, I am suggesting that the parallels between Fuller's philosophical essay and Alcott's work of fiction are more detailed, specific, and precise than others have previously considered and that tracing them illuminates both works.

7. That is, *more* than what Fuller described as a "household partnership." Meg and John's marriage eventually hints at one of Fuller's most progressively astonishing statements in her essay, considering the time period: her assertion "Male and female represent the two sides of the great radical dualism. But, in fact, they are perpetually passing into one another.... There is no wholly masculine man, no purely feminine woman" (756). Fuller may not have seen marriages like this in her time, but she clearly predicted or at least hoped for it. And this combination of expected female qualities blended with expected male qualities in a person, this disruption of "separate spheres," describes the individuals in the Marmee/Mr. March marriage, the Meg/John marriage to some extent, and most certainly Jo and Friedrich as well. Alcott again puts into action Fuller's suggestion, moving the ball forward as she does.

8. Reviews reprinted in Clark and attributed to "C" in a Massachusetts newspaper and Mrs. Henry Ward Beecher in *The Mother at Home and Household Magazine*.

9. Estes and Lant's now-classic essay from *Children's Literature* 17 (1989), reprinted in Eiselein and Phillips's *Norton Critical Edition*, summarizes in a footnote many of the arguments on Jo's marriages up to that time (see Alcott, *Little Women* 565n2).

10. Fuller at this point also raises the issue of women's education, which Alcott does not take up in *Little Women* but does, very strongly, two decades later in *Jo's Boys*.

11. While Jo was about to be twenty-five, it is interesting to note that Alcott herself was of similar age to Fuller when considering this meditation; she was thirty-six, and Fuller would have been thirty-three when writing "The Great Lawsuit."

Works Cited

Alcott, Louisa May. *The Journals of Louisa May Alcott*, edited by Joel Myerson, Daniel Shealy, and Madeleine B. Stern, Little, Brown, 1989; U of Georgia P, 1997.

Alcott, Louisa May. *The Selected Letters of Louisa May Alcott*, edited by Joel Myerson, Daniel Shealy, and Madeleine B. Stern, Little, Brown, 1987; U of Georgia P, 1995.

Alcott, Louisa May. *Little Women, or, Meg, Jo, Beth and Amy*, edited by Anne K. Phillips and Gregory Eiselein, Norton Critical Edition, W. W. Norton, 2004.

Alcott, Louisa May. Flyleaf notation in *Wilhelm Meister's Apprenticeship*, by Johann Wolfgang von Goethe, Edinburgh, 1824 (Houghton Library Item ID: AC 85.Al194. Zz824g).

Alcott, Louisa May. "Recollections of My Childhood" (1888). Rpt. in *Alcott in Her Own Time*, edited by Daniel Shealy, U of Iowa P, 2005, pp. 32–39.

Capper, Charles. *Margaret Fuller: An American Romantic Life*, 2 vols. Oxford UP, 1994, 2002.

Clark, Beverly Lyon, editor. *Louisa May Alcott: The Contemporary Reviews*. Cambridge UP, 2004.

Doyle, Christine. *Louisa May Alcott and Charlotte Brontë: Transatlantic Translations*. U of Tennessee P, 2000.

Emerson, Ralph Waldo. "Self-Reliance." *The American Transcendentalists: Essential Writings*, edited by Lawrence Buell, Modern Library, 2006, pp. 208–31. First published 1841.

Estes, Angela M., and Kathleen Margaret Lant. "Dismembering the Text: The Horror of Louisa May Alcott's *Little Women*" (1989). Rpt. in Phillips and Eiselein, *Little Women*, pp. 564–83.

Fuller, Margaret. "The Great Lawsuit: Man *versus* Men. Woman *versus* Women" (1843). Rpt. in *The Norton Anthology of American Literature, Vol. B, 1820–1865*. 9th ed., edited by Robert S. Levine, W. W. Norton, 2017, pp. 725–59.

Keyser, Elizabeth. *Whispers in the Dark*. U of Tennessee P, 1993.

Kornacki, Katie. "'A Loving League of Sisters': The Legacy of Margaret Fuller's Boston Conversations in Alcott's *Work*." *Critical Insights: Louisa May Alcott*, edited by Gregory Eiselein and Anne K. Phillips, Salem Press/Grey House Publishing, 2016, pp. 143–58.

LaPlante, Eve. *Marmee and Louisa*. Free Press, 2012.

Phillips, Anne K. "The Prophets and the Martyrs: Pilgrims and Missionaries in *Little Women* and *Jack and Jill*." *"Little Women" and the Feminist Imagination: Criticism, Controversy, Personal Essays*, edited by Janice M. Alberghene and Beverly Lyon Clark, Garland, 1999, pp. 213–36.

Rigsby, Mary Bortnyk. *Margaret Fuller's Feminist Aesthetic: A Critique of Emersonian Idealism in the Works of Fuller, Alcott, Stowe, and Freeman*. 1991. Temple U, PhD dissertation. *ProQuest*.

Rioux, Anne Boyd. *Meg, Jo, Beth, Amy: The Story of "Little Women" and Why It Still Matters*. W. W. Norton, 2018.

Shealy, Daniel. "'Wedding Marches': Louisa May Alcott, Marriage, and the Newness of *Little Women*." *Women's Studies*, vol. 48, no. 4, 2019, pp. 366–78.

Smith, Daniel Scott. "Family Limitation, Sexual Control, and Domestic Feminism in Victorian America." *Clio's Consciousness Raised: New Perspectives on the History of Women*, edited by Mary S. Hartman and Lois Banner, Harper and Row, 1974, pp. 119–36.

Stanton, Elizabeth Cady, Susan B. Anthony, and Matilda Joslyn Gage. *History of Woman Suffrage, Vol. 1, 1848–1861*. Fowler and Wells, 1881; Ayer, 1935.

Theriot, Nancy M. *Mothers & Daughters in Nineteenth-Century America: The Biosocial Construction of Femininity.* UP of Kentucky, 1996.

Wayne, Tiffany. *Woman Thinking: Feminism and Transcendentalism in Nineteenth-Century America.* Lexington Books, 2005.

Louisa May Alcott, Ethel Turner, and Some Little Women Down Under

Joel Myerson

Writing in her journal in May 1868, Louisa May Alcott voiced her concerns about the new book she was writing: "Marmee, Anna, and May all approve my plan. So I plod away, though I don't enjoy this sort of thing. Never liked girls nor knew many, except my sisters; but our queer plays and experiences may prove interesting, though I doubt it" (*Journals* 165–66).[1] The result, of course, was *Little Women*. Published in two volumes in 1868 and 1869, the work was immediately popular and sold nearly 600,000 copies for its publisher, Roberts Brothers of Boston, before the firm was bought by Little, Brown in 1898 (Myerson and Shealy 69). In her book *The Afterlife of "Little Women,"* Beverly Lyon Clark explains that the book's continued success and place in American life is due to its being "a mutable text" that "speaks differently to different readers, and differently to the same reader at different times" (2).[2] Other writers, spurred on by Alcott's success, published their own books about childhood, often dealing with their own countries and the issues facing children in them.[3] One such writer was the Australian Ethel Turner (1872–1958).

Turner wrote one of the most popular books in Australian literature, *Seven Little Australians*, which has sold over two million copies since its publication in 1894 (Saxby 222). It is also a classic Australian children's book because it deals with urban life and not the bush; because it portrays Australian children in an Australian environment, not a British children's book transplanted down under; and because it has a female lead rather than a male one as was normal for the adventure books written for boys at the time.[4] And for the purposes of my essay, it can be compared to *Little Women*. The English *Publishers' Circular and Booksellers' Record* proclaimed that Turner's book "deserves a place on our children's shelves" near *Little Women* (Review of *Little Women* 272), and the *Detroit Free Press* decided it had "all the freshness and wholesomeness of Louisa May Alcott's Works" (Review of *Seven Little Australians*, xxxix). The publishers of the work wrote its author, Ethel Turner, that they were "very glad to be associated with the Louisa Alcott of Australia" (Turner, *Diaries* 100, 30 Nov. 1893), advertisements at the end of the first edition promote the book as one with "all the simple domestic interest of Miss Alcott's 'Little Women'" (Bradford, "(Re)Constructing" 331), and a notice in the sixteenth edition of the book (1912) states that everyone considered it "to be comparable to that world-famous book 'Little Women'" and that its author is "known everywhere as Miss Alcott's true successor" (6).[5] And, like *Little Women*, *Seven Little Australians* has been adapted as a play, a movie, a television series, and a musical; has been translated into many languages; and has remained in print since its publication.[6]

There are also many personal similarities between Alcott and Turner: both wrote to be financially independent, edited childhood magazines, published children's stories and sentimental short fiction at the beginnings of their careers, were personally involved in choosing the illustrations for their first books, declined a flat payment for their work and to their great advantage chose royalties instead,[7] and used the name "Marmee" to refer to, respectively, a mother and a mother-in-law (see Turner, *Diaries* 67).

Little Women and *Seven Little Australians* also have similarities, but they differ in many ways as well. I will examine the books and their authors—one a colonial writer confronting colonialism and the other a postcolonial writer reinforcing personal values after the Civil War—and suggest why they ultimately had different approaches to their subjects. While Alcott, writing three years after the American Civil War, metaphorically presents the healing of a house divided against itself (brother against brother, Amy against Jo, Jo against Meg's marriage) through the guidance of loving parents, especially Marmee, Turner, composing her novel at the end of the nineteenth century as Australia was beginning to create its own national identity, gives her readers a family whose ineffective parents symbolize an insufficiently nurturing parent country.

The plot and characters of *Little Women* are well known, so I will begin by discussing *Seven Little Australians*. The book was published in 1894 by twenty-two-year-old Ethel Turner. Like *Little Women*, its popularity sparked sequels, but I will discuss only Alcott's first volume in comparison. Turner's book centers on the Woolcot family, and the action takes place mainly at "River House," located a few miles north of Sydney in the suburb of Parramatta, which is unofficially called, because of the actions of the children, "Misrule." Six of the seven little Australians were born to Captain Woolcot and his unnamed first wife, who died soon after the birth of the youngest one. Within a few years, the Captain married Esther Hassal, with whom he had one child. The seven children are, from youngest to oldest: the General, whose real name was Francis Rupert Burnand; Baby, a four-year-old; six-year-old Bunty; Elinor, who is ten and always called Nell; Helen, called Judy, who is thirteen, and only called Helen by her father and then only when he's mad at her, and is a tomboy who instigates most of the family's troubles; fourteen-year-old Philip, always called Pip; and Margaret, called Meg, the eldest at sixteen. I will focus on Meg and Judy, who are the central characters.

The first part of the book involves a series of pranks that result in Pip receiving a thrashing and Judy being sent away to boarding school, a prospect she dreads because it means separation from her family and being taught to perform as a "proper" young lady. Meg then falls in with a pretentious and romantic girl who introduces her to a "fast" crowd, and she learns about substance and show. Judy runs away from boarding school and hides out in a boat shed at home while the children secretly bring her furnishings and food. The Captain's anger at discovering her is tempered when he finds her ill and coughing up blood. Because Judy needs a drier climate for her health, Esther's parents invite the whole brood up to their sheep station, Yarrahappini (an Aboriginal name meaning "native bear rolling down a hill"), and all but Captain Woolcot go. One day, Judy, who is in charge of the General, notices him crawling toward a falling tree and rushes to cover his body with hers, just as the tree crashes down. The General survives unscathed, but Judy is mortally injured and dies a few hours later.

By examining these two books, their similarities and their differences, we can see how antipodean attitudes helped shape Turner's fiction whereas American civic and moral values shaped Alcott's work.

While the two novels are different in many ways, there are also points of similarity, and there should be: Turner was rereading *Little Women* in March 1893, two months after she began to write *Seven Little Australians* (Niall, *Seven Little Billabongs* 66; Turner, *Diaries*, 92, 16 Mar. 1893, 27 Jan. 1893). Surely it's not accidental that "Woolcot" suggests "Alcott," as "Judy" does "Jo," and that there are two "Meg"s. Indeed, the *Sydney Morning Herald*'s review of Turner's book explicitly connects her characters to Alcott's: "Just as Judy is moulded after Jo, of Miss Alcott's 'Little Women,' so is Meg patterned after her namesake among the March girls" ("Current Literature" 4).

The Judy/Jo and Meg/Meg comparisons indicate that these two little Australians are more important than the others. One would assume that Judy is the more important of the two. After all, she is the irrepressible tomboy who leads the others and acts as their conscience, whereas Meg is an artist figure who constantly swoons over romances. Brenda Niall expertly sums up these characters' similarities: both Megs are "pretty, slightly vain and worldly, impatient with the family's genteel poverty, almost ready for love and marriage, and finally guaranteed as good wives in the making," while Judy and Jo take "the rebel role; they are quick-tempered, clever, strong-willed and disdainful of the ladylike ways they associate with growing up" (*Australia through the Looking-Glass* 82). However, when Judy goes off to boarding school, she pretty much disappears from the novel and the focus shifts to Meg and a possible romance; and even when Judy returns, she's isolated in the boat shed. The restorative trip to Yarrahappini centers mainly on Meg, not Judy. And she dies in the end! Clearly, Turner needs Judy to be offstage for the main character of the book to develop, and after a promising beginning, Judy is inexorably steered toward her demise.[8]

We are introduced to Judy in terms reminiscent of Jo March, especially the latter's desire to run, which she shared with her creator. Alcott's Meg says to Jo, "You have been running. . . . When *will* you stop such romping ways?" (*Little Women* 126).[9] Turner's Judy was "never seen to walk. . . . If she did not dash madly to the place she wished to get to, she would progress by a series of jumps, bounds, and odd little skips" (*Seven Little Australians* 5). Turner calls her "the worst of the seven, probably because she was the cleverest" (5), also an apt description of Jo. Even though she had been christened "Helen," she was called Judy, because, according to Bunty, "she was always popping and jerking herself about like the celebrated wife of Punch" (5). Alcott's "Josephine" also adopts another name, hers an androgynous one.

Judy, like Jo, doesn't conform to stereotypical girlish traits. After she and Pip ride a roller coaster, Judy thinks it "heavenly" but Pip feels sick. She continues to ride while he watches, "waving gaily" while he has "his heart in his mouth." Both ride the merry-go-round, but Judy finds it too "tame" and, instead, runs beside it as long as she can, a reversal of him being frozen in fear as she rides the roller coaster (*Seven Little Australians* 39–40). There are many, many references in *Little Women* about Jo wanting to be a boy or acting like one,[10] even to the point of wishing to marry Meg to "keep her safe in the family" (161).

Turner makes clear that Judy's headstrong ways will lead to trouble. They will endanger her in a world where strong women must be sacrificed to maintain order and social values. Turner even adds a narrative aside after the Captain says Judy is "being ruined for want of a firm hand," saying that was "indeed" in "a measure true" (*Seven Little Australians* 47). The Captain recalls that her own mother had been concerned for Judy's future because her "restless fire" would either make her "a noble, daring, brilliant woman," or "it would flame up higher and higher and consume her" (24). Jo, on the other hand, seemingly develops from being a tomboy to a little woman, as can be seen from Mr. March's reaction when he returns home and sees the changes in her: "I don't see the 'son Jo' whom I left a year ago. . . . I see a young lady who pins her collar straight, laces her boots neatly, and neither whistles, talks slang, nor lies on the rug, as she used to" (*Little Women* 176). Still, as Daniel Shealy has noted, "Jo's exuberant spirit and unconventional manners remain intact, and her reluctance to accept Meg's courtship with John Brooke indicates there is more growth to come" (*"Little Women": An Annotated Edition* 290n16). Judy, the rebel, was not reformed by going to boarding school; she is sacrificed so that Meg, the socially responsible one, can take a place in society. Additionally, to Bradford, "through this drastic closure Turner solves the narrative problem of a female character who resists the gendered expectations of the world of the novel but for whom there exists no alternative model of female subjectivity" ("Ether Turner" 396). Jo, on the other hand, assumes a more traditional role in society after marrying the older Professor Bhaer, and in growing up loses many of those traits that had defined her as the Jo of the first volume of *Little Women*—in a way, the original Jo must conform as well.[11]

Judy's death scene is markedly different from the one when Beth appears to have died in the first part of *Little Women*. Alcott's depiction reflects the prose of the period: "The fever flush, and the look of pain, were gone, and the beloved little face looked so pale and peaceful in its utter repose, that Jo felt no desire to weep or to lament. Leaning low over this dearest of her sisters, she kissed the damp forehead with her heart on her lips, and softly whispered, 'Good-by, my Beth; good-by!'" (151). Turner, on the other hand, refuses to rely on religiosity and sentimentality. Judy acknowledges her lack of churchgoing when she attempts to say a final prayer: "Meg, I'm so frightened! I can't think of anything but 'For what we are about to receive,' and that's grace, isn't it? And there's nothing in Our Father that would do either. Meg, I wish we'd gone to Sunday school and learnt things. Look at the dark, Meg! Oh, Meg, hold my hands!" (*Seven Little Australians* 188). This also differs from Alcott's portrayal of the actual death of Beth, the traditional "Angel in the House," in the second half of *Little Women*. Judy's death,[12] in which she desperately and belatedly tries to find consolation in religion while Meg is unable to help her, is a far more realistic portrayal of children trying to deal with a catastrophic event than is Alcott's more sentimental approach. Turner's insistence that Judy's death, like Alcott's portrayal of Beth's death, fails to deliver a moral lesson is unlike other lugubrious and didactic deaths in children's literature at the time. For Niall, "*Seven Little Australians* looks back to *Little Women*, and improves on it by more realistically observed children and comparatively little moralizing" (*Seven Little Billabongs* 65).

The other character whose name parallels one in Alcott's book is Meg, who, like her New England counterpart, is taken up in a social whirl. She is introduced as a good-natured girl who, it was "generally believed, . . . wrote poetry and stories, and even kept a diary" (*Seven Little Australians* 6). Like Meg March, she wants to be accepted by what she considers high society, and after exchanging chocolates, hair ribbons, and confidences, she falls in with Aldith MacCarthy, who starts to call Meg "Marguerite." Within a couple of months, the previously unpretentious Meg is putting up her hair in papers each night, washing her face with oatmeal daily, using "freckle lotion" to help her complexion, tightly lacing her corset to slim her waist, and nightly rubbing Vaseline on her hands. In all this, she is similar to Meg in *Little Women*, who, Alcott says, "soon began to imitate the manners and conversation of those about her; to put on little airs and graces, use French phrases, crimp her hair, take in her dresses, and talk about the fashions, as well as she could" (*Little Women* 72–73).

Turner's reader is under no illusions concerning the silliness of Meg's makeover, as the dialogue in her French lessons demonstrates. Twice weekly,

Aldith and Meg went to town to "learn how to inquire, in polite French, 'Has the baker's young daughter the yellow hat, brown gloves, and umbrella of the undertaker's niece?'" to which they answered, "No, but the surgeon had some beer, some mustard, and the dinner-gong" (56).

Aldith also sweeps Meg up into the romantic world of "beaus." Disaster results, though, when she tries to change the time for a meeting Aldith has set up with two boys. The letter she writes to Andrew, the boy Aldith sets her up with, is, to put it mildly, poorly thought out: "Dear Mr. Courtney," she writes, "Let us go later, when it is quite dark. It will be *ever* so much nicer, for no one will be able to see us. And let us meet at the end of the paddocks where the bush grows thickly, it will be more private." And she adds this postscript: "I must ask you, please, not to kiss me. I should be very angry indeed if you did. I don't like kissing at all" (*Seven Little Australians* 70). Needless to say, everything that could go wrong does. Aldith, who is ill, writes letters to all three friends cancelling the meeting, but the one to Meg is never delivered, with the result that Andrew's brother Alan reads Meg's letter and arrives alone for their clandestine rendezvous. After thoroughly shaming her with such comments as "I know you *said* you did not want to be kissed; but then, girls always say that, don't they?—even when they expect it most," Alan soon gets to the point: "Miss Meg, you used to seem such a nice little girl, . . . what have you let that horrid MacCarthy girl spoil you for? . . . I imagined how I should feel if my little sister . . . began to flirt and make herself conspicuous, and I wondered would you mind if I spoke to you about it. Are you very angry with me, Miss Meg?" (79–80). Meg sobs, he apologizes, she promises to reform, and they part friends. This event is reminiscent of Meg March's taking on airs at a ball and being deflated by Laurie's comment, "I don't like fuss and feathers" (*Little Women* 79), in the confusion over Laurie's faking a love letter to her from John Brooke—and of her later recognition that she is rich in "things more precious than any luxuries money could buy; in love, protection, peace and health, the real blessings of life" (146). Both Megs grow toward maturity in their books as few of the Woolcot children do.

While both authors deliver moral lessons, Turner, as a rule, applies them to specific situations while Alcott applies them to life in general. When a series of pranks lead the Captain to bar the children from attending a show, they all act especially good in a chapter titled "Virtue Not Always Rewarded." The Woolcots only try to be good when they wish to attain a goal because when the Captain refuses to reconsider his ban, Turner notes that "the young

Woolcots determined never again to assume virtues that they had not" (*Seven Little Australians* 25). In Alcott's world, virtue *is* rewarded. After the girls give up their breakfast for the Hummels, Mr. Laurence sends over a "little feast" for them to "make up for the bread and milk breakfast" (*Little Women* 26). Later, Meg vocalizes a basic Alcott family concept: "Do your duty; and you'll get your reward" (119). The Woolcots are very different. When Bunty believes he fails to get all the credit he deserves for scrounging food for Judy when she hides in the boat shed, he gets grumpy and rats her out. Indeed, after Judy returns, her siblings don't forego their own food to help her so much as pilfer food from the pantry. Compare this to Alcott's comments about self-sacrifice: "We ought not to spend money for pleasure, when our men are suffering so in the army" (11), or "Let's each get [Marmee] something for Christmas, and not get anything for ourselves" (14), and, of course, Jo's cutting off her hair to raise money for her ill father.

There are also a number of general categories that the authors share that deserve examining: using an omniscient narrator; discussing the families' residences; employing books and reading; addressing political issues; and attacks on the books' use of language and, in Alcott's case, religion.

Both Alcott and Turner employ an omniscient narrator who comments on the action, often in asides to the reader. Beginning a new chapter, Turner self-referentially states, "It was a day after 'the events narrated in the last chapter,' as story-book parlance has it" (*Seven Little Australians* 31). Alcott begins her first chapter by saying, "As young readers like to know 'how people look,' we will take this moment to give them a little sketch of the four sisters" (*Little Women* 13).[13] When Turner describes the death scene with Judy, she intrudes into the story to say, "It is so hard to write it. My pen has had only happy writing to do so far, and now!" (*Seven Little Australians* 181). Alcott opens the chapter when Marmee returns home from nursing Mr. March with the sentimental "I don't think I have any words in which to tell the meeting of the mother and daughters" (*Little Women* 158). When the March women gather by the fireside for their second Christmas alone, with the promise of Mr. March coming home, Alcott writes, "Now and then, in this work-a-day world, things do happen in the delightful story-book fashion, and what a comfort that is" (173). Both Alcott and Turner, in concluding their books, suggest the possibility of a sequel. Turner writes, "My pen has been moving heavily, slowly for these last two chapters; . . . so I will lay it aside, or I shall sadden you. [¶] Some day, if you would care to hear it, I should like to tell you of my young Australians again, slipping a little space of years. [¶] Until then, farewell and adieu" (*Seven Little Australians* 195). Alcott is more upbeat: "So grouped the curtain falls upon Meg, Jo, Beth, and Amy. Whether it ever rises again, depends upon the reception given to the first act of the domestic drama, called 'LITTLE WOMEN'" (*Little Women* 185). Both authors directly appeal to the reader to request another book about their respective families.

The different families' residences are described in such a way that the authors are able to comment on their mutual inhabitants. The prosaic River House is called "Misrule," an apt description of the events inside, but "mis" is a pejorative prefix, suggesting something is wrong or amiss—had the children just been unruly, then a more appropriate name would have been "Unrule." Whether you take Alcott's own dwelling by its formal name of Orchard House, suggesting a fruitful existence, or "Apple Slump," her humorous nickname that suggests an off-kilter apple tree or a sweet dessert, either is better than "Misrule." Both use descriptions of their houses' interiors to reflect differences in familial relations: at "Misrule," the children are kept upstairs and the domain of the adults is downstairs; in *Little Women*, while the children's bedrooms are upstairs, the focal point of the house is the reception room downstairs where all gather. This distribution of space may explain why the Woolcot children band together upstairs against the adults downstairs, while the Alcott children consider themselves members of a complete family unit in the parlor.

Books and reading are important factors in both novels. The library at River House, like Jay Gatsby's library in *The Great Gatsby*, is mainly for display, whereas the libraries at Aunt March's and Mr. Laurence's houses are actually used by the girls. Generally speaking, there is much play and very little reading going on in *Seven Little Australians*. Mr. Gillet at Yarrahappini has a library of German and English literary works that impresses Meg, but the only other substantive use of books is when Aldith lends saccharine sentimental novels to Meg, who herself reads moral and domestic novels, including, of course, works by Louisa May Alcott.[14] The Marches' world is populated with books.[15] *Little Women* uses the many references to John Bunyan's *Pilgrim's Progress* to demonstrate the Puritan sprit of striving to avoid temptation and to become better: Alcott adapts some lines from the book as the poetic preface to her novel, has the girls recall playing out scenes from it, and even titles the chapter in which Meg gets her arriviste comeuppance from Laurie as "Meg Goes to Vanity Fair." The plays the girls put on, the issues of the "Pickwick Portfolio" they write, Jo's aspirations as a writer, and her actual publications, all show the educational value of books and thus lead Alcott to fully embrace the concept of republican motherhood, dating from the American Revolution, which holds that with the men away as diplomats or fighters, it was up to the women, who now ran the households, to educate children to be responsible adults and citizens, a task at which Marmee excels (see Kerber 187–205).

Alcott and Turner both address political matters. If the rigid Captain is symbolic of the colonialism of the British Empire, then there is an interesting coincidence that the first Australian constitutional convention was held in 1890—attended by seven representatives.[16] Whether this is intended or coincidental, the book does suggest that the revolt of the children against a father's rule, if you will, his "misrule," which Turner earlier described as their "sparkle of joyousness and rebellion" (*Seven Little Australians* 1), is closely tied to the revolt against the home country inherent in an Australian confederation: both sets of offspring are rebelling against the overbearing but distant parent. In Alcott's book, the more positive family relations can be seen as foreshadowing the promise of better times ahead, a promise based on the civic and transcendentalist virtues of the past and a note of optimism during and after the destabilization of the post-Civil War years.

Both books were attacked for their use of language and, in Alcott's case, a lack of religion. In its review of *Seven Little Australians*, the *Sydney Morning Herald* complained about Pip's crying "My oath!" and urged Turner to excise this vulgarity from the next edition ("Current Literature" 4)—which it was, with "My word!" substituted for it until the original reading was restored in 1994. Complaints about Alcott's use of colloquial language continued throughout her career. In reviewing *Little Women*, the *Graphic* wrote, "She is mistaken in making her young heroines . . . express themselves in such an unpleasing style. . . . Miss Alcott's book would be quite as interesting and amusing if her good 'Little Women' expressed themselves in more lady-like language" (Review of *Little Women*, 26 Nov. 1870). When *Little Women* was given a new and revised edition in 1880, changes were made in punctuation, spelling, capitalization, hyphenation, and paragraphing; plus Alcott's use of slang was eliminated by "correcting" it, resulting in what the modern editors of the book have called "a more polished, conventional, middle-class narrative."[17]

Reviewers must have thought that Turner was implicitly criticizing Judy's lack of religious training when describing her death scene, because I have been unable to locate any reviews that mention it other than to complain that the central character was killed off. Not so with Alcott. Some contemporary reviews of *Little Women* complained of its lack of religious values. Comments like these were common: "It is not a Christian book" because it is "religion without spirituality, and salvation without Christ," and thus "is not a good book for the Sunday school library" (Review of *Little Women*, *Ladies' Repository*); and, in describing Beth's death, regretting that *Pilgrim's Progress* "gives a semi-saintly lustre to the scene, though fainter than it would have been had the Word of God [i.e., the Bible] been a lamp unto her feet, and a light unto her path" (Review of *Little Women*, *Zion's Herald*).

While the novels' similarities clearly demonstrate that Turner was influenced and inspired by Alcott's novel, we also know *Seven Little Australians* will be quite different than *Little Women* from the very beginning. Alcott's opening lines show themes that will permeate the book: self-sacrifice— "'Christmas won't be Christmas without any presents,' grumbled Jo"—and the importance of family—"'We've got father and mother, and each other, anyhow' said Beth" (11). Like Alcott does elsewhere, Turner begins by speaking frankly of her characters' personal failings:

> If you imagine you are going to read of model children, with perhaps a naughtily inclined one to point a moral, you had better lay down the book immediately.... Not one of the seven is really good, for the very excellent reason that Australian children never are....
>
> It may be that the land and the people are young-hearted together, and the children's spirits not crushed and saddened by the shadow of long years' sorrowful history....
>
> There is a lurking sparkle of joyousness and rebellion and mischief in nature here, and therefore in children. (*Seven Little Australians* 1)[18]

The introduction to the children themselves comes through not a quiet didacticism but a noisy playfulness: they are taking nursery tea with "a minimum of comfort and a maximum of noise, so if you can bear a deafening babel of voices," says Turner, "I will ... introduce them to you" (*Seven Little Australians* 2).[19]

While Turner's children may not be "crushed and saddened by the shadow of long years' sorrowful history," their ahistorical spiritedness contrasts sharply with Alcott's children's sense of history, one that comes from learning and adapting the lessons of America's past, lessons that also come, in great measure, from their family, and especially their mother, "Marmee," whose ideas and values are congruent with those of her absent husband, Mr. March. Many of these values are summed up in the idea that work is better than play, as when Marmee tells the girls, "Work is wholesome, and there is plenty for every one; it keeps us from *ennui* and mischief; is good for health and spirits, and gives us a sense of power and independence better than money or fashion" (*Little Women* 99). To one author, writing during a period when Australia was beginning to create a separate identity for itself from Great Britain, freedom from the past results in play—children will be children—but to the other, American history gives lessons to shepherd the little women into adulthood or into, as the second part of *Little Women* was called in Great Britain, *Good Wives*.

While Alcott's characters balance work and play, Turner's children play so much because, unlike Alcott's, they have poor role models. Alcott's descriptions of Marmee suggest that sainthood is warranted: she is introduced as "a stout, motherly lady, with a 'can-I-help-you' look about her," all in all, "the most splendid woman in the world" (*Little Women* 15). And, later reflecting on Meg's possible marriage, Mrs. March says of Meg (and, by implication, herself, both in the novel and in real life) that to be "rich in the possession of a good man's heart . . . is better than a fortune" (162). While Turner's first Mrs. Woolcot must have done a good job in raising her children, as seen by their happy demeanors, Esther Hassal Woolcot is described as a twenty-year-old "girl-wife" (*Seven Little Australians* 6), just four years older than her eldest stepdaughter and, indeed, "very little steadier and very little more of a housekeeper" than her. She treats the General "more as if it were a very entertaining kitten than a real live baby" (3). Esther feels she has disappointed her husband by not organizing their household and has failed the children by not providing them with more guidance, and her attempts to encourage them often backfire. When Meg tries to have a smaller waist by tightening her corset, Esther, remembering when she was sixteen and a tiny waist was extremely desirable, compliments Meg on her nice figure. Encouraged, Meg redoubles her efforts and eventually faints because she can't breathe.[20] One can never imagine Alcott saying of Marmee what Turner says of Esther: "Her heart told her these children were not receiving a mother's care at her hands" (86).

The two authors present very different portrayals of husbands and fathers. Even though Mr. March is absent for most of the novel, there's no doubt that the March family works together toward common goals and that

Mr. March is understood to be the head of the household, through moral suasion not sheer strength.[21]

Turner's head of household is a more problematic figure. He is always called "Captain" or "Captain Woolcot" and not provided with a given name. The various brief descriptions of him lack sympathy. He is "a very particular and rather irritable father" (*Seven Little Australians* 2), he does "not understand children at all," and he was "always grumbling at the noise they made, and the money they cost" (6). Indeed, the Captain's attitude toward money and how it influences his feelings about his children runs throughout the book in a very non-Alcottian manner. For example, his expenses for keeping horses cause the children to go about in shabby and worn clothes. His relations with his children are awkward at best. Regarding the baby called only "General," he "generally laugh[s] when he [sees] it, tosse[s] it in the air, and then ask[s] someone to take it quickly" (3). All these examples confirm that his first wife was primarily responsible for raising their children.

Not even the Captain's thoughts about the family as a whole endear him to the reader. Before moving to River House, they had stayed in the barracks, but complaints from fellow officers about the children's pranks forced them to relocate, causing the Captain considerable bitterness. When a doctor instructs him to send Judy away to recover from her illness in a better climate, he ponders what he considers a number of unattractive options because all involve either spending too much money or leaving him with a set of unruly children. When the invitation from Esther's parents arrives for all the children to come to Yarrahappini, he grasps at it with "the air of a man released from a nightmare" (*Seven Little Australians* 132). And after he says good-bye to the family when they board the train, he walks down the platform with "almost a jaunty air, as if the prospect of two months' bachelordom was not without its redeeming points" (135).

The two books provide us quite different views of the parents and the ways in which the children react with them. In *Seven Little Australians*, the children form a bond against their father, who represents discipline and punishment, and seem to adopt Esther as an older sibling rather than as a parent who might provide guidance. The Captain keeps order by corporal punishment, and there are a number of scenes in which Bunty gets thrashed. Alcott's view of family is right there on the first page, as voiced by Beth: "We've got father and mother, and each other" (*Little Women* 11). And moral suasion, not physical power, enforces the rules; indeed, when

Amy is punished with some light "tingling blows" on her palm for sneaking pickled limes into the schoolroom, Alcott notes that "for the first time in her life she had been struck" (59–60).

Another marked difference between the books is how they treat people of color—African Americans in the United States and Aboriginals in Australia. Even though Concord was a stop on the underground railroad, and even though Alcott's family had strong abolitionist sentiments, African Americans are almost absent from *Little Women*. However, Alcott does have Jo respond to one of Marmee's moralizing tales by repeating (incorrectly) the mimicry of black speech in Harriet Beecher Stowe's famous novel: "We needed that lesson, and we won't forget. If we do, you just say to us as Old Chloe did in Uncle Tom,—'Tink ob yer marcies, chillen, 'tink ob yer marcies'" (43).[22]

Few Aboriginals appear in *Seven Little Australians*. There are none around River House and the ones at Yarrahappini are generally anonymous stockmen on the sheep station. The most detailed character is Tettawonga, who does little else but smoke and give daily opinions on the weather, a position rewarded him for earlier killing a bushranger who attacked Mrs. Hassal and Esther. And, like so many writers of this period, Turner struggles with Aboriginal dialect: "Plenty fellow rabbit longa scrub, budgery way north, budgery way south; budgery way eblywhere" (151).

After the fifth edition of 1896, a fairly long—about a thousand words—section dealing with Aboriginals was deleted from the book. This important deletion shows Turner sympathetic to the continent's original inhabitants. As the children are being driven to the picnic at Yarrahappini, Mr. Gillet tells them an Aboriginal tale about the kookaburra and the snake, beginning in typical Western fashion:[23] "Once upon a time . . . when this young land was still younger, and incomparably more beautiful, when Tettawonga's ancestors were brave and strong and happy as careless children, when their worst nightmare had never shown them so evil a time as the white man would bring their race, when—" but he is interrupted by Pip's "Oh, get on!" (*Seven Little Australians* 163–64). Gillet then continues the story in a straightforward fashion. The omission is odd: the story itself is a benign myth. There are, I believe, three possible reasons for the deletion. First, Gillet's prologue is highly sympathetic to Aboriginals, and parents might have been concerned that children reading *Seven Little Australians* would ask why and how the whites brought evil to the native peoples. Second, Turner uses the term "Koorie" to describe the blacks, choosing a word preferred by Aboriginal peoples of her part of New South Wales to call themselves, rather than a term (and probably a derogatory one) used by whites to describe them. And third, as Clare Bradford has noted, it eliminates the "shadow" of the "long years' sorrowful history" under which Turner had earlier said Australian children do not labor (Bradford, *Reading Race* 5).

In a general comparison of these two books, we can say that while both books are their author's first published children's novel, Alcott's is far more sophisticated. She had tried her hand at writing a novel in the late 1840s with *The Inheritance* (first published in 1997), and she published numerous short stories (including her "blood and thunder" tales) in the 1850s; an autobiographical work, *Hospital Sketches*, in 1863; and *Moods* in 1864. For Turner, although she had written short stories and sketches earlier, *Seven Little Australians* was her first novel. The first volume of *Little Women* is about ninety thousand words long, as compared to Turner's book, which is only half that length, allowing Alcott twice as much space to develop her characters and themes. Turner merely describes family life—and especially its failures—in an outpost of the British Empire, while Alcott, brought up by parents who challenged the American educational, political, and class system, embodies *their* values in her work. While Mrs. Alcott and the first Mrs. Woolcot both raised their children successfully, Esther Woolcot lacks oversight of and guidance to her children; and while Mr. March (who is present only at the end of the book) embodies moral values, Captain Woolcot (who is absent during most of the second half) is shown to be an indifferent and self-centered father. Finally, in *Seven Little Australians* the children are allowed to remain children until they become adults in the sequels, whereas in *Little Women* the maturation process is ongoing, making it, I think, a work of more permanent value.

Perhaps, too, the books are the result of the difference between two colonial writers. One is an Australian writing a century after her country was founded by convicts, using her book, at a time when a type of separation from the mother country is being proposed by confederation, to reinforce the idea that Australians are a different breed from the English. The other is an American, writing a century after people seeking religious and political freedom successfully fought a war with the mother country to achieve independence, using her book, in her contemporary post-Civil War world when nostalgia for the past is more comforting than the present or the promise of the future, to depict the genuine American values with which she has been brought up.

Notes

1. I thank Beverly Lyon Clark for her help in researching this essay and Clark, Richard Flynn, Greta Little, and Daniel Shealy for comments on an earlier draft.

2. See also Rioux.

3. Clark identifies such followers as "the British Mrs. George de Horne Vaizey's (Jessie Mansergh's) *Sisters Three* (1900), and, in the United States, Marion Ames Taggart's *The Little Women Club* (1905), May Hollis Barton's *Four Little Women of Roxby, or The Queer Old Lady Who Lost Her Way* (1926), and the four books in Gabrielle E. Jackson's Three Little Women series (1908–14)" (*Afterlife* 58, 60).

4. For an excellent summary of the historical importance of *Seven Little Australians*, as well as a concise examination of its parallels to *Little Women*, see the sketch of Turner by Bradford, "Ethel Turner," esp. 394–96.

5. When the British *Girl's Realm* asked its readers for their favorite female characters, Jo March finished first and, from *Seven Little Australians*, Meg and Judy Woolcot third and twelfth, respectively (the former possibly because of the sequels to the book), and when a 1904 poll in the London *Westminster Budget* asked "between 3,000 and 4,000 girls of the educated classes" to name their favorite female fictional characters, Jo March finished first and Judy Woolcot tenth ("My Birthday Party," qtd. in Niall, *Seven Little Billabongs* 77; "Girl Favourites in Fiction," 32).

6. However, it sold poorly in the United States, unlike *Little Women*, which did well in Britain. *Seven Little Australians* seems to have had only one contemporary American edition, that by David McKay in 1909 (Carter and Osborne 130–32).

7. Coincidentally, British editions of *Little Women* in 1871 and 1878 were published by Ward, Lock, who was also Turner's publisher.

8. Perhaps this reflects a comment in Turner's diary that her stepfather had declared "he would rather bury me than see me married" (5 Oct. 1889; and see also the entry for 16 June 1892, *Diaries* 20, 80). Alcott felt that Jo "should have remained a literary spinster" but yielded to her readers' desire to marry her off, though, in the end, she "went & made a funny match for her" (20 Mar. [1869], *Selected Letters* 125). Indeed, many readers of *Little Women* have agreed with Alcott that Jo should have remained a literary single woman.

9. In her "Recollections of My Childhood" (1888), Alcott wrote, "It was such a joy to run. No boy could be my friend till I had beaten him in a race." A friend of Alcott's recalled that she "could run like a gazelle. She was the most beautiful girl runner I ever saw" (both qtd. in *"Little Women": An Annotated Edition* 215n14).

10. See, for example, Jo's complaint that "I can't get over my disappointment in not being a boy" (13).

11. Others see Jo's marriage as a positive step: see *"Little Women": An Annotated Edition*, 584n19, n20, and Shealy, "Wedding Marches."

12. Turner wrote in her diary that she had "killed Judy to slow music" (18 Oct. 1893, *Diaries* 98). In a letter to her sister, Turner wrote of her earlier children's stories that "I was never happy unless my favourite character or characters had died on beautiful death-beds to slow music" ("Dedicatory Letter" 7).

13. This is similar to Turner's beginning, where she states, "I will . . . introduce [the children] to you" (2).

14. Aldith "lent Meg novels, *Family Herald Supplements, Young Ladies' Journals*, and such publications, and the young girl took to them with avidity, surprised at the new world into

which they took her; for Charlotte Yonge and Louisa Alcott and Miss Wetherell had hitherto formed her simple and wholesome fare" (*Seven Little Australians* 52–53). Both Yonge and Elizabeth Wetherell [Susan Warner] wrote religious novels in, respectively, England and America. Turner herself was, in her youth, an "avid reader" of these three authors (204).

15. For more on this, see Matteson's introduction to *"Little Women": An Annotated Edition* (Alcott xvi–xvii).

16. The representatives were from New South Wales, Queensland, South Australia, Tasmania, Victoria, Western Australia, and New Zealand.

17. Alcott, *Little Women*, ed. Phillips and Eiselein, 391. See also Shealy's "Note on the Text," which discusses the changes, Alcott's possible involvement in them, and how language "correctness" in the 1880s might have affected the linguistic revisions in the book (Alcott, *"Little Women": An Annotated Edition* ix–xi).

18. For this edition, "a number of corrections were made to the text to bring it closer in line with the first edition, which was more faithful to Ethel Turner's original manuscript" (*Seven Little Australians*, ed. Poole 201).

19. The response of the *New York Times* to Turner's children was to generalize, "What a precious lot of trouble they must have in Sydney if the Woolcot family is to be taken as a sample!" ("Trouble in Australia").

20. In a similar fashion, Alcott writes in "Meg Goes to Vanity Fair" that "They laced her into a sky-blue dress, which was so tight she could hardly breathe" (76). See also her comments on dress reform in *"Little Women": An Annotated Edition* 42n29.

21. As Shealy observes in "Wedding Marches," "By stating that anger is something she has to suppress all the time, Marmee suggests that a volatile temper is part of her personality. She tells Jo that her own mother 'used to help me,' but after her death, 'I was too proud to confess my weakness to any one else.' Once they are married, Mr. March helps her by his own example and by his suggestion that his wife 'must try to practise all the virtues I would have my little girls possess.' While some readers may see Mr. March's advice as overbearing patriarchal authority, Marmee does not view it that way" (373).

22. As Shealy points out, she is here misquoting a passage from chap. 11 in Harriet Beecher Stowe's *Uncle Tom's Cabin* (*"Little Women": An Annotated Edition* 91n42).

23. He says, "Mine is only got at second-hand" from an Aboriginal "and freely translated," which helps explain the "once upon a time" beginning (163).

Works Cited

Alcott, Louisa May. *The Annotated "Little Women,"* edited by John Matteson, W. W. Norton, 2015.

Alcott, Louisa May. *The Journals of Louisa May Alcott*, edited by Joel Myerson, Daniel Shealy, and Madeleine B. Stern, Little, Brown, 1989; U of Georgia P, 1997.

Alcott, Louisa May. *Little Women, or, Meg, Jo, Beth and Amy*, edited by Anne K. Phillips and Gregory Eiselein, Norton Critical Edition, W. W. Norton, 2004.

Alcott, Louisa May. *"Little Women": An Annotated Edition*, edited by Daniel Shealy, Belknap Press of Harvard UP, 2013.

Alcott, Louisa May. "Recollections of My Childhood" (1888), Rpt. in *"Little Women": An Annotated Edition*, edited by Daniel Shealy, Harvard UP, 2013.

Alcott, Louisa May. *The Selected Letters of Louisa May Alcott*, edited by Joel Myerson, Daniel Shealy, and Madeleine B. Stern, Little, Brown, 1987; U of Georgia P, 1995.
Bradford, Clare. "Ethel Turner." *Australian Literature 1788–1914*, edited by Selina Samuels, Gale, 2001, pp. 393–400.
Bradford, Clare. *Reading Race: Aboriginality in Australian Children's Literature*. Melbourne UP, 2001.
Bradford, Clare. "(Re)Constructing Australian Childhood: The Pound Collection at the State Library of Victoria, Australia." *The Lion and the Unicorn*, 22 Sept. 1988, pp. 327–37.
Carter, David, and Roger Osborne. *Australian Books and Authors in the American Marketplace 1840s–1940s*. U of Sydney P, 2018.
Clark, Beverly Lyon. *The Afterlife of "Little Women."* Johns Hopkins UP, 2014.
Clark, Beverly Lyon, editor. *Louisa May Alcott: The Critical Reception*. Cambridge UP, 2004.
"Current Literature," *Sydney Morning Herald*, 6 Oct. 1894, p. 4.
"Girl Favourites in Fiction," *Westminster Budget*, 1 Apr. 1904, p. 32.
Kerber, Linda. "The Republican Mother: Women and the Enlightenment—An American Perspective." *American Quarterly*, 28, summer 1976, pp. 87–205.
"My Birthday Party," *Girl's Realm*, Mar. 1903, p. 441.
Myerson, Joel, and Daniel Shealy. "The Sales of Louisa May Alcott's Books." *Harvard Library Bulletin*, n.s., 1, spring 1990, pp. 47–86.
Niall, Brenda. *Australia through the Looking-Glass: Children's Fiction 1830–1980*. Melbourne UP, 1984.
Niall, Brenda. *Seven Little Billabongs: The World of Ethel Turner and Mary Grant Bruce*. Melbourne UP, 1979.
Review of *Little Women*, by Louisa May Alcott. *Graphic*, 26 Nov. 1870.
Review of *Little Women*, by Louisa May Alcott. *Ladies' Repository* [Cincinnati], Nov. 1868.
Review of *Little Women*, by Louisa May Alcott. *Publishers' Circular and Booksellers' Record*, no. 1472, 15 Sept. 1894, p. 272.
Review of *Little Women*, by Louisa May Alcott. *Zion's Herald*, 20 May 1869.
Review of *Seven Little Australians*, by Ethel Turner. *Detroit Free Press*, qtd. in advertising circular inserted at the beginning of *The American Church Almanac and Year Book for 1895*. New York: James Pott, 1895, p. xxxix.
Rioux, Anne Boyd. *Meg, Jo, Beth, Amy: The Story of "Little Women" and Why It Still Matters*. W. W. Norton, 2018.
Saxby, Maurice. *Offered to Children: A History of Australian Children's Literature 1841–1941*. Scholastic, 1998.
Shealy, Daniel. "'Wedding Marches': Louisa May Alcott, Marriage, and the Newness of *Little Women*." *Women's Studies*, vol. 48, no. 4, 2019, pp. 366–78.
"Trouble in Australia," *New York Times*, 9 Sept. 1894.
Turner, Ethel. "Dedicatory Letter. To My Sister Lilian." *The Camp at Wandinong*, by Turner, Ward, Lock, 1898, 7.
Turner, Ethel. *Diaries of Ethel Turner*, edited by Philippa Poole, Collins, 1987.
Turner, Ethel. *Seven Little Australians*. Ward, Lock, 1912.
Turner, Ethel. *Seven Little Australians*, edited by Philippa Poole, National Library of Australia, 2005.

LOUISA MAY ALCOTT, MAJOR AUTHOR
Little Women and Beyond

GREGORY EISELEIN

INTRODUCTION: LITERARY JUDGMENTS AND ROCK 'N' ROLL

In 2018 for the first time, historically significant songs, not just artists, were honored in the Rock & Roll Hall of Fame. The 1963 version of "Louie Louie," for instance, was enshrined in the Rock Hall in 2018 for its influence on garage rock, which is cool for the Kingsmen, who are not otherwise getting in. Their second most significant work is either their "Jolly Green Giant" (1965) novelty song or their cameo in an Annette Funicello movie, *How to Stuff a Wild Bikini* (1965; Graff; Deming). Likewise, in 2019, "Tequila" (1958) also earned a spot in the Rock Hall, and while it is clearly significant as one of the first rock 'n' roll songs to use Latin rhythms, it is perhaps more famous now for its association with *Pee-wee's Big Adventure* (1985), where Pee-wee Herman dances to it inside a biker bar, than its association with the Champs, who released it as the B side of their "Train to Nowhere" single (Haidet; Ruhlmann).

While the move to include significant songs has given the Rock Hall another way to preserve music history, the museum leadership has emphasized that these singles aren't actually being "inducted" into the Hall of Fame in the same way that a Chuck Berry or Roxy Music have been (Smith).

Instead, the singles category is a way to acknowledge an important popular song without having to induct the artist. If there had been such a category before 2018, perhaps songs like "I Only Have Eyes for You" (1959) or "Why Do Fools Fall in Love?" (1955) would have been included in the Rock Hall rather than their lesser-known performers, the Flamingos and Frankie Lymon and the Teenagers. In both cases, the songs endure, though neither artist has the body of work or renown of a typical inductee ("Flamingos"; "Frankie").

The Rock & Roll Hall of Fame is a prominent example of a cultural institution that preserves the history of a cultural form in terms of its major artists and in terms of culturally relevant instances of the art. The process generates controversies about who is in, who should be in, and who made it but should not have. This conversation promotes the history of rock 'n' roll and in doing so preserves this history for fans and successive generations. And the museum and its many projects help draw attention to artists like Little Richard and Van Morrison and Patti Smith for those who may not have heard their music when first released.

Literary historians perform a similar cultural function. The uses of literary criticism are manifold, of course, and I don't mean to suggest that cultural preservation or the introduction of new audiences to significant works and artists of the past are the only important functions of literary scholarship. Arguments about importance, significance, excellence, impact, greatness, and value are, moreover, ever-changing controversies that reflect the cultural educations and social biases of those doing the arguing. The situated nature of these perspectives should be acknowledged and fed back into those arguments about excellence, impact, and value. Yet, it is often in these controversies and at the boundaries of these ever-shifting debates that the critical conversation becomes most perceptive and stimulating. Such arguments are, moreover, always already a part of a mission to preserve and educate—to preserve by noting and recording what's critical to our cultural history and to educate by introducing new audiences to some extraordinary aesthetic experiences. In doing so, literary critics identify extraordinary artists and memorable moments generated by minor artists.

Identifying major artists and minor ones, and historically or aesthetically significant works by minor artists, is an imprecise sort of criticism that tries to identify artists with a large, extraordinary, and significant body of work. The project of identifying major and minor artists—Bob Dylan versus the Kingsmen, Toni Morrison versus Samuel Woodworth ("The Old Oaken

Bucket")—doesn't let a specific reader know in advance which individual texts will please them most. Such a critical project only identifies artists that have been beloved by more than one generation and regarded as significant and influential by scholars, critics, or those in the field. They help those new to a genre know where they might want to start or what they should try to get to before they die. They help those who are experienced know whose work might be profitably and pleasurably explored in depth, beyond a single text, or whose body of work might be explored with more pleasure or satisfaction or joy than disappointment.

In this essay, I would like to make the case for defining Louisa May Alcott as a major author, as an artist with a significant, substantial, and excellent body of work and not merely as the writer behind one fondly remembered book. Her career, I think it can be shown, is *not* like the Kingsmen's career. If there were a literary hall of fame, Alcott should be in it.

Even some of the theorists and critics most responsible for creating the academic situation for revaluing Alcott's texts have overlooked the possibility that she might be a major author. Let me examine two brief examples, both theorists whom I admire and respect deeply. In the late 1980s and early 1990s, Jane Tompkins and Catharine Stimpson powerfully shaped our ideas about what ought to be taught in US literature classes and why. They are important to my own intellectual development and to the history of literary theory. Tompkins's *Sensational Designs* (1985) drew attention to the historical significance and cultural work of women writers. Stimpson, the founding editor of *Signs*, made multiple contributions to feminist theory and literary studies, but she might be most famous among Alcott scholars for her 1990 article on "Reading for Love," where she introduced the notion of a "paracanon" of books that are beloved, books that should be read and studied and valued because they were deeply loved. She uses *Little Women* (1868–69) as her chief example, and it serves her purposes well. I am grateful to Stimpson not only for her insights into Alcott but also for her efforts to use "the concept of the paracanon [to reclaim] love and pleasure for criticism" (962).

As field defining as their work has been, it is time to rethink the ways we use their theories or similar ones to justify the teaching of Alcott or to explain the value of her writings. These arguments, once very important, are perhaps no longer doing justice to Alcott. Even though *Little Women is* a much beloved text, the affection that readers have had for it is only one of many reasons to admire the book. It is more appropriate now to acknowledge that *Little Women* is a canonical text, not a merely paracanonical one. It is also time to move beyond Tompkins's work, which values women's texts for the cultural work they did during their era. I feel as if her assumption is that aesthetic analysis of Alcott's books might show that they are perhaps artistically embarrassing, which is not the case.

Alcott is remarkable for her texts' cultural work in their era, but she is also worthy of attention for artistic reasons that deserve more than slighting attention. Moreover, her work is as vital to us now as it was in the 1860s. In what follows, I want to outline the case for thinking of Alcott as a major author, as someone to be read, remembered, and studied not for just one masterpiece, *Little Women*, but for her whole complex and varied career of work. She is a writer with a large and sometimes remarkable body of work, one whom all kinds of readers might want to know and whose career might be explored with interest and pleasure, and the kind of writer who might be taught in a university-level course devoted to one extraordinary author with a large, varied, and significant body of work.

The Case for Treating Alcott as a Major Author

Definitions of what constitutes a major author vary. Some critics, like Christopher Ricks, have argued that the terms "major" and "minor" are not especially illuminating. Some have poked fun at the critical effort, as in E. B. White's hilarious "How to Tell a Major Poet from a Minor Poet" (1930, 23–24). And some, such as Jay B. Hubbell in *Who Are the Major American Writers* (1972), have ventured into the project of valuing and ranking authors without much explicit consideration of what constituted a major or minor author. Other critics have provided some ideas or criteria, but often the designation of a writer as a major author proceeds from a kind of metajudgment, an analysis or synthesis of other previous critical judgments. For example, T. S. Eliot wants, it seems, to emphasize the role of genuineness but leave final judgments about greatness to "Time" (16). David Hume similarly acknowledges the role that time plays, noting that we should perhaps not examine "each particular beauty" in a work of literature or art but instead "the durable admiration, which attends those works, that have survived all the caprices of mode and fashion" (271). Other critics and writers have noted the importance of range, originality, and technique. Pragmatically, the definition perhaps most often in play is an institutional one. From this perspective, a major author is simply a writer who typically gets taught as a major author in secondary schools, colleges, and universities. This idea is reminiscent of Arthur Danto's theory of art, which emphasizes that art cannot be understood or defined apart from its context within the social institutions of art (theories, museums, schools and education, the art market, etc.); "to see something as art requires something the eye cannot decry—an atmosphere of artistic theory, a knowledge of the history of art: an artworld" (580). Likewise, then, perhaps the notion of a major author cannot be adequately explained as anything beyond those writers who are treated as major authors by schools, universities, professors, writers, bookstores, and so on. This changes over time, of course, as can be documented by a look at course curricula, trends in criticism, or college textbooks and anthologies.

Still, it's worth pondering what makes the literary world embrace any specific writer as a major author. I would like to suggest that the following five criteria or conditions would help us determine who we might want to consider a major author.

1. A major author is canonical.
2. There exists a substantial body of criticism about a major author.
3. A major author has had a noteworthy influence on literary history and a reputation that endures beyond their own generation or century or period.
4. A major author has a sizable and varied body of writing.
5. The works of a major author, or at least some of them, have been deemed by those in the literary world as artistically excellent or aesthetically important, even if the criteria for that artistic excellent varies over time.

I realize that there are other criteria to consider. In ways utterly consistent with Modernist standards, W. H. Auden, for example, proposes "an unmistakable originality of vision and style" (16). I have elected to blend Auden's consideration into my ideas about influence (my third criterion above) and aesthetics (my fifth) and not separate it out. And my first measure, canonicity, is mostly tautological and not really generative of new knowledge, but I include it briefly to emphasize the role of metajudgments in identifying major authors. The next three criteria tell us a bit more about those features of a writer's career and critical reputation that make them major authors. The fifth and final category is perhaps the most subjective and most dependent on critics' judgments or on accounts of subjective aesthetic engagements with that author's texts.

All five of these measures identify Louisa May Alcott as a major author, even if some additional critical work needs to be done in terms of the fifth category, and I will take up each criterion in order and devote the most attention to the fifth element.

(1) *Canonicity*. Although returning to a discussion of a literary "canon" may feel like a flashback to the culture wars, one of the central insights from the theorization of the literary canon during the 1990s was that canons are hardly stable or immune from the power dynamics and cultural changes of their social worlds. Canons are expressions of those social power relationships, and their ever-changing constitutions could never be separated from the cultural changes that shape those canons. In what is perhaps the most important theorization of the idea of literary canon formation, *Cultural Capital* (1993), John Guillory reminds us that we never really get away from canons. Instead, we constantly reshape them, and schools play a key role: "Every construction of a syllabus *institutes* once again the process of canon formation" (31). Moreover, canon debates are really interesting sites of cultural struggle and illuminating pieces of evidence about cultural historical change. These debates can often be heated (the culture wars of the 1990s, for example), and they can sometimes be entertaining (the perennial debates related to halls of fame, for example). But as I suggested in the opening discussion about the Rock & Roll Hall of Fame, critically self-aware engagements in such conversations can play an important role in education by helping us to identify the cultural values in play, by spurring us to preserve important artifacts or texts in our cultural history, and by introducing new audiences to extraordinary aesthetic experiences.

While literary scholars do not have church councils or an exact equivalent for the Rock & Roll Hall of Fame to adjudicate issues of canonicity, the field does have ever-evolving anthologies of US literature and classic book series, which seem to function, unofficially and without consensus, as the barometers that indicate who is in the canon. According to the major author criteria that I have suggested, the late 1980s and early 1990s are the moment when Alcott became a major author, which is also when her work was embraced in major US literature anthologies: the second edition of *The Norton Anthology of American Literature* (Baym 1985) and *The Heath Anthology of American Literature* (Lauter 1990). Since then her work has been included in several canon-defining literary series, such as the Norton Critical Editions (Alcott, *Little Women* 2004) and the Library of America series (Cheever 2014; Showalter 2005). Alcott's masterpiece *Little Women* has also been lavished with critical attention and canonical confirmation in the form of two prestigious annotated editions (Matteson, *Annotated* 2015; Shealy, *Little Women* 2013). And Alcott's life and complete career, not just her one famous work, has been the subject of several biographies, including a PBS American Masters documentary, *Louisa May Alcott: The Woman behind "Little Women"* (Porter 2008). These types of inclusion are not pure proofs of canonicity, and her place in the canon may still be debated, but they might be the closest thing to corroborating or proxy evidence we have.

(2) *Criticism.* The 1990s is also the decade in which scholarly criticism on Alcott balloons. According to the *MLA International Bibliography*, the 1990s produced about 150 journal articles, monographs, or other scholarly resources devoted to Alcott, more than all previous decades combined. In the two subsequent decades, critical attention to Alcott has continued to expand steadily. There is now, without question, a substantial body of criticism and scholarly work devoted to Alcott. We should also take note of the truly excellent scholarly and critical work produced since then. To mention just a few examples: Beverly Lyon Clark's *The Afterlife of "Little Women"* (2014), Shealy's annotated edition of *Little Women* (2013), Eve LaPlante's edition of the *Writings of Abigail May Alcott* (2012), Richard Francis's *Fruitlands* (2010), and John Matteson's Pulitzer Prize-winning *Eden's Outcasts* (2007). This recent work is dependent on the scholarly editions of her letters and journals edited by Shealy, Myerson, and Stern in the late 1980s, and it is clearly informed by feminist criticism from the 1970s and early 1980s—essays by Nina Auerbach (1976), Judith Fetterley (1979, 1983), and Elizabeth Keyser (1982), among several others, come to mind.

Alcott's work also receives a remarkable amount of commentary and critical attention in important nonacademic or nonscholarly venues. During the 150th anniversary celebration of the publication of *Little Women*, for example, a host of newspapers and magazines ran stories on the novel, the author, and the sharp uptick in TV, film, and book adaptations. A quick search of Google News for 2018–19 produces hundreds of results, from the *New York Times* and the *Washington Post* to *Vanity Fair* and the *New Yorker*, among seemingly countless others. Moreover, Alcott has become a popular topic in a range of distinctively twenty-first-century venues, including Twitter accounts, listservs, podcasts, Facebook groups ("Louisa May Alcott: A Group for Fans,

Readers, & Scholars," to mention one), and blogs (Susan Bailey's rich "Louisa May Alcott Is My Passion," for example), among others.

It might be possible to date the explosion of Alcott criticism to an earlier moment. Clark, for example, uses the 1960s as her chronological marker, noting that "since 1960 scholarship addressing *Little Women* has exploded—by one measure more than a hundredfold" (*Afterlife* 198). Still, taking into account the important critical work that paved the way, the sheer quantity and range of critical work, both peer-reviewed academic work and popular criticism and commentary, on Alcott from the 1990s on is markedly different than what was available earlier.

(3) *Influence*. *Little Women* has left a distinct mark on literary history. Since its initial publication, it has been much loved and much imitated. *Little Women* and its successors such as *Little Men* (1871) and *Jo's Boys* (1886), but also her other novels for children such as *Eight Cousins* (1875) or *Rose in Bloom* (1876), introduced a powerful if typically ordinary realism into not only the subsequent history of children's literature but also the history of literary realism in the late nineteenth century. By writing *Little Women*, Alcott provided us one of the urstories of US literature—this one about four young women with divergent personalities and talents whose interactions with each other help them discover who they are and who they want to become—that has been a model for many others. Recent examples that come to mind are *The Poisonwood Bible* (1998), *The Penderwicks* (2005), and the HBO series *Girls* (2012–17). I won't rehearse the long list of leaders, thinkers, and writers who have acknowledged Alcott's influence (see instead Clark, *Afterlife* and Rioux), except to quote the author of the Harry Potter series, J. K. Rowling: "My favorite literary heroine is Jo March. It is hard to overstate what she meant to a small, plain girl called Jo, who had a hot temper and a burning ambition to be a writer" (BR8). It's equally hard to imagine Hermione Granger without first a Jo March.

This enduring influence of *Little Women* on US and even world culture from its initial publication to the present has been well documented by Clark's *The Afterlife of "Little Women"* (2014) and Anne Boyd Rioux's *Meg, Jo, Beth, Amy: The Story of "Little Women" and Why It Still Matters* (2018). Both Rioux and Clark worry, however, about the book's imminent and possible disappearance from childhood reading practices and popular culture. Rioux notes the book's disappearance from classrooms and schools: "*Little Women*, it turns out, is barely on teachers' and students' radars" (161). She also reveals the deeply sexist but widespread assumptions among teachers, school librarians, families, and young readers that *Little Women* is not a book for boys but for girls only. Rioux challenges those assumptions powerfully, of course, and notes the many male readers who have embraced the book. She also outlines the moral reasons boys and men should also be reading the novel, quoting at one point Jane Roland Martin: "Given that the ability to take the point of view of another is a basic element of morality itself, it is unconscionable—I would say positively immoral—to deprive them of the opportunity of identifying with the other half of humanity" (qtd. in Rioux 179). In *Kiddie Lit*, Clark wonders if Alcott's growing acceptance within academic circles and university classrooms isn't related to a decline in interest among young readers. Clark notes, "Anecdotal evidence suggests that she does not have the same riveting appeal for young women now in their teens and twenties as she had for their predecessors, that fewer young women now would say, with Anna Quindlen, '*Little Women* changed my life'" (126). While such a trend may be disheartening for some, Clark convincingly shows that Alcott's place within the literary canon and university curriculum has improved dramatically over the past three decades (see *Kiddie Lit* 122–27). Moreover, there seems to be ample evidence that even if the nature of *Little Women*'s place in US culture may be changing or evolving in unexpected ways, away from a children's literature classic commonly read by children, the novel continues to inspire readers, remakes, and new versions of Alcott's original urstory, as a recent special issue of *Women's Studies*, "The Newness of *Little Women*," documents in part. *Little Women* continues to appear on best-books-ever lists: in a 2014 list published by the *Atlantic* (Meyer), for example, or, more recently, scoring a top ten position in PBS's "The Great American Read." Moreover, as the mash-up craze of 2009–10 with books like *Little Vampire Women* and *Little Women and Werewolves* (see Daly-Galeano) or the rush of recent film remakes (Vanessa Caswill's 2017 BBC miniseries, Clare Niederpruem's 2018 *Little Women* film with its modernized version of the story, Greta Gerwig's 2019 feature film) all seem to suggest, *Little Women*'s place in popular reading and the popular imagination isn't so much disappearing as changing and perhaps growing.

(4) *Body of work*. *Little Women* is clearly Alcott's masterpiece. It is her longest and most complex work, the one that altered her career and the history of young adult literature forever after, and her most famous, most reprinted, most translated, and most studied work. Without the literary historical event that is *Little Women*, it is difficult to imagine even wondering whether or not Alcott is a major author. Nevertheless, including but beyond *Little Women*,

it is clear that Alcott has a large, varied, and aesthetically interesting body of writing across genres, styles, and decades. A nonexhaustive overview of her four-decade oeuvre summarizes this range:

- The seven young adult novels published by Roberts Brothers in the "Little Women" series from 1868 to 1886: *Little Women, An Old-Fashioned Girl, Little Men, Eight Cousins, Rose in Bloom, Jack and Jill,* and *Jo's Boys*
- The scores of stories published in periodicals but also often collected and reprinted in the *Aunt Jo's Scrap-Bag* series (six volumes from 1872 to 1882), the *Lulu's Library* series (three volumes from 1886 to 1889), or in individual story volumes like *Spinning-Wheel Stories* (1884) and *A Garland for Girls* (1889), among others
- The more than three dozen fairy tales and fantasy stories (Shealy's *Louisa May Alcott's Fairy Tales and Fantasy Stories* [1992] is the outstanding scholarly collection of Alcott's work in this genre)
- The two novels for adult audiences—one written in a transcendentalist mode, *Moods* (1864, revised 1882), and the other in a realist mode, *Work* (1873)
- The poetry, which she wrote throughout her life (nicely assembled in the Ironweed edition of *The Poems of Louisa May Alcott* [2000])
- The enormous variety of nonfiction, including her sketches, feminist essays, and autobiographical work, including the career-changing *Hospital Sketches* from 1863 (also collected in an Ironweed edition, *The Sketches of Louisa May Alcott* [2001])
- Her juvenilia, which would include, among other texts, the plays she wrote with her sister Anna (who collected and edited them in *Comic Tragedies* [1893]), her first published short stories ("The Rival Painters" [1852] and "The Rival Prima Donnas" [1854]), and her first novel (*The Inheritance*, written when she was seventeen but not published until 1997)
- Her very funny travel writings—such as "Letters from the Mountains" (1863), or "Up the Rhine" (1867), or *Shawl-Straps* (1872), among others
- The novel-length melodramatic romances—*The Long Fatal Love Chase* (written in 1866 but not published until 1995), *Behind a Mask* (1866), and *A Modern Mephistopheles* (1877)

- And, of course, the thirty or so shorter thrillers or sensation stories she wrote in the 1860s (Stern's *Louisa May Alcott Unmasked: Collected Thrillers* [1995] is the most comprehensive collection of Alcott's work in this style)

In other words, Alcott wrote a lot, which is Auden's first criterion for a major author (15). She demonstrated considerable range, from thrillers to domestic and nondomestic realisms, from autobiographical satire to sentimental poems and stories and novels, from fairy tales and fantasy stories to dark gothic sensation tales, from drama to creative nonfiction and participant observer sketches, to travel writing and political commentaries, and so much more. I think it's Madeleine Stern and Leona Rostenberg's groundbreaking research on the thrillers in the 1940s that established the fact that Alcott was a writer with stylistic range (see Rostenberg). But Showalter's editing work in her *Alternative Alcott* anthology (1988) and Keyser's fascinating and brilliant *Whispers in the Dark* (1993) helped cement in the late 1980s and early 1990s our understanding of the dark and experimental range of Alcott's writings across her career. In other words, though we knew about Alcott's body of work for decades, the late 1980s and early 1990s again appears to be the moment when, within our academic practices, Alcott becomes a major author.

(5) *Aesthetic value*. Part of the case for a major author ought to include analysis and appreciation of the author's writings in terms of their artistic, formal, and aesthetic merit. The complexity and nuance of a masterpiece like *Little Women* is not often explicitly acknowledged. Yet since at least the 1960s, critics have continued to find new ways of interpreting and appreciating this novel from a variety of new critical and theoretical vantages, opening new ways of seeing and experiencing the text. This suggests, I would argue, that *Little Women* offers the kind of rich and nuanced aesthetic experience that "resonates" across generations and across time (to invoke Wai Chee Dimock's concept from her "Theory of Resonance").

Critical work on Alcott tends to be historical, though some critics have explicitly brought aesthetic concerns to bear on *Little Women* and other texts or incorporated those concerns into an otherwise historical approach. Monika Elbert's critical work has drawn important attention to Alcott's strategic and imaginative use of gothic and theatrical conventions ("Divas") and elsewhere highlighted the aesthetics of poverty in Alcott's Christmas stories ("Charitable"). I have argued that Alcott's modernity (Eiselein, "Modernity") and her use of contradiction and paradox (Eiselein, "Contradiction") are important elements of her aesthetic. Some critics have examined her masterly use of realism (Griffis; Rioux 135–45) and sentimentalism (Eiselein, "Sentimental"; Hendler; Proehl), while other have noted the influence of German Romantic and transcendentalist aesthetics (Doyle; Rigsby; Walls). Moreover, numerous scholars have noted or explored Alcott's thematic use of art or her depiction of artists, from her earliest published story ("The Rival Painters") to her thrillers ("A Marble Woman" [1865]) to her depictions of groups of female artists in *Little Women* (Meg, Jo, Beth, and Amy each have their own artistic gift) or *An Old-Fashioned Girl* (1870; in chap. 13, "The Sunny Side"), and much more ("Psyche's Art" [1868] or the unfinished "Diana and Persis" [first published 1978], for example).

Nevertheless, the aesthetic aspects of Alcott's works have been undervalued, and her place in the history of literary aesthetics and her works' connections to the work of other great writers have been understudied. I think there are some key reasons for this lack of attention, such as the dominant historical emphasis within US literary criticism and also perhaps the (misguided) sense that Alcott was not so great artistically. James Baldwin, for example, famously lumps together *Little Women* and *Uncle Tom's Cabin* (1852) as examples of "very bad" novels that deploy sentimentality, which he defines as "the ostentatious parading of excessive and spurious emotion" (579). To redress this gap in a small way but to also illustrate how not only *Little Women* but also Alcott's lesser-studied texts lend themselves to both an aesthetic analysis and a placement in a history of literary aesthetics, I would like to examine in detail Alcott's artistically significant use of contraries, which she learned partly from Charles Dickens but creatively adapted to her own varied uses throughout her career. My first four criterion for major author status can be empirically demonstrated. This fifth and final measure is an interpretive judgment and a clear example of where more work on Alcott needs to be done. For those reasons, I will explore this aspect of Alcott's work in further detail in the following section.

Alcott's Aesthetic: Dickens and Contraries

Alcott's writings disclose a deep attachment to Dickens and an extensive familiarity with his work, from *Sketches by Boz* (1836) to *Edwin Drood* (1870). There are numerous examples in *Little Women*, for instance: the March girls' secret society and their newspaper, "The Pickwick Portfolio" (85), or the comparison of Amy's schoolmaster to Dr. Blimber from *Dombey and Son* (1848; 8). Previous critics have noted this intertextual debt. The *Biographical Dictionary of Literary Influences*, for example, acknowledges that Dickens is the most important influence on Alcott, and it cites her frequent allusions to *Oliver Twist* (1839), *Dombey and Son*, *David Copperfield* (1850), *Bleak House* (1853), and *The Pickwick Papers* (1837; Casper 17). Still, few critics have studied carefully the connection between the two writers, and no one has systematically examined Alcott's use of Dickens. Her first biographer Ednah Cheney says, "She was a great admirer of Dickens's writings ... although she has never imitated him" (396). The statement is true, but Cheney goes no further to examine the connections. Others have acknowledged Dickens's influence but sought to separate Alcott from the dark or sordid elements in his books. Caroline Dall writes in her review of *Eight Cousins* (1875), "It is very like what Charles Dickens did, except that she seldom carries us into the company of squalor, filth, and crime, as he too often did" (Clark, "Eight Cousins" 244). Despite the attempts to downplay the relationship, I think it would be fair to say that most scholars would readily allow that Dickens had a significant impact on Alcott's work, though the subject remains surprisingly underexamined.

To redress this gap in our understanding of Alcott and draw attention to noteworthy aesthetic elements in her work and her place in a history of literary aesthetics, I would like to outline what I see as a key but overlooked lesson Alcott gleaned from reading Dickens. She learned from his works how to use contraries as her chief stylistic and structural principle, how to combine or yoke together apparent opposites for sentimental, comic, dramatic, or intellectual effect. From him, she learned how to render, to quote from *Hospital Sketches*, the "darkness made visible" (22).

Dickens is an artist who mastered the use of contraries to create vivid scenes and unforgettable characters. As the narrator of *The Old Curiosity Shop* (1841) tells us, "Everything in our lives, whether of good or evil, affects us most by contrast" (399). While he used contraries in different ways—highlighted differences, contradictions, complements, contrasts, oppositions, and so forth—I want to examine just two important types of Dickensian contraries.

The first is juxtaposition, where he takes two very different things and places them side by side or in the same setting. For instance, in chapter 11 of *The Old Curiosity Shop*, Dickens puts the brutal and disgusting Daniel Quilp—the novel's villain who creepily proposes to marry fourteen-year-old

Little Nell "when Mrs. Quilp the first is dead" (43)—in the bed of the pretty and innocent Little Nell. Just after she hurries herself out of her bedroom, Quilp decides, "The bedstead is much about my size. I think I shall make it *my* little room." He then takes over Nell's bed "by throwing himself on his back upon the bed with his pipe in his mouth, and then kicking up his legs and smoking violently" (86–87). The scene's placement of Quilp in Nell's bedroom is part of the novel's overt melodrama. Yet the scene also joins together the middle-aged dwarf and the undersized child in terms of their similar stature. Dickens's main point may not be to emphasize their similarity or even their differences, but instead to surprise us with a rather bizarre image of innocence and degeneracy, malice and kindness.

While such an example highlights synchronous juxtaposition, Dickens also uses sequential juxtaposition in his organization of chapters. For instance, the chapters narrating the deaths of Nell (chap. 71) and Quilp (chap. 72) appear one after the other in the same installment (30 Jan. 1841). In *David Copperfield*, the chapter (chap. 8) that narrates one of the happiest days of David's life—an afternoon he spent with his mother, Peggoty, and his new baby half brother—is quickly followed by a chapter (chap. 9) on an equally "memorable" (110) day, when he learns of his mother's death. The sharp contrasts between chapters emphasize differences (good/evil, joy/sadness) as well as similarities (death, mother), but the purpose of the juxtaposition seems to me to be more affective and aesthetic than thematic or moral.

Perhaps even more interesting than his use of juxtaposition is Dickens's deployment of contradiction, a literary form that holds together opposites. Consider David Copperfield, for instance, a character defined in terms of his "strong powers of observation" (136). Yet he is also utterly clueless about James Steerforth's selfish, manipulative, and destructive behavior, just as he seems to have no way of seeing how mismatched he and Dora Spenlow are. In *Dombey and Son*, Paul Dombey the son is young (a child, the son, and his small size emphasizes his youth) but usually described as "old" or "old-fashioned" (76). Such contradictions abound in Dickens but not just in the characters. Knitting—a productive, creative practice with generally pleasant and domestic associations—becomes in *A Tale of Two Cities* (1859) an image of destruction, vengeance, and revolution. A humorous catchphrase like "Barkis is willin'" also serves as Barkis's last words (378); thus, the very sentence that has prompted so much laughter throughout the first half of *David Copperfield* now elicits tears.

Dickens's influence on Alcott can be seen in most of her work, including, for example, her quasiautobiographical narrative of life as a Union nurse, *Hospital Sketches*. The title connects her to Dickens's first book, *Sketches by Boz*, and to their use of the same literary form, the sketch. The name of the book's protagonist—Tribulation Periwinkle—is another overt nod to Dickens. The name suggests a combination of travail and good humor. The blue periwinkle flower is a symbol of friendship (as opposed to romance), a reminder perhaps of the heroine's happily unmarried status. I hear "wink" in her last name, a gesture perhaps that this solemn business of nursing the war wounded is perhaps not always so serious or a sign that she is letting us in on her inside joke about her service as a nurse. I love this name not only because the apocalyptically miserable first name is usually shortened to a cute nickname, Trib, but also because Alcott has deliberately joined the superserious Tribulation to the lighthearted Periwinkle, bringing together the earnest and comic opposites that define our protagonist.

Beyond genre and character naming, *Hospital Sketches* discloses its debt to Dickens with three overt references to Sarah or Sairey Gamp (2, 33, 46)—the disheveled nurse who enjoys snuff, spirits, and drinking toasts in *Martin Chuzzlewit* (1844)—including the book's epigraph, which quotes "Sairy Gamp" [sic] as saying, "Which, naming no names, no offence could be took" (2). Alcott also alludes to *The Pickwick Papers* and *Bleak House* and even mentions Dickens himself, whom she refers to as "the god of my idolatry, though he does wear too much jewelry and talk slang" (94). Moreover, this narrative, like *Little Women* and *The Old Curiosity Shop*, has a beautiful deathbed scene, though the innocent soul who bravely faces death here is not a Little Nell or Beth, the shyest of the four little women, but instead a large and masculine, bearded soldier named John, "the brave Virginia blacksmith" (65)—an interesting but characteristically Alcott-like gender twist on the Dickensian deathbed scene.

Nevertheless, the Dickensian technique that is most important to the style and structure of *Hospital Sketches* is contraries. For instance, Alcott juxtaposes the "Day" chapter with the "Night" chapter, and our narrator tells us, "Curious contrasts of the tragic and comic met one everywhere" (40) in this army hospital known as Hurly-Burly House (another Dickensianism) that makes Trib both a nurse and a patient (another pulling together of opposites to define a single character). In fact, Alcott saturates the narrative with all kinds of contraries like these. In chapter 4, to focus on just one example, "Night," Trib is on duty when "a certain Pennsylvania gentleman," who had a leg amputated and had been suffering with a "wound-fever," goes on "a drunken campaign and hops over to salute her, touching the military cap which formed a striking contrast to the severe simplicity of the rest of his decidedly *undress* uniform" (51). She describes him:

> balancing himself on one leg, like a meditative stork. . . . scantily draped in white, its one foot covered with a big blue sock, a dingy cap set rakingly askew on its shaven head, and placid satisfaction beaming in its broad red face, as it flourished a mug in one hand, an old boot in the other, calling them canteen and knapsack, while it skipped and fluttered in the most unearthly fashion. (52)

While her description of the drunk solider from Pennsylvania is meant to get a laugh, Alcott ends this same paragraph with a heart-wrenching visit to the side of a twelve-year-old "drummer boy," Teddy, who is sobbing in his bed. The injured Teddy had been saved by Kit, another wounded soldier at the Battle of Fredericksburg. By the time they arrived at the hospital, Kit has died. And now Teddy, waking from a dream that Kit was still alive, weeps inconsolably and imagines himself responsible for Kit's death: "Oh! if I'd only been as thin when Kit carried me as I am now, maybe he wouldn't have died; but I was heavy, he was hurt worser than we knew, and so it killed him; and I didn't see him, to say good bye" (53–54). I wonder about the level of taste in Alcott's decision to caricature the drunken, one-legged soldier and to put his "supremely ridiculous" (52) figure alongside the image of a wounded boy "sobbing" in his bed and "pining" for a dead friend who saved his life (53). On the other hand, such a juxtaposition of the grotesque with the sentimental seems to me to be a characteristically Dickensian maneuver.

Alcott's novel *Work* is also replete with signs of Dickens's influence. The novel has a supremely reasonable female protagonist, who reminds us of Agnes Wickfield from *David Copperfield*, and an array of minor, comic characters, who speak dialect. The novel's themes seem pretty Dickensian—the difficulty of selecting a suitable romantic partner, the world of work, the contrast of urban and rural settings, fallen women, hidden identities, suicide, the hypocrisy of the affluent classes, theater, and the catastrophic nature of economic hardship. There are two direct references to Dickens, including the theatrical adaptations of Dickens in which Christie performs, and multiple allusions to his novels, including *Martin Chuzzlewit*.

Still, it is the contraries that make *Work* an interesting example of Alcott's distinctive reformulation of Dickens's technique. A novel about the relationship of the self to others, *Work* is the story of a young woman who leaves home to find herself, her independence, and her vocation. In the process of searching for "independence and self-culture" (10), Christie spirals downward through a succession of jobs until she ends up as a seamstress in a large sweatshop overseen by Mrs. King and Miss Cotton. In the antebellum moment depicted in this novel, these names signify in a Dickensian manner the tyrannical nature of this shop and their affiliation with the enslavement of African peoples in the South. King and Cotton conspire to publicly reveal that Christie's girlfriend, Rachel, is a fallen woman, whom they then fire. In the process, Christie loses her girlfriend, quits her job, and experiences "the saddest [year] [she] had ever known" (115). "Her heart was empty" (115), and she considered herself "a failure after all" (119). She begins to regret her attempt to find herself and her independence, prompting her to wish that she has "stayed with Aunt Betsey or married Joe" (119). Joe is "rough Joe Butterfield" (208), her first heterosexual suitor, whom she considers marrying at one point "in sheer desperation" (13). Things get so bad, so lonely, so pointless, Christie contemplates suicide (124–25). Thus, it seems that in the process of trying to find herself, she utterly loses her sense of self to the point that she is planning self-destruction. In the second half of *Work*, we see the opposite movement. Christie finds her sense of purpose and self by abandoning herself to feelings of "self-sacrifice" (279) and the work of helping others—at first the Sterling family, then her daughter Ruth, then the newly emancipated "Freed people" (327), and finally the cause of working women, in the rousing and radical final chapter (chap. 20).

Numerous other contraries also proliferate. There are juxtapositions, such as the placement of Christie's joy about her relationship with Rachel (103–6) right up against the loss of Rachel (chap. 6.) and Christie's subsequent depression and near suicide (chap. 7). There are also a number of contradictions. For instance, although love and work function as oppositions in this novel (in the opening chapter, she rejects marriage in order to pursue work, for example), the novel repeatedly sees the workplace as the context, occasion, or situation for romance to grow: Phillip Fletcher falls in love with Christie, when she is working as a governess (chap. 4); the sweatshop is where Christie and Rachel meet and fall in love (chap. 6); and in the gardens at Mrs. Sterling's place, work facilitates Christie's romance with David (chap. 11).

Examining Alcott's creative appropriation of Dickens's use of contraries can help us better understand the function of contraries in Alcott's work and the pervasive place of what we might call the dark side in Alcott's writings. Many readers and critics have a way of skipping over the "squalor, filth, and crime" in Alcott's work. Dickens's explorations of the dirty, disagreeable, destructive, and despicable aspects of society and human behavior are regularly acknowledged, much discussed, and frequently admired (by Fyodor Dostoevsky, for example; see Lary; MacPike). Yet Alcott's readers are often so eager to acknowledge the wholesomeness of her fiction that they overlook the dark, disordered, or unpleasant aspects, which she almost always joins directly to the delightful, the beautiful, and the good. I am not saying that we shouldn't admire Trib's desire to serve her country and heal the wounded, but we should also acknowledge her less noble motivations, as when she confesses, "Having a taste for 'ghastliness,' I . . . rather longed for the wounded to arrive" (32).

Critics who have studied the darker side of Alcott's writing and seen the "squalor, filth, and crime" there are usually drawn to her anonymously authored thrillers with their overtly violent, dark gothic elements. These critics have often tried to divide her career into what Ann Douglas calls Alcott's "double literary life" (vii). On the one hand, these critics argue, she cultivated a secret or hidden career represented by her adult thrillers filled with violence, insanity, sexual manipulation, and drug addiction. On the other hand, she had a well-known public career with wholesome transcendentalist narratives and popular domestic children's fiction. These critics often see the first as a more authentic Alcott and the second as a less original artist who had an unfortunate capitulation to market pressure.

An examination of Alcott's *Hospital Sketches* and *Work* (or *Little Women* or dozens of other texts by Alcott) in light of Dickens provides us with a different approach, a way of understanding how she does not so much alternate between the dark and the light or the sentimental and the gothic as consistently blend and juxtapose them. Alcott's artistic chiaroscuro reveals, then, not a schizophrenic sense of authorship but an ambivalent fascination with love *and* work, with violence *and* noble reform efforts designed to make the world better and more peaceful, with modernity *and* family, and with the complex mix of decent *and* corrupt motivations that motor so much human activity. Her use of contraries makes most of her literary work not only artistically interesting and dramatic but also complex and profound.

Teaching Alcott as a Major Author

The aesthetic study of Alcott's texts is far from finished, but I hope that my extended example of her use of contraries, in addition to the previous work on Alcott's aesthetics, suggests that her work can be reasonably considered artistically excellent and aesthetically important. Even if we consider the aesthetic examination of Alcott's work as in development, I think it is fair to say that it has become permissible this century, if not yet normal, to teach Alcott as a major author. I first taught Alcott in a major authors context in 2004 and then again in 2010 and 2013. In all three instances, I paired Alcott with Mark Twain, which became a way to scrutinize literary designations such as "classic," "popular," "best-selling," "canonical" and "noncanonical," "artistic," "trashy," "masterpiece," and so on. The course let us examine the parallel careers of Alcott and Twain from their early travel sketch writing to their autobiographical writings and most famous classic works. We read each author's darker and lesser-known writings, such as Alcott's early thrillers and Twain's scathing late essays. In 2018, Anne Phillips and I taught our university's major authors course as an Alcott-only class, an approach that allowed for additional attention to Alcott's incredibly rich cultural context and her enduing influence on US culture.

This teaching experience tells me, however, that arguments about who to consider a major author is not simply about canonicity, criticism, influence, oeuvre, and aesthetics. It must also be pedagogically pragmatic: What does the inclusion of Alcott within the major author course format allow one to teach and our students to learn? For me, the value in a major authors approach is the chance to see an author's life and body of work *comprehensively*. Students can read a wide range of an author's work, not just the famous masterpiece, and start to see how a writer's career emerges, develops, and evolves. But there is also in these courses the chance for exciting theoretical and historical comprehensiveness.

For example, in a major authors course, it is not just one or two theoretical approaches that can be taught, modeled, and encouraged, but a whole range of approaches. One student might write a psychoanalytic critique of *Rose in Bloom* and another a deconstruction of "Transcendental Wild Oats" (1873) and another a New Historical examination of "Marjorie's Birthday Gifts" (1876) and so on. Such critical pluralism is a way for the class to witness the complexity of an author's work and a way to allow students to invest themselves in the author and course, regardless of their interests, proclivities, or theoretical denominations.

The major authors course is also a great way to see to how an author's life and career intersect with literary, social, and cultural history. The author is this fascinating node that provides us with a way to see how earlier writers, events, and conditions shape, determine, and influence literary texts: How did German Idealism shape *Little Men*? The author as a node is also a way to understand how subsequent texts, trends, and events depend on an earlier author's work: What do we learn by studying the ways Alcott is the muse for *Sex in the City* (1998–2004)? Authors courses provide us with a way to study how cultural trends and contexts shape the authors' work: How did her family's involvement with the antislavery movement influence Alcott's writings? It is also a chance for students to see how writers shape their worlds: In what ways did Alcott contribute to the nineteenth-century women's movement or to subsequent developments in the feminist movement?

But, most of all, I think a major authors course is a way to open up new perspectives and new avenues for study. The study of a major author is a method for imagining new combinations, new insights, and the scholarly work that still needs to be done. Examining an author's body of work in context with other readers and students/scholars makes us see new things and revalue and reappreciate what we think we knew well. To use another rock 'n' roll analogy, one might think the Beatles' *Sgt. Pepper's* (1967) is the greatest album of all time, as *Rolling Stone* does ("500 Greatest"), until one listens to all of the Beatles' albums together and realizes that it's really probably their third or fourth best album. "Stairway to Heaven" might seem a likely candidate for one of the greatest rock songs ever, unless one listens to it in the context of the untitled *Led Zeppelin IV* (1971) and remembers that—awesome as it is—"Stairway to Heaven" is only the third best of the four songs on the A side of the album.

Conclusion: Alcott and the Twenty-First-Century Public Sphere

We should also teach and study Alcott as a major author because her work is more relevant to us now than ever. *Little Women* and Alcott's writings in general are often considered material for nostalgic longing, and nostalgia no doubt plays a role in her enduring popularity. But Alcott's work matters now not because of its glimpse into an unrecoverable past but because of its extraordinary relevance to our own era.

Alcott's work makes a compelling case for the empowerment of women, youth, the marginalized, and those who live on modest means. For instance, in a *USA Today* article from 2018, Harriet Reisen reminds us that well before our era's #MeToo movement, Alcott had shared her own story of sexual harassment in "How I Went Out to Service" (1874). Alcott defends those who love the arts, learning, and families. She champions antiracist and feminist reforms, and she meditates in complex ways on the importance of religious tolerance and tolerant religion. At the dawn of the "Gilded Age," novels like *An Old-Fashioned Girl* and *Little Women* provided warnings about the dangers of making wealth, social status, and material things the measures we use to value our lives, the people in our lives, and our social worlds. Alcott sees such attitudes not only as unwise but also as a threat to democratic ideals such as liberty and equality. While her warnings may have gone partly unheeded then and now, her works still provide readers with practical strategies for surviving, thriving, and protecting oneself and others in an era of brutal and expanding inequality.

Alcott's work matters. And it is a testimony to her ambitious imagination, her creative energy, and her talent that her work continues to resonate with and shed light on our contemporary situation. Teaching *Little Women* as a significant literary masterpiece and teaching Alcott herself as a major author in the classroom but also treating her as a major author in our critical work, both academic and broadly public, make that point clearly and powerfully.

Works Cited

"The 500 Greatest Albums of All Time." *Rolling Stone*, 11 Dec. 2003, pp. 83–178.

Alcott, Louisa May. *Hospital Sketches*. James Redpath, 1863. *HathiTrust*, https://babel.hathi trust.org/cgi/pt?id=duh1.ark:/13960/t4dn4zw6t;view=1up;seq=7.

Alcott, Louisa May. *The Journals of Louisa May Alcott*, edited by Joel Myerson, Daniel Shealy, and Madeleine B. Stern, Little, Brown, 1989; U of Georgia P, 1997.

Alcott, Louisa May. *Little Women, or, Meg, Jo, Beth and Amy*, edited by Anne K. Phillips and Gregory Eiselein, Norton Critical Edition, W. W. Norton, 2004.

Alcott, Louisa May. *An Old-Fashioned Girl*. Roberts Brothers, 1870.

Alcott, Louisa May. *The Poems of Louisa May Alcott*, introduction by Robert S. Nelsen, Ironweed, 2000.

Alcott, Louisa May. *The Selected Letters of Louisa May Alcott*, edited by Joel Myerson, Daniel Shealy, and Madeleine B. Stern, Little, Brown, 1987; U of Georgia P, 1995.

Alcott, Louisa May. *The Sketches of Louisa May Alcott*, introduction by Gregory Eiselein, Ironweed, 2001.

Alcott, Louisa May. *Work: A Story of Experience*, edited by Joy S. Kasson, Penguin, 1994. First published Roberts Brothers 1873.
Auden, W. H. "Introduction." *Nineteenth-Century British Minor Poets*, edited by Auden, Dell, 1966, pp. 15–26.
Auerbach, Nina. "Austen and Alcott on Matriarchy: New Women or New Wives?" *Novel*, vol. 10, no. 1, 1976, pp. 6–26.
Bailey, Susan. "Louisa May Alcott Is My Passion," https://louisamayalcottismypassion.com.
Baldwin, James. "Everybody's Protest Novel." *Partisan Review*, vol. 16, no. 6, 1949, pp. 578–85.
Baym, Nina, editor. *The Norton Anthology of American Literature*. 2nd ed., 2 vols. W. W. Norton, 1985.
Casper, Scott E. "Alcott, Louisa May." *Biographical Dictionary of Literary Influences: The Nineteenth Century, 1800 –1914*, edited by John Powell et al., Greenwood, 2001, pp. 17–18.
Cheever, Susan, editor. *"Work," "Eight Cousins," "Rose in Bloom," Stories & Other Writings*, by Louisa May Alcott, Library of America, 2014.
Cheney, Ednah D. *Louisa May Alcott: Her Life, Letters, and Journals*. Roberts Brothers, 1889.
Clark, Beverly Lyon. *The Afterlife of "Little Women."* Johns Hopkins UP, 2014.
Clark, Beverly Lyon, editor. "Eight Cousins; or, The Aunt-Hill (1875)." *Louisa May Alcott: The Contemporary Reviews*, Cambridge UP, 2004, pp. 233–62.
Clark, Beverly Lyon. *Kiddie Lit: The Cultural Construction of Children's Literature in America*. Johns Hopkins UP, 2003.
Daly-Galeano, Marlowe. "'Oh dear, yes!': Mashing Up *Little Women*, Vampires, and Werewolves." *Women's Studies: An Interdisciplinary Journal*, vol. 48, no. 4, 2019. Taylor & Francis Online, https://doi.org/10.1080/00497878.2019.1614871.
Danto, Arthur. "The Artworld." *The Journal of Philosophy*, vol. 61, no. 19, 1964, pp. 571–84.
Deming, Mark. "The Kingsmen." *AllMusic*, https://www.allmusic.com.
Dickens, Charles. *David Copperfield*, edited by Jerome H. Buckley, W. W. Norton, 1990. First published 1850.
Dickens, Charles. *Dombey and Son*, edited by Alan Horsman, Oxford UP, 1982. First published 1844.
Dickens, Charles. *The Life and Adventures of Martin Chuzzlewit*, edited by Michael Slater, Everyman, 1994. First published 1844.
Dickens, Charles. *The Old Curiosity Shop*. Dodd, Mead, 1943. First published 1841. *HathiTrust*, https://babel.hathitrust.org/cgi/pt?id=mdp.39076006935725;view=1up;seq=13.
Dickens, Charles. *A Tale of Two Cities*, edited by Richard Maxwell, Penguin, 2003. First published 1859.
Dimock, Wai Chee. "A Theory of Resonance." *PMLA*, vol. 112, no. 5, 1997, pp. 1060–71.
Douglas, Ann. "Introduction." *Little Women*, by Louisa May Alcott, Signet Classic, 1983, pp. vii–xxvii.
Doyle, Christine. "Singing Mignon's Song: German Literature and Culture in the March Trilogy." *Children's Literature*, vol. 31, 2003, pp. 50–70.
Eiselein, Gregory. "Contradiction in Louisa May Alcott's *Little Men*." *The New England Quarterly*, vol. 78, no. 1, 2005, pp. 3–25.
Eiselein, Gregory. "Modernity and Louisa May Alcott's *Jo's Boys*." *Children's Literature*, vol. 34, 2006, pp. 83–108.
Eiselein, Gregory. "Sentimental Discourse and the Bisexual Erotics of *Work*." *Texas Studies in Literature and Language*, vol. 41, no. 3, 1999, pp. 203–35.
Eiselein, Gregory, and Anne K. Phillips. "The Newness of *Little Women*." *Women's Studies: An Interdisciplinary Journal*, vol. 48, no. 4, 2019, pp. 363–65.

Elbert, Monika. "Charitable (Mis)givings and the Aesthetics of Poverty in Louisa May Alcott's Christmas Stories." *Enterprising Youth: Social Values and Acculturation in Nineteenth-Century American Children's Literature*, edited by Elbert, Routledge, 2008, pp. 19–38.

Elbert, Monika. "Divas, Drugs, and Desire on Alcott's Gothic Stage." *Critical Insights: Louisa May Alcott*, edited by Gregory Eiselein and Anne K. Phillips, Salem Press/Grey House Publishing, 2016, pp. 128–42.

Eliot, T. S. "What Is Minor Poetry?" *The Sewanee Review*, vol. 54, no. 1, 1946, pp. 1–18.

Fetterley, Judith. "Impersonating 'Little Women': The Radicalism of Alcott's *Behind a Mask*." *Women's Studies: An Interdisciplinary Journal*, vol. 10, no. 1, 1983, pp. 1–14.

Fetterley, Judith. "*Little Women*: Alcott's Civil War." *Feminist Studies*, vol. 5, no. 2, 1979, pp. 369–83.

"The Flamingos." *Rock & Roll Hall of Fame*, https://www.rockhall.com/inductees/flamingos.

Francis, Richard. *Fruitlands: The Alcott Family and Their Search for Utopia*, Yale UP, 2010.

"Frankie Lymon and the Teenagers." *Rock & Roll Hall of Fame*, https://www.rockhall.com/inductees/frankie-lymon-and-teenagers.

Graff, Gary. "Rock and Roll Hall of Fame Inducts Songs for the First Time, Including 'Born to Be Wild' & 'Louie.'" *Billboard*, 14 Apr. 2018, https://www.billboard.com/articles/columns/rock/8333912/rock-and-roll-hall-of-fame-inducts-songs-born-to-be-wild-louie-louie.

"The Great American Read." *Public Broadcasting Service*, 2018, http://www.pbs.org/the-great-american-read/home/.

Griffis, Rachel B. "Stories for 'Good Young Girls': Louisa May Alcott, Gender, and Realism." *Women's Studies: An Interdisciplinary Journal*, vol. 45, no. 3, 2016, pp. 263–74.

Guillory, John. *Cultural Capital: The Problem of Literary Canon Formation*, U of Chicago P, 1993.

Haidet, Ryan. "2019 Rock and Roll Hall of Fame Induction Ceremony as It Happened." *WKYC*, 29 Mar. 2019, https://www.wkyc.com/article/entertainment/music/rock-hall/2019-rock-and-roll-hall-of-fame-induction-ceremony-as-it-happened-real-time-updates/95-29cc6170-6f4b-4a67-b8f6-9ae46f2e58c6.

Hendler, Glenn. *Public Sentiments: Structures of Feeling in Nineteenth-Century American Literature*, U of North Carolina P, 2001.

Hubbell, Jay B. *Who Are the Major American Writers? A Study of the Changing Literary Canon*. Duke UP, 1972.

Hume, David. "Of the Standards of Taste." *Essays Moral, Political, and Literary*, edited by T. H. Green and T. H. Grose, 2 vols. Longmans, Green, 1875, vol. 1, pp. 266–86. First published 1757.

Keyser, Elizabeth L. "Alcott's Portraits of the Artist as Little Women." *International Journal of Women's Studies*, vol. 5, no. 5, 1982, pp. 445–59.

Keyser, Elizabeth Lennox. *Whispers in the Dark: The Fiction of Louisa May Alcott*. U of Tennessee P, 1993.

LaPlante, Eve, editor. *My Heart Is Boundless: Writings of Abigail May Alcott, Louisa's Mother*. Free Press, 2012.

Lary, N. M. *Dostoevsky and Dickens: A Study of Literary Influence*. Routledge, 1973.

Lauter, Paul et al. *The Heath Anthology of American Literature*, 2 vols. Heath, 1990.

"Louisa May Alcott: A Group for Fans, Readers, & Scholars." *Facebook*, https://www.facebook.com/groups/133575067326419/.

MacPike, Loralee. *Dostoevsky's Dickens: A Study of Literary Influence*. George Prior, 1981.

Matteson, John, editor. *The Annotated "Little Women."* W. W. Norton, 2015.

Matteson, John. *Eden's Outcasts: The Story of Louisa May Alcott and Her Father.* W. W. Norton, 2007.
Meyer, Robinson. "The 100 Books Facebook Users Love." *The Atlantic,* 8 Sept. 2014. *The Atlantic.com,* https://www.theatlantic.com/technology/archive/2014/09/the-100-books-that-facebook-users-love/379797/.
Porter, Nancy, director. *Louisa May Alcott: The Woman behind "Little Women."* Public Broadcasting Service, 2008.
Proehl, Kristen. "Sympathetic Jo: Tomboyism, Poverty, and Race in Louisa May Alcott's *Little Women.*" *Sentimentalism in Nineteenth-Century America: Literary and Cultural Practices,* edited by Mary G. De Jong, Fairleigh Dickinson UP, 2013, pp. 105–19.
Reisen, Harriet. "Long before 'Little Women,' Louisa May Alcott Had a Painful #MeToo Moment." *USA Today,* 20 May 2018, https://www.usatoday.com/story/opinion/2018/05/20/before-little-women-louisa-may-alcott-metoo-moment-column/620525002/.
Ricks, Christopher. "Notes away from the Definition of Major and Minor." *Ploughshares,* vol. 4, no. 3, 1978, pp. 115–21.
Rigsby, Mary Bortnyk. *Margaret Fuller's Feminist Aesthetic: A Critique of Emersonian Idealism in the Works of Fuller, Alcott, Stowe, and Freeman.* 1991. Temple U, PhD dissertation. *ProQuest,* https://search-proquest-com.er.lib.k-state.edu/docview/303962496.
Rioux, Anne Boyd. *Meg, Jo, Beth, Amy: The Story of "Little Women" and Why It Still Matters.* W. W. Norton, 2018.
Rostenberg, Leona. "Some Anonymous and Pseudonymous Thrillers of Louisa M. Alcott." *The Papers of the Bibliographical Society of America,* vol. 37, no. 2, 1943, pp. 131–40.
Rowling, J. K. "J. K. Rowling: By the Book." *The New York Times Sunday Book Review,* 14 Oct. 2012, p. BR8.
Ruhlmann, William. "The Champs." *AllMusic,* https://www.allmusic.com.
Shealy, Daniel, editor. *"Little Women": An Annotated Edition,* by Louisa May Alcott, Belknap P of Harvard UP, 2013.
Shealy, Daniel, editor. *Louisa May Alcott's Fairy Tales and Fantasy Stories.* U of Tennessee P, 1992.
Showalter, Elaine, editor. *Alternative Alcott.* Rutgers UP, 1988.
Showalter, Elaine, editor. *Little Women, Little Men, Jo's Boys,* by Louisa May Alcott, Library of America, 2005.
Smith, Troy L. "Rock Hall to Continue Honoring Songs at 2019 Induction Ceremony." *The Plain Dealer/cleveland.com,* 15 Jan. 2019, https://www.cleveland.com/news/2019/01/rock-hall-to-continue-honoring-songs-at-2019-induction-ceremony.html.
Stern, Madeleine, editor. *Louisa May Alcott Unmasked: Collected Thrillers.* Northeastern UP, 1995.
Stimpson, Catharine R. "Reading for Love: Canons, Paracanons, and Whistling Jo March." *New Literary History,* vol. 21, no. 4, 1990, pp. 957–76.
Tompkins, Jane. *Sensational Designs: The Cultural Work of American Fiction, 1790–1860.* Oxford UP, 1985.
Walls, Laura Dassow. "The Cosmopolitical Project of Louisa May Alcott." *ESQ: A Journal of the American Renaissance,* vol. 57, nos. 1–2, 2011, pp. 107–32.
White, E. B. "How to Tell a Major Poet from a Minor Poet." *The New Yorker,* 8 Nov. 1930, pp. 23–24.

About the Contributors

Beverly Lyon Clark was Professor of English and Women's & Gender Studies at Wheaton College in Massachusetts and published numerous scholarly articles on children's literature. She also published a dozen books, including *Kiddie Lit: The Cultural Construction of Children's Literature in America* (2003) and the coedited *"Little Women" and the Feminist Imagination* (1999). Her last recent book was *The Afterlife of "Little Women"* (2014).

Christine Doyle, Professor of English, Emerita, at Central Connecticut State University, has published numerous articles on children's literature. In 2006, she served as guest editor, along with Anne K. Phillips, for *Children's Literature* (vol. 34), an issue of the journal devoted entirely to Louisa May Alcott. She is also the author of *Louisa May Alcott and Charlotte Brontë: Transatlantic Translations* (2000).

Gregory Eiselein, Professor of English and University Distinguished Teaching Scholar at Kansas State University, is the author of *Literature and Humanitarian Reform in the Civil War Era* (1996). With Anne K. Phillips, he has coedited four books on Alcott, including *The Louisa May Alcott Encyclopedia* (2001) and the *Norton Critical Edition of "Little Women"* (2004). His most recent book is *Critical Insights: Louisa May Alcott* (2016).

John Matteson, Distinguished Professor of English at John Jay College of Criminal Justice, was awarded the Pulitzer Prize for Biography in 2008 for

Eden's Outcasts: The Story of Louisa May Alcott and Her Father. A Fellow at the Massachusetts Historical Society and former deputy director of the Leon Levy Center for Biography, he is also the author of *The Lives of Margaret Fuller: A Biography* (2012). In 2015, he edited the W. W. Norton version of *The Annotated "Little Women."* His latest book, *A Place Worse than Hell: How the Civil War Battle of Fredericksburg Changed a Nation*, was published by W. W. Norton in February 2021.

Joel Myerson was Carolina Distinguished Professor of American Literature, Emeritus, at the University of South Carolina. He published over fifty books on such authors as Ralph Waldo Emerson, Margaret Fuller, Nathaniel Hawthorne, Emily Dickinson, and Walt Whitman, among others. He also coedited five books on Alcott, including *The Selected Letters of Louisa May Alcott* and *The Journals of Louisa May Alcott*. His most recent coedited books were *Ralph Waldo Emerson: The Major Prose* (2015) and *Picturing Emerson: An Iconography* (2016).

Sandra Harbert Petrulionis is Distinguished Professor of English and American Studies at Pennsylvania State University, Altoona. Her books include *To Set This World Right: The Antislavery Movement in Thoreau's Concord* (2006), *Thoreau in His Own Time* (2012), and, with Joel Myerson and Laura Dassow Walls, *The Oxford Handbook of Transcendentalism* (2010). A past president of the Louisa May Alcott Society, she has directed National Endowment for the Humanities Summer Institutes on "Transcendentalism and Reform in the Age of Emerson, Thoreau, and Fuller." With Noelle A. Baker, she is currently editing *The Almanacks of Mary Moody Emerson: A Scholarly Digital Edition*.

Anne K. Phillips, Professor of English at Kansas State University, has published numerous scholarly articles on children's literature. A past president of the Louisa May Alcott Society, she has coedited, with Gregory Eiselein, four books on Louisa May Alcott, including the Norton Critical Edition of *Little Women* (2004). Their most recent book is *Critical Insights: Louisa May Alcott* (2016), and to mark the sesquicentennial of *Little Women*, they cocurated the blog "Little Women 150" (https://lw150.wordpress.com).

Daniel Shealy, Professor of English at the University of North Carolina-Charlotte, has published twelve books and numerous articles on Louisa May Alcott. With Joel Myerson, he coedited *The Selected Letters of Louisa May Alcott* (1987) and *The Journals of Louisa May Alcott* (1989). In 2008, he edited *Little Women Abroad: The Alcott Sisters' Letters from Europe, 1870–71*. His most recent book is *"Little Women": An Annotated Edition* (2013), published by Harvard University Press.

Roberta Seelinger Trites, Distinguished Professor of English at Illinois State University and former President of the Children's Literature Association (2006–2007), is the author of numerous scholarly essays and five books, including *Disturbing the Universe: Power and Repression in Adolescent Literature* (2000) and *Twain, Alcott, and the Birth of the Adolescent Reform Novel* (2007). Her most recent book is *Twenty-First-Century Feminisms in Children's and Adolescent Literature* (2017).

Index

References to illustrations appear in **bold**.

Adamo, Mark, 9, 69
aesthetics, 152, 181, 183–85, 189–93, 198
Afterlife of "Little Women," The (Clark), 15, 162, 186, 187
agency, 25, 83, 108–9
Alcott, Abba, 6, 22, 24, 29, 41, 69–73, 140, 162; work at employment agency, 22, 71–73, 119
Alcott, Anna, 6, 29, 69, 119, 140, 145, 162, 189
Alcott, Bronson, 4–6, 10, 21–22, 28, 33, 35, 37, 38–39, 41, 55–56, 69, 119, 140–41
Alcott, Lizzie, 28–31, 140
Alcott, Louisa May: attitude toward servants, 69–85; childhood, 3, 22–23, 37, 39, 69, 140; journal entries, 7–8, 12, 15, 22, 29–31, 39–41, 56, 114, 119, 137, 141–42, 145, 151, 162; as major author, 15, 182–200; on nature, 5, 13, 38–40, 46, 49, 52–54, 57–60, 119, 142–43, 154; nephews, 119–20; other occupations, 29, 35, 69–71, 85, 89, 194, 200; subversion of conventional expectations, 13–14, 116; use of contradiction, 13, 15, 55, 116, 123, 191–98; use of juxtaposition, 192–97; use of language, 13, 38, 46, 49–50, 53–60, 117, 157, 169, 171; use of omission, 13, 116–17, 134; use of paradox, 191; use of triangulation, 13, 116, 121–22; view of family, 13–14, 16, 21–22, 27–31, 33, 35, 46–47, 52, 55–56, 68–71, 89–90, 105, 116, 119–21, 124, 126, 146, 169, 171–75, 197, 199; views on death, 30–31
Alcott, May, 6, 90, 140, 145, 162
Allsopp, Sophie, 90
Allyson, June, 10
Alternative Alcott (Showalter), 190
American Sunday School Union, 43
American Tract Society, 43
American Woman's Home (Beecher and Stowe), 72
Anthony, Susan B., 104
Armstrong, Gillian, 10, 69
Atlantic, 188
Auden, W. H., 184, 190
Auerbach, Nina, 66, 186
Aunt Jo's Scrap-Bag (Alcott), 189

Bailey, Peter, 95
Baldwin, James, 191
Bang, Molly, 131
Beatles, 199
Bedell, Madelon, 73

Beecher, Catherine, 72
Beecher, Mrs. Henry Ward, 7
Behind a Mask (Alcott), 11, 189
Bernard, Dorothy, 3
Berry, Chuck, 180
Bhaer, Friedrich, 12, 34–35, 47–48, 54, 74–75, 100–102, 115–17, 120–29, **130**, 133–34, 151, 153, 155–58, 166
Bhaer, Josephine. *See* March, Josephine (Jo)
Billings, Hammatt, 127, 132
Biographical Dictionary of Literary Influences, The (Powell), 192
Blaisdell, Elinore, 13, 91, **92**, 109
Bleak House (Dickens), 192, 194
Bly, Nellie, 104
Boston, MA, 4, 22, 33, 71–73, 89, 119
Boston Daily Evening Transcript, 6
Bowlby, Rachel, 105–6
Bradford, Clare, 166, 176
Brady, William A., 3
Brodhead, Richard, 68
Brooke, John, 27, 29, 47, 74, 82–84, 93, 102, 117–18, 146, 156, 166, 168
Brooks, Geraldine, 10
Brundage, Frances, 132–34, **135**, **136**
Bunyan, John, 12–13, 38, 40–45, 47, 49–52, 59–60, 170

Campbell, Donna M., 115–16
Capper, Charles, 144
Carlyle, Thomas, 39
Carrol, Mary (Aunt Carrol), 32, 148, 154
Champs, 180
Chandler, Marilyn, 105
charity, 12, 19–20, 23–35, 66, 69–71, 74
Cheney, Ednah Dow, 11, 192
Cherry Ripe (Millais), 94
Child, Lydia Maria, 72
children's literature, 8, 11, 167, 187–88, 197
Chopin, Kate, 115
Civil War, 4, 8, 10, 15, 29, 43, 49, 85, 144, 146, 163, 171, 176
Clark, Beverly Lyon, 14, 15, 132, 162, 186–87, 188
Cohoon, Lorinda B., 67
colonialism, 15, 19, 163, 171, 176
Comic Tragedies (Alcott), 189

community, 14, 18, 32, 56, 66, 115–16, 119, 121, 126–27, 130–32, 134
Concord, MA, 3–4, 10, 41, 89, 140, 141, 175
Cooney, Barbara, 95
critics and reviews, 6–9, 12, 33, 46, 56, 67, 94, 126, 151, 157, 165, 171–72, 181–85, 187, 190–92, 197
Cukor, George, 9, 69
Cultural Capital (Guillory), 185
culture, 3, 9, 15, 19, 32, 66, 72, 102, 140, 143, 181–83, 185, 187–88, 196, 198–99
Curse of Kehana, The (Southey), 144

Dalke, Anne, 120
Dall, Caroline, 46
Danto, Arthur, 184
David Copperfield (Dickens), 192, 193, 195
Dawson, Janis, 68
de Certeau, Michel, 98
Deese, Helen, 44
de Remusat, Madame, 141
Detroit Free Press, 163
Dial, 142, 143
"Diana and Persis" (Alcott), 191
Dickens, Charles, 15, 56, 103, 191–97
Dimock, Wai Chee, 190
Dolan, Kathryn, 77
Dombey and Son (Dickens), 192, 193
Dostoevsky, Fyodor, 197
Douglas, Ann, 197
Dylan, Bob, 181

"Each and All" (Emerson), 44
Early Lectures (Emerson), 43
Eclectic Magazine, The, 7
Eden's Outcasts (Matteson), 186
education, 35, 40, 73–75, 78, 80, 140, 144, 147, 155–56, 171, 176, 181, 184–85
Edwin Drood (Dickens), 191
Eight Cousins (Alcott), 187, 189, 192
Eiselein, Gregory, 123
Elbert, Monika, 190
Elbert, Sarah, 44, 45, 67
Elementary English Review, 10
Eliot, T. S., 183
Emerson, Ralph Waldo, 12–13, 22, 32, 37–47, 49–54, 56–60, 140, 142–44, 156

Engels, Friedrich, 12, 20, 21–23, 27–28, 30
English, Mark, 13, 90, 100–101, 103, 108–9
Essays (Emerson), 142
Estes, Angela M., 114, 151
ethnicity, 25, 73–75
"Experience" (Emerson), 37–38, 44, 46–47, 49–50, 54

Felski, Rita, 104–5
feminism, 11, 56, 60, 105, 107, 140–41, 151, 157, 182, 186, 189, 199–200
Fetterley, Judith, 186
Flamingos, 181
Flower Fables (Alcott), 5, 16
Foote, Stephanie, 67–68
Foster, Shirley, 68
Francis, Richard, 186
Frankie Lymon and the Teenagers, 181
Fruitlands (Francis), 186
Fruitlands experiment, 21–22, 28, 33, 35, 41, 140
Fuller, Horace B., 5
Fuller, Margaret, 33, 37, 39, 44, 140–58; death in shipwreck, 140–41, 142, 144; series of Conversations, 142, 157
Funicello, Annette, 180

Gabbey, Terry, 106–8
Gannon, Susan, 127, 132
Garland for Girls, A (Alcott), 189
Geronimo Stilton series, 102–3
Gerwig, Greta, 10, 69, 188
Gilbert, Sandra M., 38
Girls (HBO series), 187
Godolphin, Mary, 43
Goethe, Johann Wolfgang von, 39, 142, 144
Graphic, 171
"Great American Read, The," 10, 188
Great Gatsby, The (Fitzgerald), 170
"Great Lawsuit, The" (Fuller), 142–43, 145, 151–53
Gubar, Susan, 38
Guillory, John, 185

"Happy Women" (Alcott), 118, 154
Harris, Susan K., 116
Hart, John Seely, 16

Hawthorne, Julian, 3, 9, 11
Hawthorne, Nathaniel, 3, 8
Heath Anthology of American Literature, The (Lauter), 185
Heilbrun, Carolyn, 114
Hepburn, Katharine, 9
Higginson, Mary E. Channing, 4
Higginson, Thomas Wentworth, 4
History of American Housework (Strasser), 71
History of Women's Suffrage (Stanton et al.), 140
Hospital Sketches (Alcott), 5, 30, 85, 176, 189, 192, 194–95, 197
Houdyshell, Jayne, 69
"How I Went Out to Service" (Alcott), 70, 85, 200
How to Stuff a Wild Bikini, 180
"How to Tell a Major Poet from a Minor Poet" (White), 183
Hubbell, Jay B., 183
Hume, David, 183
Hummels, 12, 23–26, 66, 69–70, 74, 80, 107, 169

illustrators and illustrations, 13, 14, 30, 73, 89–109, 116, 127–34; Amy and Laurie, 90–91, **92**, 93–94, 109, 127, 163; Camp Laurence expedition, 91, 103; doorways, 107–8; female illustrators, 90, 105; houses, 13, 89, 102–8; Jo and Beth at the seashore, 127–28, **128**; Jo and Professor Bhaer, 90, 100–102, 127–29, **129**, **130**, 133, **135**; Jo on train to New York, 96–99, **100**, **101**; Jo writing, 90, 94; male illustrators, 90, 105, 108; Plumfield, 130–34, **131**, **133**; wedding of Meg and John, 93
immigrants, 22, 72–73, 97; German, 12, 24, 72, 74; Irish, 69, 72–74, 97–99, **100**, **101**, 147
imperialism, 97–98
individualism, 14, 116, 126
Inheritance, The (Alcott), 176, 189
interdependence, 14, 32, 118, 120, 126, 132
"I Only Have Eyes for You," 181

Jack and Jill (Alcott), 189
Jambor, Louis, 90, 99

James, Derek, 91
James, Henry, 37, 47, 56
Johnson, Nicholas, 91
"Jolly Green Giant," 180
Jo's Boys (Alcott), 4, 35, 157, 187, 189

Kessler-Harris, Alice, 68
Keyser, Elizabeth, 81, 84, 114, 151, 186, 190
Kiddie Lit (Clark), 188
King, Gordon, 107–8
Kingsmen, 180, 181–82
Kornacki, Katie, 141

Lahey, Sarah, 74, 77
Laird, Susan, 67, 78
Langland, Elizabeth, 115
"Language" (Emerson), 53, 58–59
Lant, Kathleen Margaret, 114, 151
LaPlante, Eva, 186
Laurence, James (Mr. Laurence), 23, 26, 53, 66, 74–75, 78, 80–81, 120, 169, 170
Laurence, Theodore (Laurie), 3, 48, 69, 80–81, 84, 90–91, 93–95, **95**, 99, 104, 105, 107, 109, 126, 142, 145, 154, 168, 170; relationship with Amy, 35, 93–94, 114–17, 122, 127, 148–51, 155–56; relationship with Jo, 7, 14, 114–17, 120–24, 137, 147–49, 151, 155–56
Ledger, The, 154
Led Zeppelin IV, 199
Leigh, Janet, 10
Leroy, Mervyn, 69
Leslie, Frank, 5–6
"Letters from the Mountains" (Alcott), 189
literary criticism, 11–12, 15, 33, 46, 181, 191, 198
Little, Brown, 8, 162
Little Machinery (Liddell), 102
Little Men (Alcott), 142, 187, 189, 199
Little Richard, 181
Little Vampire Women (Messina), 188
Little Women (Alcott): 1984 abridgment, 107; Adventure Classics edition, 108; "Beth's Secret," 58, 128; "Burdens," 73, 75–76, 117; "Calls," 32; "Castles in the Air," 48, 125; Christmas, 9, 18, 24–26, 48, 66, 71, 77, 107, 146, 149, 169, 172; "Domestic Experiences," 83; "Experiments," 66, 75–77; "Harvest Time," 125–26; "Heartache," 122; as intertextual palimpsest, 12–13, 37–38, 46–53, 60; Ladybird Children's Classics abridgement, 106–7; "Literary Lessons," 152; "Meg Goes to Vanity Fair," 145, 154, 170; "New Impressions," 148–49; "On the Shelf," 147; part 1, 12, 43, 55, 60, 65, 75, 77, 84, 142, 145, 148, 154, 166, 176; part 2, 7, 29–30, 43, 54, 82–84, 117–18, 121, 127, 137, 142, 145–46, 158, 173; "The P. C. and the P. O.," 75; "Playing Pilgrims," 125; "Pleasant Meadows," 49; publication, 4–9, 16, 43, 103, 158, 162, 187; reception, 5, 7–11, 170; revised edition, 76; sales, 6–9; social vision, 12, 18–35; "Surprises," 122; "Tender Troubles," 122; "Under the Umbrella," 117; "The Valley of the Shadow," 52. *See also individual characters*
Little Women (film): 1917 silent film, 9; 1918 silent film, 9; 1933 RKO film, 9, 69; 1949 Technicolor film, 9, 69; 1994 Armstrong film, 10, 69; 2018 Clare Niederpruem film, 188; 2019 Greta Gerwig film, 10, 69, 188; Nippon Animation Japanese film, 39; Paramount-Artcraft film, 3
Little Women (opera): 1998 opera, 9; *Little Women, an Operetta in Three Acts*, 9, 69
Little Women (stage): 2001 stage version, 69; Broadway play, 3, 9
Little Women (television): 2017 BBC miniseries, 69, 188; PBS *Masterpiece* series, 10
Little Women and the Feminist Imagination (Alberghene and Clark), 11
Little Women and Werewolves (Grand), 188
Little Women: The Musical, 9
Lonette, Reisie, 13, 94–95, 109
Long Fatal Love Chase, The (Alcott), 189
"Louie Louie," 180
Louisa May Alcott's Fairy Tale and Fantasy Stories (Shealy), 189
Louisa May Alcott: The Woman behind "Little Women," 186
Louisa May Alcott Unmasked (Stern), 190
Lulu's Library series (Alcott), 189

major author criteria, 184–91; aesthetic value, 184, 190–91; body of work, 184,

188–90; canonicity, 184–86; criticism, 184, 186–87; influence, 184, 187–88
Manual of American Literature, A (Hart), 16
March (Brooks), 10
March, Amy, 18, 25, 30, 31–32, 34, 48, 50, 59, 74, 78–80, 84, 93–94, 96, 107, 132; artistic career in Europe, 33–35, 83, 89, 93–94, 99, 147–48, 154–56; Bess, 132, 134, 150–51; burning Jo's manuscript, 148, 152–53; limes incident, 31, 59, 73–75, 97, 175; relationship with Laurie, 84, 109, 114–17, 122, 127, 148–51, 155–56
March, Beth, 18, 48–49, 59, 53, 75, 106, 172, 174; domestic abilities, 67, 76, 78–79, 117; illness and death, 30–32, 34, 50, 52, 57, 77, 80–82, 84, 90, 100, 107, 114, 121, 125, 147, 148, 150, 153, 155–56, 158, 166–67, 172, 194; at the seaside with Jo, 54, 127–28, **128**
March, Josephine (Aunt March), 23, 26–27, 32, 76, 80, 120, 148, 170
March, Josephine (Jo), 18, 21, 23, 24–25, 31–32, 34–35, 47–54, 56–57, 73, 75–76, 78–81, 83, 84, 95–96, 99, 106, 107–9, 117, 145, 148, 150, 169, 172, 175; adulthood, 114–37, 154; literary aspirations and career, 4, 33–35, 54–55, 58–59, 152–53, 155–57, 170–71; motherhood, 115–17, 120, 126, 131–32, 134, 157; in New York, 89, 94, 95–102, **100**, 121, 147, 154–56; popularity with readers, 8–9, 11, 187; relationship with Friedrich Bhaer, 14, 33, 74, 115–17, 120–29, **130**, 133–34, 151, 155–58, 166; relationship with Laurie, 7, 14, 91, 114–17, 120–24, 137, 147–49, 151, 155–56; at the seaside with Beth, 54, 127–28, **128**
March, Margaret (Mrs. March, Marmee), 12, 13, 19, 23–25, 27–30, 34, 47–48, 50–51, 53, 57–58, 65–71, 73, 75–85, 94, 99, 100, 107, 117, 120, 126, 130–32, **133**, 134, **136**, 145, 146–47, 163, 169, 171, 173, 175
March, Meg, 18, 29, 48, 71, 74–76, 78–81, 84, 90, 121, 132, 145, 167, 168, 169, 170; children, 29, 83–84, 93–95, 109, 121, 132, 134, 147; having hair curled by Jo, 23, 125; jelly incident, 29, 74, 83–84, 146; relationship with John Brooke, 27, 29, 82–84, 93, 102, 116–18, 145–47, 154, 156, 166, 168, 173

March, Robert (Mr. March), 10, 18, 27, 34, 47, 49, 57–58, 76, 80, 108, 117, 120, 146, 152, 166, 169, 173, 176; illness, 68, 73, 77, 81, 100, 107, 169
"Marjorie's Birthday Gifts" (Alcott), 198
marriage, 14, 21–23, 27, 116–19, 122, 137, 140–58, 165; Amy and Laurie, 33, 34, 84, 114–17, 122, 148, 150–51, 155–57; equality, 14, 146, 148, 150–51, 154–56, 158; Jo and Friedrich, 14, 33, 74, 115–17, 120–29, 134, 151, 155–58, 166; Meg and John, 27, 29, 93, 116–18, 145–47, 154, 156, 173; Mr. and Mrs. March, 14, 146, 156; spinsterhood, 115, 145, 151–54, 194
Martin, Jane Roland, 188
Martin Chuzzlewit (Dickens), 194, 195
Massé, Michelle, 117
Massey, Doreen, 105, 108
materialism, 18–19, 52
Matteson, John, 186
Matthiessen, F. O., 54
May, Joseph, 10
May, Samuel, 115
McCullers, Carson, 8
Meg, Jo, Beth, Amy (Rioux), 15, 187
Merrill, Frank, 13, 73, **79**, 90, 93–94, **95**, 96, 99, **100**, 108–9, 127–32, **128**, **129**, **130**, **131**, **133**, 134
Merry's Museum, 5–6
metajudgments, 183–84
Methven, Eleanor, 69
Millais, John Everett, 94
MLA International Bibliography, 186
mobility, 89–90, 95, 105–6, 108–9; gendering of, 13, 89–90, 93–95, 102–4, 108
"Model of Christian Charity, A" (Winthrop), 12, 19–21
Modern Mephistopheles, A (Alcott), 189
Moebius, William, 132–33
Moods (Alcott), 12, 37–38, 40, 41, 43–46, 55–56, 118, 142, 152, 176, 189
morals and morality, 19–21, 24, 27, 30, 34–35, 40–53, 55, 76, 85, 96, 164, 167–68, 170, 172–76, 188, 193
Morning-Glories, and Other Stories (Alcott), 5–6
Morrison, Toni, 181

Morrison, Van, 181
Mother at Home and Household Magazine, The, 7
motherhood, 115–16, 118, 120, 134, 171
Mott, Luther, 43
Mullet, Hannah, 13, 65–85, **79**, 107, 117
Myerson, Joel, 15, 186

Nature (Emerson), 39–40, 53–54, 143
New York Times Book Review, 8
Niall, Brenda, 165, 167
Niederpruem, Clare, 188
Niles, Thomas, 5–7, 115, 127
Norton Anthology of American Literature (Baym), 185
nostalgia, 103–4, 108, 176, 199–200

O'Brien, Margaret, 10
Old Curiosity Shop, The (Dickens), 192–94
Old-Fashioned Girl, An (Alcott), 189, 191, 200
Oliver Twist (Dickens), 192
op de Beeck, Nathalie, 102
Orchard House, 6, 10, 89, 105–6, 170
Origin of Family, Private Property and the State, The (Engels), 12, 20, 22, 30

paracanon, 182–83
Parker, Alison M., 116
Patterson, Elizabeth, 69
Peabody, Elizabeth Palmer, 33, 39
Pee-wee's Big Adventure, 180
Penderwicks, The (Birdsall), 187
philanthropy, 19, 22, 26, 33–35, 150
Phillips, Anne K., 47, 198
philosophy, 4, 13, 37–40, 45, 47, 51–52, 54–56, 58–60, 143, 156
Pickwick Papers, The (Dickens), 192, 194
Pilgrim's Progress, The (Bunyan), 12–13, 37–60, 65, 157, 170, 172
Pilgrim's Progress in Words of One Syllable, The (Godolphin), 43
Plumfield, 26, 33–35, 120, 125–26, 130–32, **131**, 142, 156
Poems of Louisa May Alcott, The (Alcott), 189
Poisonwood Bible, The (Kingsolver), 187
Pooley, Colin, 95

Powell, Elizabeth, 115, 118, 151
Pratt, John Bridge, 119
Proehl, Kristen, 74
"Prophets and the Martyrs, The" (Phillips), 47
Prunier, Jame's, 99
Publishers' Circular and Booksellers' Record, 163
Pugh, Florence, 10

Quindlen, Anna, 188

race, 69, 73, 96, 115, 175
realism, 8, 55, 158, 167, 187, 189–91
Reisen, Harriet, 200
religion, 12, 19–21, 24, 29, 34, 38–42, 44–53, 57–58, 72, 171–72, 200
Richter, Amy, 95
Ricks, Christopher, 183
Rigsby, Mary, 152
Rioux, Anne Boyd, 15–16, 151, 187–88
"Rival Painters, The" (Alcott), 189
"Rival Prima Donna, The" (Alcott), 189
Roberts Brothers Publishers, 5–8, 131, 162, 189
Rock & Roll Hall of Fame, 180, 185
Rolling Stone, 199
Ronan, Saoirse, 10
Roosevelt, Theodore, 8
Rose Family, The (Alcott), 5
Rose in Bloom (Alcott), 187, 189, 198
Rostenberg, Leona, 190
Rowling, J. K., 8, 9, 187
Roxy Music, 180
Ruskin, John, 34
Ryder, Winona, 10

Sand, George, 39
Sands-O'Connor, Karen, 73
Schultz, April, 70
Scott, Walter, 43
Sedgwick, Catharine, 72
Selected Letters (Alcott), 141
self-reliance, 32–33, 44, 51, 53, 143, 153
"Self-Reliance" (Emerson), 56, 142–43
Sensational Designs (Tompkins), 182
Seven Little Australians (Turner), 14–15, 162–76; Aboriginals, 175–76; adaptations, 163; Aldith, 167–68, 170; Baby, 164; Bunty,

164, 169, 174; Captain Woolcot, 164, 166, 168, 171, 174, 176; Captain Woolcot's first wife, 164, 173–74, 176; Elinore (Nell), 164; Esther Hassal Woolcot, 164, 173–74, 175, 176; Francis Rupert Burnand (the General), 164, 173–74; Helen (Judy), 164–67, 169, 171–72, 174; Margaret (Meg), 164–68, 170, 173; Philip (Pip), 164, 166, 171, 175; River House, 164, 170, 174, 175; "Virtue Not Always Rewarded," 168–69; Yarrahappini, 165, 170, 174, 175
Sex in the City (television show), 199
Sgt. Pepper's Lonely Hearts Club Band, 199
Shakespeare, William, 39
Shawl-Straps (Alcott), 189
Shealy, Daniel, 15, 115, 151, 166, 186, 189
Shelley, Lorna, 95
Showalter, Elaine, 190
Simons, Judy, 68
Sketches by Boz (Dickens), 191, 194
Sketches from Concord and Appledore (Stearns), 7
Sketches of Louisa May Alcott, The (Alcott), 189
Skilton, David, 103
slavery, 22, 73, 144, 196, 199
Smith, Jessie Wilcox, 90
Smith, Patti, 8, 181
social class, 12, 13, 15, 18–27, 65, 67–68, 70–74, 76, 78–79, 81, 85, 90, 93, 97, 101–2, 165, 171, 176, 200
Society of Illustrators Annual Exhibition, 100
Soileau, Hodges, 13, 93
Southey, Robert, 144
Spinning-Wheel Stories (Alcott), 189
Springfield Daily Republican, 7
"Stairway to Heaven," 199
Stanton, Elizabeth Cady, 140, 142
Stearns, Frank Preston, 7
Steinem, Gloria, 8
stereotypes, 28, 69, 72–73, 107, 166
Stern, Madeleine B., 11, 15, 186, 190
Stimpson, Catharine, 182
Stone, Lucy, 119
Stoneley, Peter, 67
Stowe, Harriet Beecher, 7, 30, 72, 175

Strasser, Susan, 71
Streep, Meryl, 10
Strickland, Charles, 119
Sydney Morning Herald, 165, 171

Tale of Two Cities, A (Dickens), 193
Taylor, Elizabeth, 10
"Tequila," 180
Thiede, Adolf, 95
Thoreau, Henry David, 22, 37, 43, 140, 143, 154
Tompkins, Jane, 182–83
"Train to Nowhere," 180
transactional economy, 12, 28
transcendentalism, 4, 12, 14, 23, 37–39, 41, 43–46, 51–53, 55–57, 60, 140, 143, 152, 156, 171, 189, 191, 197
"Transcendental Wild Oats" (Alcott), 198
transportation, 13, 89–91, 93–95, 106, 108; bicycles, 90, 102–4; boats, 90–91, 93, 94, 108; carriages, 90, 93–94, 106, 108; horses, 90, 93–94, 106; omnibuses, 95–96, 124; sleighs, 106–7; trains, 90, 94, 95–102, **100**, **101**, 109; wagons, 90
Tudor, Tasha, 13, 99, **101**
Turner, Ethel, 14–15, 162–76
Twain, Mark, 198

Uncle Tom's Cabin (Stowe), 56, 73, 175, 191
"Up the Rhine" (Alcott), 189
urstories, 187–88
USA Today, 200

Verschaffel, Bart, 104

Wadsworth, Sarah, 123
Watson, Emma, 10
Wayne, Tiffany, 157
Whispers in the Dark (Keyser), 190
White, E. B., 183
Who Are the Major American Writers (Hubbell), 183
"Why Do Fools Fall in Love?," 181
Wilhelm Meister (Goethe), 39
Wilhelm Meister's Apprenticeship (Goethe), 142, 144
Winthrop, John, 12, 19–21, 32, 34

Woman in the Nineteenth Century (Fuller), 142
Woman's Journal, 119
women, 12, 21–22, 42, 53, 56, 67, 73, 95, 103–4, 108, 115–17, 121, 125–26, 142–45, 152–53, 158, 166, 191; employment, 66–68, 71–72, 85; empowerment, 15, 60, 104, 200; femininity, 91, 95, 102, 114, 117, 125, 134, 149, 156; rights, 140, 142, 144, 199; spirituality, 43, 46; suffrage, 38, 119–20; writers, 38, 152, 182–83
Women's Studies, 188
Woodworth, Samuel, 181
Work (Alcott), 30, 74, 85, 122, 126, 142, 189, 195–97
Writings of Abigail May Alcott (LaPlante), 186

Youth's Companion, The, 5–6

www.ingramcontent.com/pod-product-compliance
Lightning Source LLC
Chambersburg PA
CBHW030622230426
43661CB00053B/2101